# War & Conflict

# War & Conflict

## Selected Images from the National Archives
## 1765–1970

Edited by
Jonathan Heller

National Archives and Records Administration
Washington, D.C.
1990

PUBLISHED FOR THE
NATIONAL ARCHIVES AND RECORDS ADMINISTRATION
BY THE NATIONAL ARCHIVES TRUST FUND BOARD
1990

Library of Congress Cataloging-in-Publication Data

   War and conflict : selected images from the National Archives /
edited by Jonathan Heller.

   ISBN 0-911333-77-0
   1. United States — History, Military — Pictorial works. 2. War
photography — United States. I. Heller, Jonathan. II. United
States. National Archives and Records Administration.
E181.W27            973'.022'2 — dc20       89-39644

Designed by Serene Feldman Werblood, National Archives

*Frontispiece: Photo 729*

# TABLE OF CONTENTS

# PREFACE

Since it began operations in 1935, the National Archives has been accessioning the permanently valuable photographic records of the federal government. Still growing after half a century, this national resource now includes almost 6 million photographic prints, negatives, transparencies, and other visual materials in the Still Picture Branch, and more than 10 million aerial photographs in the Cartographic and Architectural Branch. Supplementing the holdings of these Washington area units are the photographic materials held by such National Archives facilities outside Washington as the 9 presidential libraries and 11 regional archives.

The images in *War & Conflict* have been selected only from those held by the Still Picture Branch. The catalog format has been adopted to increase the visibility of the branch's holdings and, at the same time, to simplify the process of ordering reproductions of many of the best pictures in the National Archives. Past efforts to enhance access to pictorial documentation in the National Archives have included select lists of photos of such subjects as the American West, Indians, the Revolutionary War, the Civil War, naval ships, and American cities. Photographs have been featured in a number of exhibits mounted in the National Archives Building, including, in particular, the major photographic exhibition of a decade ago, *The American Image*.

In presenting more than 1,500 images relating to American participation in war from the Revolution through Korea and Vietnam, this catalog highlights the widest variety of imagery from some of the Archives' more popular holdings. It features the work of U.S. military photographers, but also includes images from nongovernment artists and photographers. The photographs, prints, paintings, drawings, and posters presented in *War & Conflict* convey not only the variety of the records in the Still Picture Branch, but also the breadth of the wartime experience of the American people. We hope that you, the reader, will turn often to *War & Conflict* as a source of memorable images of events from history and your own experience.

DON W. WILSON
*Archivist of the United States*

# Acknowledgments

*War & Conflict: Selected Images from the National Archives* could not have been completed without the participation and help of many National Archives staff members. The entire staff of the Still Picture Branch, Office of the National Archives, enthusiastically assisted in the initial selection of pictures from which the images for this catalog and another to follow were chosen. Several people spent many more hours searching for photos on various subjects, military campaigns, or from important series of records. Thanks go to James H. Trimble, Holly Reed, Karen Yaffe, Barbara Lewis Burger, Deborah M. Edge, Sue McDonough, Paul White, Jerry L. Thompson, Sheila V. Mayo, Joan S. Clemens, Ouida W. Brown, Sharon Culley, Robert Ellis, Geraldine Evans, Patricia Richter, Annie G. Smith, Rutha M. Dicks, Tim Stanley, Edward J. McCarter, and Elizabeth L. Hill.

William H. Cunliffe, Director of the Special Archives Division, also helped to gather images, reviewed the final selections, and shared his extensive knowledge of the history of World War II.

I am grateful for the encouragement, guidance, and patience of the current and past chiefs of the Still Picture Branch, Elizabeth L. Hill and Jack Saunders, throughout this project.

The National Archives Photo Lab, under the direction of Bobbye West, did a skillful job in reproducing many of the pictures for *War & Conflict*. Amy Young ably took on the big job of making several thousand copy negatives; Nancy Olds and Susan Amos made high quality prints to ensure the best reproductions; and Susan also copied all of the posters. Connie McCabe deserves mention for her preservation work on several of the photographs before they could be copied.

The work of the Publications Division, Office of Public Programs, was crucial to the preparation and completion of this book. Serene Feldman Werblood did a wonderful job of designing it and supervising its production. Her input in page layout and her overall enthusiasm were invaluable. Thanks also are due to Sandra Tilley, Sherry King-Anderson, and Mary C. Ryan for their work in meticulously proofreading all of the captions and text. Dennis R. Means helped in the initial stages of this project, and Richard B. Smith guided *War & Conflict* through the publication process.

Sharon Gibbs Thibodeau of the Archival Publications Staff edited the text for *War & Conflict* and made many helpful suggestions to refine the written part of this book.

The staff of the National Archives Library and various reference archivists who helped locate source materials were most helpful in caption and historical research. I also appreciate the research assistance I was given by the staffs of the Library of Congress Prints and Photographs Division, the Copyright Office, particularly Victor Martin, and the National Portrait Gallery.

My own family, my parents and brothers, are also picture professionals whose insights into the use and history of photography and war were of great help toward my understanding of the subject.

Finally, I owe a special thanks to my assistant for much of this project, Holly Reed, whose uncomplaining and diligent hard work made the completion of *War & Conflict* possible.

JONATHAN HELLER
*Still Picture Branch, National Archives*

# INTRODUCTION

## STILL PICTURE BRANCH

Even before the staff moved into the brand new National Archives Building in 1935, the decision was made to establish a separate division to administer still photographic archives, reproduction, and research. Although in the beginning the primary emphasis of this unit was on copying paper records in the Archives, microfilming projects, and documenting the new facilities, efforts moved quickly into accessioning the permanently valuable photographic records of the U.S. government.

At the time the National Archives opened, it was sponsoring the Survey of Federal Archives with the Works Progress Administration (WPA). This survey of federal records identified some 2,750,000 still photographs held by government agencies in the Washington, DC, area. The earliest accessions included photos from the War, Navy, and Interior Departments, pictures from World War I, photographs of American Indians, and some aerial photographs.

Later, as the responsibilities of the photo archives expanded to include posters and other pictorial records, transfers from earlier accessions were made from other branches of the Archives. Aerial photography eventually came within the purview of the Cartographic Archives.

While not all of the millions of photos examined in the 1930s were deemed to be permanently valuable and worthy of retention, many were eventually added to the Archives' holdings. The end of the Depression and the closing of the many New Deal agencies brought in large numbers of photographs. The end of World War II saw a similar surge of photos as many civilian war agencies concluded their work.

Among the largest accessions of the Still Picture Branch were those from the various branches of the military. Navy photographs in the National Archives account for more than three-quarters of a million items. Almost the same number are from the Army Signal Corps, almost 150,000 from the Marine Corps, and about 50,000 from the Coast Guard. These photos cover most of the military history of the United States, but most of them are from World War I, World War II, and the Korean War.

The Still Picture Branch receives photographic records that are no longer needed for the operations of federal agencies. The eligibility of records for transfer to the National Archives has been variously interpreted throughout the government. Differing interpretations may explain why the Archives has not accessioned the bulk of World War II photos taken by the Army Air Forces, and why none of the armed services has transferred its photographs covering the Vietnam War.

The holdings of the Still Picture Branch extend to more than 175 record groups — each encompassing the records of a different government agency. Selections from 43 of these groups, including both civilian and military records, were chosen for *War & Conflict*. The images include a variety of types of still pictures — photographs, posters, drawings, prints, and copies of works of art.

The Still Picture Branch will continue to accession records, including photographs of the many aspects of war. Through these images from the National Archives, this catalog presents both a nostalgic and grimly realistic look back at the wars America has fought since its struggle for independence.

## SCOPE AND SELECTION

When it was suggested in the summer of 1987 that the Archives publish a picture catalog from its holdings, the intent was to reproduce photos from existing select lists on American Indians, the Revolutionary and Civil Wars, the West, and cities, supplemented by a few additional subjects. The Still Picture Branch decided, however, that it would be more valuable to start anew and present what were considered to be the best images from its holdings.

An energetic 3-month search was undertaken with the help and suggestions of all Still Picture Branch staff members. As tens of thousands of pictures examined dwindled into more manageable piles totaling more than 12,000 paper copies, it became apparent that there were too many outstanding images for just one book. After an exhilarating and difficult process of elimination, the final selections were made, some 3,000 of them. These were divided into two groups: the first relating to war; the second, to all other subjects. The first group is presented in *War & Conflict* and the second will appear in a subsequent catalog.

*War & Conflict* opens with the Revolutionary War and closes with the Korean War. Because the Still Picture Branch holds few photos of the Vietnam War, that war, significant as it was, has been included with other 20th-century conflicts that took American troops to foreign lands. Other strictly foreign hostilities, such as the Spanish Civil War, despite the participation of American volunteers, or the presence of photos in our records, were omitted. We made no attempt to track down photos of every war or military action in which Americans or American troops participated, but tried to include only those conflicts that featured prominently or uniquely in American history or in the holdings of the Still Picture Branch.

It must be admitted that the overall selection process was a subjective one. Because it would have taken years to review all of the war-related photos in the Still Picture Branch, the searches were supplemented by shortcuts, including existing lists, finding aids, exhibit checklists, published works that featured photos from the National Archives, and selections already made by the agencies or branches of the military. Whenever possible, we searched the records for specific subjects, personalities, or locations of importance. We also searched through specific important series of photos. And, when possible, we just took boxes off the shelves and browsed. Unfortunately, some collections, such as very large series of photos arranged numerically, did not lend themselves to easy searching. Smaller series and those arranged by subject were easier to survey.

In the end, it was decided not to try to fill every subject gap, not to see every campaign or theater of operations equally represented, and not to include every well-known personality. A volume so inclusive would have been an endless task. Instead, we relied on the visual impact of each image, the subject it showed, and the emotional response to it, whether seeing it for the first or the hundredth time. We apologize for any inadvertent omissions, but the selection process was such that each image was judged on its own qualities. The images were arranged after most of these final selections were made.

We made an exception for the pictures of World War II, which make up the largest part of the catalog. The World War II chapter is indeed repre-

sentative of the most used and popular records in the Still Picture Branch. It seemed necessary to include the most important campaigns, homefront activities and issues, and top-level personalities of the era. A recent accession of Marine Corps photos also made continuing additions to this group essential. As we reach the 50th anniversary of World War II, interest in the greatest conflict in history continues unabated.

Much of the photography in this catalog was the work of U.S. government and military photographers. Government agencies also acquired the work of private or commercial photographers to help document the wars in which the United States was involved. The armed services, in particular, collected photographs of artwork that depicted the early military history of the United States.

Practical considerations of space and layout for *War & Conflict* eliminated some images. Some would not have reduced well, others were too graphic or bizarre, and others were repetitive. A few nongovernment pictures were still under copyright protection.

Many of the images in this catalog will be familiar. Others will not. Many have appeared in books, newspapers, or magazines; some were censored during wartime; some were not chosen by contemporary picture editors; and some once considered ordinary now seem extraordinary from a historical perspective.

Choosing 1,500 images for this catalog still leaves hundreds of thousands or even millions for the dedicated researcher to find. There are gems still to be discovered. Whether searching for images of the vast scope of war or of a more personal view, and whether searching for images of war or of peace, the National Archives remains the place to come for pictures and *War & Conflict* is among its most important sources for the best of them.

# WAR AND PICTURES

From Washington crossing the Delaware to MacArthur wading ashore in the Philippines, pictures of war have served to inform, inspire, and instruct the American public. Over the years, patriotism has continued to influence the creation of a pictorial record of America during wartime, while additional needs have expanded the scope of coverage.

Changes over the last two centuries in the means of pictorial expression have also had a great impact on the imaging of war. The difference between what is depicted in paintings, for example, and what is shown in early war photographs is quite striking. As photography played a greater role in documenting wartime, changes in photographic technology had a major impact on the evolving ability to show nearly every facet of civilian and military activities.

Considered within the framework of the development of our nation, the pictorial depiction of war has changed as the American people have matured from an ex-colony to a world power. The sobering experience of the Civil War changed the way that armed conflict was seen and portrayed by the camera. The pride with which America took its place in world affairs in the late 19th and early 20th centuries also clearly influenced the outlook of those who photographed war scenes.

It was the relentless bloodshed and destruction of World War II, though, that altered the attitudes of many war cameramen. Eventually, particularly during the Vietnam War, a certain antiwar subjectiveness made its way into photographic documentation. The unavoidable everyday realities of war were brought into the living rooms of the American public by the television news and by photos published in the nation's magazines and newspapers.

## ART AND WAR

The colonial and revolutionary periods saw many artists plying their skills to depict the military and political struggles for independence. From the engravings of Paul Revere to the heroic paintings of John Trumbull, the most important scenes and personalities of the American Revolution were depicted in prints, paintings, and drawings. The style of art was "the then current classical style of commemorative painting [that] emphasized the glorification of heroes and great deeds."[1] This romantic tradition in battle art continued through the conflicts of the first half of the 19th century.

Some pictures of early wars that were done at the time of the events they portray are shown in this catalog. Many of the pictures shown were done later. The artist either was an eyewitness, or made a print from a sketch done at the battle by someone else, or based his or her work on historical or popular accounts. During the middle decades of the 1800s, a number of comprehensive volumes on American history were published. Artists were commissioned to create large numbers of illustrations for these books.

The battle successes of the War of 1812 and the Mexican War were also celebrated in popular prints. By the 1840s, artists like Currier and Ives in New York and others were mass marketing lithographs on a variety of subjects, including the victories in the Mexican War.

During this period a patriotic theme was still the dominant element in the creation of the images of war. This was to change with the invention of photography in 1839 and the growth of its use during the period leading to the Civil War.

## EARLY WAR PHOTOGRAPHY

The perceived nature of photography as a mirror of reality changed the way in which war could be depicted. "Battle paintings traditionally celebrated martial glory and rendered gallant death with a decorous dab of gore. The inherent naturalism of photography was bound to contradict the romantic excesses which so appealed to the armchair patriot."[2]

Another concept that gradually developed during the 19th century was that of the subjective eye of the photographer. A photograph revealed not only what was in front of the lens, but also how the photographer perceived his subject and used the various technical facets of his art to portray it. "While the painter *interprets* events and happenings, the photographer is able to *reflect* them in a precise and accurate form. The choice of the *content* . . . remains subjective, however, and the human element of selection cannot be eliminated."[3]

The earliest known photographs of war are a handful of daguerreotypes taken during the Mexican War, 1846–47. Most of these were made by an anonymous local photographer, and show American troops in and around Saltillo, Mexico.[4] Another surviving daguerreotype shows volunteer troops in Exeter, NH, preparing to leave for Mexico in 1846.[5] A British amateur photographer, John MacCosh, was the first identified war photographer. He took pictures during some of Britain's colonial wars in India and Burma, 1848–52.[6] The next known war photographer was Karl Baptist von Szathmari, who accompanied Russian troops invading what is now Romania in 1853–54 at the beginning of the Russo-Turkish wars. None of his work survives.

The first major "photo opportunity" for war photography was the Crimean War. In 1854 the British and French joined Turkey to fight the Russians. The British army was ill prepared and suffered greatly from disease, a harsh winter, and mismanagement of supplies, medical support, and military leadership. When the press reported these conditions, the public was outraged. A new government sent several photographers to show perhaps that these conditions had improved. It is the work of one of these, Roger Fenton, that is recognized as the first photographic documentation of war.

Under royal and government patronage, and financed commercially, Fenton arrived in the Crimea in March 1855. He made images of battlefields and soldiers, but none of the death and misery that made up the reality of that campaign. He used the difficult wet collodion glass negative process, and despite difficult conditions that were exacerbated by heat and insects, he succeeded in taking some 360 plates, mostly 12 by 16 inches. There were no battle scenes, as exposures needed to be from 3 to 20 seconds long. Upon his return to England, Fenton had his pictures printed, exhibited, and sold. Some were published in the *London Illustrated News* as engravings. But soon the public lost interest in the war and the collection of negatives and remaining prints was sold at auction.

## CIVIL WAR

Before the Civil War, pictures relating to important news events of the day were made available to the public through the new American pictorial press. *Frank Leslie's Illustrated Newspaper* was first published on December 15, 1855. It was followed by *Harper's Weekly* in 1857. Both of these publications achieved enormous popularity and were credited with having larger circulations than any of their competitors.[7] Illustrations took the form of wood engravings that were based on original drawings or, later, photographs.

When the Civil War began in 1861, Mathew Brady was the most famous photographer in America. His fashionable studios in New York City and Washington, DC, attracted the most noted celebrities of his time. Politicians, actors, the well-to-do, and the general public flocked in to have their portraits made. Brady was a businessman but also saw himself as a pictorial historian. He felt a great need to document the war. "I can only describe the destiny that overruled me by saying that, like Euphorion, I felt that I had to go. A spirit in my feet said 'Go'. and I went."[8] Brady had started using the wet-plate process in 1854. It had been invented by Englishman Frederick Scott Archer in 1851. Brady was visiting Europe in 1851–52 and was introduced to the new process, which would supplant the daguerreotype. Brady was probably familiar with Fenton's Crimean War photos either through later reproductions in the American illustrated press, or through his association with Alexander Gardner, who emigrated from England to the United States in 1856 to work for Brady.

Brady's ambition to document the war would be an expensive one. Although he was not attached to the U.S. Army, he received the Army's cooperation to work on all fields of battle. The photographic technology of the time still made war photography difficult, although finally, "the camera did look frankly into the face of battle."[9] "Brady's photographs also reveal the technical deficiencies of early photography: long exposures, heavy cameras, and the wet process completely robbed the pictures of spontaneity. In spite of this, Brady's assertions in his catalogue that the photos were taken during the Civil War and that they depicted its true grimness were thoroughly justified."[10]

Brady took his first war photographs at the first Battle of Bull Run in July 1861. Whereas the romantic tradition still dominated battle art at the beginning of the war, it was replaced by more realistic images in both art and photography. Mass-produced engravings in the illustrated newspapers, made after drawings and photos, fed the public's appetite for news and pictures of the conflict. Brady and many other photographers sold photographs and stereo cards by the thousands.

Brady himself managed his project more often than he actually photographed. He had a large number of photographers in the field. "I had men in all parts of the Army," he said, "like a rich newspaper... I spent over $100,000 in my war enterprises."[11] Among his more well-known photographers were Alexander Gardner and Timothy O'Sullivan. They left Brady in 1862 over a dispute concerning Brady's failure to include photographers' credit lines on the prints he sold.

Civil War photographers with the Union forces had great freedom of action, within technical limitations. There was little censorship, armies moved slowly, and the photographers could go wherever they wanted. The northern Army of the Potomac alone issued field passes to some 300 photographers. These were independent photographers who more often took portraits of the soldiers and their units stationed or fighting nearby. Among the more well-known northern photographers were George Barnard, who accompanied General Sherman during his march through the South in 1864–65, and Capt. Andrew J. Russell, attached to the U.S. Military Railroads Bureau, who may have been the only official military photographer. Some of the battles of the war resulted in extremely heavy casualties. The battlefield photographer, limited to shooting the aftermath of battle, did not shy away from showing the reality of dead bodies and ruined buildings.

As the war ended, both Brady and Gardner hoped that published selections of Civil War pictures would be a commercial success for them. Both lost money, however, for within a few years the public wanted to forget the war. Brady's financial difficulties led to the War Department's purchase of his collection of Civil War and other images, thus ensuring their preservation. In 1874, for the sum of $2,840, the government bought about 6,000 of Brady's negatives, sold for nonpayment of storage charges at auction. Comprising portraits and war views, this collection was widely recognized for its importance. Gen. Ulysses S. Grant spoke in 1866 of its value for future generations. Gen. James A. Garfield in 1875 valued the collection at $150,000. Gen. Benjamin Butler, Congressman from Massachusetts, felt that an injustice had been done to Brady and he pushed through Congress an appropriation of an additional $25,000 to be paid to the photographer.[12] (Unfortunately, even this windfall did not solve Brady's financial problems.)

The War Department's Brady negatives were stored in various places under different conditions until they finally found a home in the National Archives. Other large collections of Brady's work were later acquired by the Library of Congress, private collectors, and the National Portrait Gallery.

## LATER WARS

The decades after the Civil War saw a number of technical breakthroughs in photography that greatly improved the ability of the medium to illustrate war and other news events. The 1870s saw the development of the gelatin dry-plate negative, which had a faster (more sensitive) emulsion and also eliminated the messy and cumbersome apparatus and chemicals necessary to produce the collodion wet plate. The mechanical shutter had been invented earlier to replace manual exposure (removing and replacing a lens cap), but could only be used as the sensitivity of the plates increased.[13] Lenses were faster and smaller cameras were developed. Tripods were no longer essential, and flash powder made indoor shots possible. New shutter speeds of fractions of a second could finally stop action. In the United States, George Eastman's development of the Kodak box camera, the folding camera, and especially roll film helped to increase the potential of the camera and the photographer to record the realities of war.

By the time of the outbreak of the Spanish-American War in 1898, photographs had taken the place of engravings in newspapers and magazines. This was made possible by the invention of the halftone reproduction process, first used in the United States in 1880. Further improvements were needed, but by the late 1890s, most of the hundreds of illustrations published in *Harper's Weekly, Leslie's Weekly,* and the daily newspapers were made from photographs, the majority reproduced by halftone. Along with the use of the halftone, the introduction in 1896–97 of the illustrated Sunday supplement magazine by major newspapers, such as the *New York Times, New York Tribune,* and *Chicago Tribune,* would provide an important showcase for upcoming war photography.

Photographers still had unlimited access when they arrived at the battlefields of the Spanish-American War. Most of the large publishers of stereo views, such as Underwood and Underwood and B. W. Kilburn, sent photographers to cover the conflict, as did the news services run by the major New York newspapers. The latter sent artists, photographers, and correspondents into the field to send back images and stories to an information-hungry public. The competition between the newspaper chains of William Randolph Hearst and Joseph Pulitzer also fueled the demand for more coverage of the war.[14]

Although no photographer or publisher attempted to make a comprehensive photographic record of the war, the combined coverage was very complete except for scenes of battle action. For a war that lasted a mere 4 months, the number of photos taken was considerable. Indeed, there were more stereo views taken of the Spanish-American War than of any other.[15]

There were U.S. Army photographers working during the Spanish-American War, as evidenced by the large number of original glass and film negatives and vintage prints in the National Archives. There were also many amateur photographers in the field and with the fleets. Soldiers and sailors took their personal folding cameras off to war with them. Even some of the war correspondents took pictures.[16]

Most of the photographers had difficulties in adjusting to the hot and humid climate in both the Caribbean and the Philippines. By the time they figured out how to overcome their problems, the war was over. In the following few years, however, during the Philippine Insurrection and the China Relief Expedition (Boxer Rebellion), the Signal Corps produced many excellent photographs, mainly documenting its own activities, but of general military operations as well.[17] Capt. C. F. O'Keefe of the 36th U.S. Volunteer Infantry served as a photographer in the Philippines and also in China during the Boxer Rebellion, 1900–1901. His photographs show a variety of exotic scenes and American and foreign troops.

At the turn of the century, real battle action photographs as we know them today still seemed to be out of reach for the war photographer and his equipment. Some action shots were still being posed for the camera, although scenes at the front were coming closer to showing actual battle than ever before.

Cpl. C. Tucker Beckett was serving in El Paso, TX, as a photographer with the 16th Infantry when Pancho Villa's men raided the town of Columbus, NM. American troops were sent into Mexico in pursuit during the Mexican Punitive Expedition in 1916. Beckett was eager to become a war photographer. "When the Columbus atrocity occurred, I bundled my entire studio into goods-boxes, stored them in a warehouse, put a 3-A special Kodak alongside my rifle, arranged for a tank developing outfit to be forwarded later, and was ready. Ever since the European War started, I have wondered why the expert (?) war photographers of the world, with the world's wonderful appliances at their command, have not caught the tense moments of battle, or the horror of horrors—the bayonet charge. Perhaps this would be my chance."[18]

Photo 341

There was little actual fighting and the harsh desert conditions made Beckett's work difficult, but the body of work he produced is fascinating for its detailed portrayal of army life, the common soldier, and the military and civilian activities that accompanied the expedition. Beckett developed his film and made prints in the field, washing negatives in any convenient stream, making portrait prints in an adobe hut. He had great foresight as to the needs of the combat photographer, and was well aware that even after presetting it, "The best ready-made camera is not ready enough . . . All you have to do (in ordinary cases) would be to draw your camera from the case, pull down the door, pull out the bellows and fire away. Such a camera it is very easy to arrange. But if you are in deadly earnest, it would be still better if, when you pulled down the door, the bellows extended itself [and] after you shoot, the film rolls up automatically, reloading itself like a rifle. Your eye has never left the subject. Thus it is with the rifle—why not the camera?"[19] With these words, Beckett predicted the automatic features of modern cameras.

Photographers were sent to the expedition from commercial news photo agencies such as Underwood and Underwood, and there were other photographers attached to several other regiments. Beckett's photos were sent back to El Paso, where they were sold through a local studio. Other photos were sent to New York for publication.

It was at this same time that war on a much greater scale was being waged in Europe, a war that would provide a greatly enlarged perspective for war photography.

## WORLD WAR I

World War I was a conflict that touched much of the western world. When the United States entered the war in 1917, every aspect of American life became involved and was, consequently, documented by the camera. Photographic coverage on a comprehensive scale was recognized early as a necessity in recording the history of the war.

By the time of the outbreak of war, the circulations of illustrated magazines and newspapers in Europe and the United States ran into the millions. Response to the demand for war photographs, however, was limited by censorship, mainly for security reasons, especially in the European nations. Admittance to battlefields was forbidden to press photographers by both the French and German armies.[20] Official military photographers showed war scenes that suited propaganda purposes. As was the case during the Crimean War, depiction of the reality of grim frontline conditions was not considered good for morale. Official British, French, and German photos were taken and released to the press and other governments. European governments and their allies did not photograph the war on a large scale. For example, there was usually only one official Canadian photographer in the field at any one time during much of the war. (Despite that limitation, Canadian photographic output was extensive.)

Responsibility for American war photography was first given almost exclusively to the U.S. Army Signal Corps. The Signal Corps Photographic Service was established in July 1917, becoming the Photographic Division in October of that year. Its work had military, historical, and educational uses

Photo 603

and consisted of both still and motion picture photography. Military photography included aerial and land photography. Most aerial photographs were taken for reconnaissance and intelligence uses, from airplanes and observation balloons. Most of the land photography was taken for historical and educational purposes. The aerial work was the only real tactical photography in use. Historical photography consisted of documenting the Army from recruitment and training, through camp life and embarkation, to landing abroad and all military and support operations. These subjects overlapped with educational photography, which involved the provision of official photos to the Committee on Public Information for distribution at home, and the preparation of photographic materials for training purposes.

In order to train its photographers, the Signal Corps established two

*Photo 607*

schools in early 1918; one for aerial photography in Rochester, NY, another for land photography at Columbia University in New York City. Each combat division of the U.S. Army was assigned a photographic unit at embarkation, which consisted of one still photographer, one motion picture cameraman, and their assistants. Thirty-eight division units were sent overseas. At peak strength, the Signal Corps had 92 officers and 498 enlisted men engaged in photography, with a photo lab located in Paris. That unit had responsibility for procuring and storing photographic supplies, both from the United States and locally, and for the developing and printing of photos from the field. In addition, most photographic units had field darkroom facilities, either in buildings or in trucks with electric generators.

The main Signal Corps photo lab in the United States was in Washington, DC. It provided prints to the Committee on Public Information and to the public from U.S. Army photographs taken in the United States and abroad. Its work load was massive. From February 1918 to July 1919, for example, over 800,000 prints were made, 45,000 negatives developed, and almost 130,000 lantern slides prepared.

In May 1918 the Air Service, along with its aerial and other photographic operations, was separated from the Signal Corps. The Photographic Section of the Air Service and its aerial reconnaissance work was vital to military operations, especially during the major battles of the latter part of the war. Thousands of prints were made in just a few days to prepare for the offensive in the Argonne in 1918. Great attention had also been paid to creating a history of the Air Service during World War I. Photographs were widely recognized as an essential part of the Air Service's activities.

The Photographic Section came under the direction of noted photographer Edward Steichen. Originally commissioned a lieutenant in the Signal Corps, he arrived in France in November 1917 to organize aerial photography there, and later transferred to the Air Service. Photographic Section units, composed of photographers trained in Rochester, were assigned to various aero squadrons and observation groups. During the war, Air Service photographers took 18,000 photographs of enemy positions, from which over half a million prints were made. A photographic section was expected to make more than 10,000 prints a day during peak activity.

After the armistice, the mission of the photographers of the Signal Corps and Air Service actually expanded and their work and staffing increased. All fields of action were photographed on the ground for historical purposes, as were all the activities of the military services and occupation forces.

Technological developments through the war were summed up by the Chief Signal Officer of the U.S. Army. "It is a grand stride from the methods employed by Mathew Brady, who during the Civil War made his wet plates in the field . . . using a camera with a lens made from spectacle glass, taking photographs which later were developed in the shelter of some barn with uncertainty as to results — to the present-day photographer conveyed to points of vantage by motor cycle, automobile, or airplane, equipped with his graphic camera containing a lens made from the finest of optical glass, high speed shutter, dry plates, and cut film, which enable him to make both still and moving pictures of objects moving at high rates of speed, and with the aid of a portable darkroom produce a finished print of a still photograph in the field within 15 minutes."[21]

A variety of folding and single lens Graflex cameras were used. Often they were still operated on tripods, but they could be hand held as well. As many photographic supplies as possible were brought from the United States, but the demand at home made it necessary to procure cameras, lenses, plates, film, paper, and chemicals in France. Many photographic supplies were of German manufacture, which made supply difficult at times, but enough of what was needed was always found.

During World War I, war photography was no longer "the domain of the resourceful newspaper photographer of earlier, smaller wars, who roamed at will behind the lines, at the front, and sometimes even in the advance of the contending armies."[22] All American Army photography was militarized and civilians were not allowed except as war photographers accredited by the War Department. The importance of the press in disseminating information on the war to the public was recognized, but their responsibility to military security was paramount. Each publication or news service could send one photographer and correspondent into the field, upon approval of their credentials and posting of a bond. Rules concerning their clothing, equipment, and behavior had to be followed. All photos were submitted through a military censor.

Similar but less stringent rules applied to photographs taken of the military in the United States. News photo agencies and local photographers often documented the activities on the homefront. A wide variety of subjects were photographed, from food conservation and war industries to war bond drives and victory parades. Indeed, the War Department's Pictorial Section had a subject listing of photos it had collected that ran to almost 100 pages.

The photographic files of the Pictorial Section were for official use by the War Department only. Most were obtained from private sources and were not generally for public use as were the military photos. Some of the images, for example, showed "secret manufacturing processes and other confidential material," and were obtained "on the condition that the pictures should not be placed at the disposal of the public without proper authority."[23] On the other hand, military photos passed by the censors were available to the press and the public during and after the war. The price of an 8- by 10-inch print from the Signal Corps was 15 cents.

The immediate and future uses of the photography of World War I were more than adequately ensured by an American military administration that seemed to be very enlightened concerning the importance of the medium. Photographic units covered the Army and the Air Service. Other photographers were attached to the Navy, sea transport service, supply and support services, and such welfare organizations as the American Red Cross and the YMCA, which looked after the comforts and needs of American soldiers as well as refugees and other civilians in Europe.

The visual image in the form of photographs, motion pictures, posters, and combat art, was put to the greatest use up to that time in World War I. Uses for propaganda, fundraising, military operations, boosting morale, and recording history were promoted in an extremely organized and efficient manner. The military censored pictures as well as words for propaganda purposes and some action shots from the frontline trenches were occasionally posed. However, as the Chief Signal Officer put it, "The photograph preserves a faithful reproduction of events and thus gives to military history a quality of exactness that never before was able to be incorporated in it. What would the world not give for similar . . . pictures of Washington's Army or Napoleon's campaigns?"[24]

# WORLD WAR II

It is not surprising that the war that cost the lives of tens of millions of people and the equivalent of hundreds of billions of dollars and saw the wholesale destruction of hundreds of cities and towns and thousands of ships and planes also produced millions of photographs. The Second World

War employed thousands of military and civilian photographers to document combat and homefront activities in a global conflict that exceeded the vast scale of death and destruction associated with World War I.

All of the armed forces of the United States organized photographic coverage of every theater of war. The Army, Navy, Marine Corps, and Coast Guard documented their activities from training to combat to victory.* Other wartime government agencies such as the Office of War Information also took and acquired photos depicting homefront activities. They documented war production, women war workers, and rationing; and they assembled pictures of American life to send abroad.

Perhaps more well known to the American public is the wartime photography of *LIFE* magazine. *LIFE* claimed to have deployed more photographers and artists during World War II than all of the newspapers of the United States combined.[25] Most of the well-known war photographers worked for *LIFE*. Since this war was less restrictive than World War I as far as access for civilian photographers, there were cameramen representing other newspapers and magazines, the major wire services, news photo agencies, and newsreel companies in all areas of combat.

Photographers were generally fearless in pursuing their missions. Both military and civilian lensmen were also soldiers and their equipment included rifles and grenades in addition to cameras and film. Many were killed, wounded, or taken prisoner. "Combat photographers were among the first to leap ashore as invasion barges scraped the shell-scorched beaches of enemy-held territory from Africa to Borneo, from Sicily to Normandy, from Guadalcanal to Okinawa. Their nerve under fire, their technical skill and their picture sense combined have produced an outstanding pictorial record of this war — a record that is packed with dramatic action, for the combat cameramen moved the grime and fury of battle right into the front pages of the nation's press."[26]

## Army

The Signal Corps was again in charge of all U.S. Army photography, and employed thousands of still and motion picture photographers. The Army Pictorial Service (APS) administered all photographic matters for the Signal

*Air Force photography for World War II and later conflicts is not discussed because most of these records are not in the National Archives.*

Photo 868

Corps. Its chief branches in the United States were the Signal Corps Photographic Center (SCPC) in Astoria, NY, and the Signal Corps Photographic Laboratory (SCPL) in Washington, DC. The SCPC was responsible for training combat photographers at its Photographic School, and for photographic research and development at its Pictorial Engineering and Research Laboratory (PERL). The SCPC trained a great variety of specialists besides photographers, among them camera repairmen, lab technicians, editors, and photo librarians.

The photographic activities of the Signal Corps suffered from some administrative confusion and lack of cooperation from Washington during the first half of the war. There had been almost no prewar planning for photography and few people understood the photographic responsibilities of the Signal Corps. All parts of the War Department expected different things: the Bureau of Public Relations wanted dramatic pictures for public release; training officers wanted visual aids; field staff needed tactical photos for immediate strategic uses.

The photographic services of the Signal Corps amounted to only 3 percent of its total activity, but were responsible for the majority of favorable comment.[27] While motion picture footage got more attention, still pictures filled other needs—identification, detailed study, a permanent record, and publication in the press.

Occasional complaints that pictures from the field were not dramatic enough ignored the reality of the war. "The truth was that the stark actuality of the battle front was seldom photogenic. Except for landings . . . the most striking feature of the battlefield is its emptiness."[28] During the last 2 years of the war, better organization of Signal Corps photo units made it easier to cover the war on all fronts. Combat experience and better training also helped to improve the quality of U.S. Army photography.

Shortages of photographic supplies and APS Still Picture Library personnel also led to more editing of the hundreds of thousands of pictures received. A picture selected for retention had to meet a high standard for its strategic, tactical, training, intelligence, information, or historical value. During the last 2 years of the war, over 10,000 combat photos arrived at the picture library each month. By the end of the war, the library's holdings amounted to more than 500,000 images. Signal Corps photos accounted for about one-half of all pictures published in the press and in books.[29]

The prestige of Signal Corps photography increased during the last half of the war. "Combat photographers served as the eyes of the public as well as of the Army."[30] At the end of the war, the true value of U.S. Army photography was recognized both within the military and by the American people.

## Navy

U.S. Navy photography had the dual responsibilities of providing aerial reconnaissance photographs for intelligence and tactical planning, especially in the Pacific, and ground photography, both in and out of combat. Modern naval war photography had grown out of the development of naval aviation, around the time of World War I. Aerial photography had developed early, with the Army Air Service first exercising that responsibility.

Navy photographic training was centered at the Naval School of Photography at Pensacola, FL. Eventually, naval photographers would be sent out to naval facilities, ships, and battle areas around the world. There were more than 5,000 people involved in naval photography during World War II. Photographers were stationed at naval training stations, navy bases, and naval air stations, in the United States and abroad. They served in Combat Photographic Units (CPUs), accompanied the fleets, and served on carriers, battleships, cruisers, and with aviation units. Naval photography headquarters was located at the Anacostia Naval Station in Washington, DC.

Perhaps the most well known of naval photographers were the members of Edward Steichen's unit. In 1941 Steichen was again eager to serve the war effort, as he had in World War I. He volunteered his services to the Army Air Forces, but was turned down. Soon after Pearl Harbor, he was approached by the Navy and he happily accepted their offer. He proposed to establish a small unit that would document naval aviation training and help in recruitment, an area in which the Navy was competing with the Air Forces for men to become pilots. Steichen was commissioned as Lieutenant Commander in the U.S. Naval Reserve. He staffed his unit with experienced photographers who were also commissioned as officers. They had great freedom to document training activities in the United States. Although he was already 62 years old, Steichen proceeded to work with great energy.

As the Navy moved into combat operations, Steichen's unit expanded its coverage to include all of naval aviation. He and his photographers were assigned to various task groups in the Atlantic and Pacific and also worked in Alaska, North Africa, Italy, and France. Steichen himself could not resist the

*Photo 759*

lure of action, and he signed on for duty with the U.S.S. *Lexington* in 1943. Steichen's photographers had unprecedented freedom of movement throughout the theaters of war.

In Washington, DC, Steichen supervised all of the processing of his unit's work. He insisted on the highest standards for developing film, making prints, and deciding which images would become part of the permanent files. His standards were high enough to meet the demands of *LIFE* magazine and other magazines and newspapers that were always willing to feature the excellent pictures their own photographers couldn't get.[31] The unit's still photos, and motion picture footage from the *Lexington,* were used in exhibits, books, movies, and newsreels during and after the war, and Steichen also made sure to include the work of other Navy, Marine, and Coast Guard photographers.

During the last 6 months of the war, Steichen was put in direct command of all Navy combat photography. He summed up his experience: "In the Navy I started with a handful of good photographers who became experts, not only in using a lens but in photographing with their hearts and minds. The influence of that handful spread to 4,000 Navy photographers. Not all were great photographers. But they all contributed to the story of the war. And there had never been anything like the photographic story of the last war."[32]

## Marine Corps

The Marine Corps, like the Coast Guard, was administratively part of the U.S. Navy. Photographic training took place at Pensacola. The Marines had only 430 still and motion picture cameramen on combat duty in the Pacific during the war.[33] Their photographic coverage is as graphic and comprehensive for that theater of war, however, as that of the Navy or the Signal Corps. Photographs of the island-hopping Pacific campaigns were of the utmost military importance. Both still and moving pictures proved invaluable in training and planning for future island operations.[34]

Among the more well-known U.S. Marine photographic sections was the unit attached to headquarters of the Second Marine Division. The officer in charge was former movie star Capt. Louis Hayward. He and his still and motion picture photographers went in with the first waves of Marines at Tarawa, along with other civilian news cameramen. According to Captain

Hayward's second in command, Gunner John F. Leopold, "We had split up the section to make sure photographers would be in every part of the convoy. It was the first time in the history of amphibious warfare that photographers had landed to take a beachhead with initial assault waves." [35] The fighting there was intense, as it would be throughout the Pacific over the next 2 years. Leopold described the experience: "Each man had his individual, spine-chilling experiences to report. I don't believe there ever was another group of men who had been so close to death so often in such a short time. They put down their cameras only when they had to use their weapons." [36]

## Coast Guard

Almost 200 photographers covered the war for the Coast Guard. Photographic operations were run by the Coast Guard's Public Relations Division (Public Information Division after June 1945). The public relations work of the Coast Guard "started from scratch and grew with the Service during the war until it had reached a scope and excellence that warranted the highest national recognition." [37]

The aims of the Coast Guard's photographic activities were to acquaint the public with the work of the Coast Guard, counter the idea that the Coast Guard was not involved in combat, build morale among Coast Guardsmen and their families, provide historical documentation, and increase recruitment. Coast Guard photography stressed the individual; pictures and stories of Coast Guardsmen were released to many hometown newspapers. In 1945 the Coast Guard Information Division was processing photos of 330 Coast Guardsmen per day, and sending a thousand pictures daily to over 300 newspapers. Photographers were encouraged to portray the individual man or event as symbolic or representative of a massive struggle. [38]

Cameramen of the Photographic Section served aboard Coast Guard ships around the world and they participated in all amphibious operations from North Africa, Italy, and France to the islands of the Pacific. Photographers accompanied Coast Guard transports and landing craft to the beaches with the first assault waves.

Photographic processing was done both in the field and at headquarters in Washington, DC. The latter operated 24 hours a day. At the end of the war, over 80,000 images were on file, and Coast Guard photos were being published on the front pages of newspapers across the United States. [39]

## Other Agencies

Many other government agencies contributed to the photographic documentation of World War II. Besides the Office of War Information, agencies that photographed the homefront included the Department of Agriculture, Women's Bureau, Federal Works Administration, Office of Civilian Defense, Forest Service, Office of Price Administration, and War Relocation Authority. Other parts of the military services, such as the Bureau of Ships, Bureau of Medicine and Surgery, Bureau of Naval Personnel, Bureau of Aeronautics, Air Transport Command, and Office of Strategic Services (OSS), documented their particular areas of responsibility.

Additional photographic coverage of the end of the war and its consequences was undertaken by the U.S. Occupation Forces, Strategic Bombing Survey, Supreme Headquarters Allied Expeditionary Forces (SHAEF), American Commission for the Protection and Salvage of Artistic and Historic Monuments in War Areas (Roberts Commission), and U.S. Military Tribunal in Nuremberg.

## Technology

Needless to say, photographic technology had improved greatly in the period between the World Wars. Film had entirely replaced the glass plate negative. Color film was in use. Cameras were sturdier and camera controls were more advanced. Film, lenses, and shutter speeds were faster. The tripod was no longer necessary. The combat photographer could and did get into the thick of the fighting action.

The camera used most by military photographers was the Speed Graphic. It was a press-type camera that used 4- by 5-inch negatives in separate cut film or film packs of 8 or 12 exposures each. Since roll film for this camera did not exist, film packs were always used in combat. The Speed Graphic could be focused easily and quickly or could be preset for distance in action. In the hands of experienced lensmen, optimum results could be obtained under combat conditions.

The 35mm camera (the "miniature" Kodak) was not in general use in military photography, but was often supplied as a backup. Some military photographers preferred to use the Rolleiflex, a twin lens reflex which took

2¼- by 2¼-inch negatives. Some of Steichen's men, for example, shot that format.

The Speed Graphic camera still did not provide the speed of operation that modern cameras have. It and the other commercially obtained cameras were not designed for combat use. The Signal Corps' research lab had the responsibility for improving equipment that was used both for taking pictures and in the darkroom. The researchers were able to undertake many projects that resulted in short term solutions for better equipment and field darkroom facilities and greatly improved technical manuals. The other armed services had similar support groups. The most important developments, however, did not take place until the end of the war and would have to carry over to the next conflict.

Obtaining supplies was sometimes a problem. There was a tremendous demand for photographic chemicals, paper, and film, at the military photo labs both in the United States and in the theaters of operation. In fact, by late 1944, the supply needs for photographic materials far exceeded previous estimates. Only by strict controls and emergency retail purchases was crisis prevented.

Combat photographers employed color film for the first time during World War II. It was used primarily for motion picture footage, but many Kodachrome transparencies were taken, especially by U.S. Army and Navy photographers.

Combat photographers were fast, and trained to document all of the activities going on around them. It was not unusual for a photographer to go into combat with enough film for several hundred exposures. Generally, night shots were unwise and unappreciated in the field. Flash bulbs only served to draw enemy fire both on land and aboard ship.

Darkroom facilities were set up behind the front lines for fast processing of tactical photographs. Other work was sent to central photo labs run by the different services. Most often, the negatives were developed in the field or in facilities on Guam or in Pearl Harbor. Most negatives were then sent to Washington, DC, for printing and those that were not restricted were released to the press. The work of hundreds of civilian photojournalists covering the war was submitted for approval through a War Still Picture Pool.

As the war progressed, it was the goal of the military to reduce the time between the taking of the pictures and their release to the public and to staff for internal uses. Rapid air courier services, from the European and Pacific fronts, had been initiated by 1944. For example, "the first D-Day pictures were on General Marshall's desk within 24 hours."[40] The introduction of the wirephoto, the transmission of photographs by electronic means, made the process even faster. After much experimentation, the first wirephoto was radioed back to the United States from North Africa in 1943. Transmission stations were set up at central locations and at battlefronts in the theaters of operations in Europe and the Pacific. Some 600 photos were sent by wire from the Normandy invasion.[41] This technology hardly compares with the immediacy we now have from television, but the ability to see scenes of the heat of battle in newspapers or in newsreels within a day or two after the event quite amazed the World War II homefront audience.

## Censorship

Censorship during World War II was a necessity. Military security made it essential and prudent to restrict the release of a number of categories of photographs: pictures that showed aerial views of American military installations both at home and abroad; pictures that showed any other secret military activities such as those dealing with intelligence, preparations for invasion, etc.; photos that showed or included any advanced technology such as radar; photos that identified the location or strength of military units.

For reasons of privacy and out of respect for the families, photos of dead Americans were not released if faces were shown, or if death or injury was too graphically portrayed. On the other hand, bloody corpses of the enemy enjoyed no such restrictions.

Photographs that were of poor quality or of no documentary value tended not to be released. Pictures that were embarrassing to individuals or to the military, such as those relating to troublemakers and criminal behavior among servicemen, were restricted. Much medical photography was not released, for example, pictures of men suffering from shell shock.

During most of the war, however, censorship did not deprive the American public of information on the course of the war. Some failures, as well as the successes, were acknowledged in the media. Indeed the horrors of modern warfare tended more to inspire the war effort than to turn people against the excesses of war.

Often security or privacy requirements were met by censoring of photo captions rather than by restricting release of the photos themselves. A phrase such as "somewhere in Europe" could very well satisfy American security needs.

## Summary

Photography in World War II was closer to the action than in any previous American war. Photographs were used, along with motion pictures, written accounts, posters, and artwork, to fully document all activities of war. Thousands of people were involved. Hollywood filmmakers participated in photography throughout the services—Frank Capra and John Huston in the Army, Louis Hayward in the Marine Corps, and John Ford in the Office of Strategic Services. Americans received most of their visual information on the war from the military services.

"This had been the most photographed of all wars and the combat cameramen proved their mettle in compiling a monumental visual history that cannot be over-praised." "On land, in the air, on the sea, the combat cameramen, wearing the insignia of every service, have gone into the thick of battle with more concern for their equipment than their necks. Recognition of their deeds has been too slow and too infrequent, but no final appraisal of the war can well omit the men who brought back the visual record of fighting on every front. That there could not be more personal credit to individual photographers is to be regretted, but credit for over-all superb coverage of one of the biggest assignments in history can and should be emphasized." [42]

# KOREA AND VIETNAM

Changes in America's outlook on war influenced the photography of the wars in Korea and Vietnam. As the Korean War progressed, it became less popular, and public interest in war photographs from Korea diminished. However, the images taken were considered then, as now, to be of the highest quality.

Armed services cameramen were trained at the Signal Corps Photo Center at Fort Monmouth, NJ; the Photo Branch of the U.S. Navy and the Photo Section of the Marine Corps at Pensacola, FL; and the Air Force Photo School in Denver, CO. Many World War II military photographers had become noted photojournalists working for magazines or news services. Most had changed over to 35mm photography by that time. Ironically, they usually were using German cameras fitted with new Japanese lenses.

For the most part, the military still equipped its photographers with the Speed Graphic camera with its 4- by 5-inch negatives. This format was much more valuable for the detail necessary in the tactical uses of war photography as aerial and ground photographic reconnaissance still played a vital role during the Korean conflict. Improvements in cameras and other equipment that had been developed by the end of World War II went into use in Korea. Photographic facilities were considerably better than those of World War II, and there were more and improved portable photo labs.

All military pictures were released through the Pictorial Branch, Office of Public Information, Department of Defense, and censorship was similar to that of the previous war. Criticism was made that the reality of death on the battlefield was not adequately portrayed. Such photos were being taken, but the censors restricted their use.

By the time America became involved in Vietnam in the 1960s, both military and civilian photography had switched to 35mm or medium format cameras. With television reporting every favorable and unfavorable aspect of the war, censorship of images coming from the field was reduced. Military security was still the main consideration, but death and destruction, as well as the lives of America's fighting men, were openly portrayed and discussed in the nation's communications media.

Color film was as easy to obtain and use as black and white film. The 35mm roll film allowed photographers to shoot hundreds or thousands of exposures, whereas the old 4- by 5-inch cameras and film packs were much more limited. High film and shutter speeds and motorized film advance (as Beckett had predicted) allowed an event that may have lasted only a few seconds to be documented on film in dramatic detail, and with a great sense of presence, emotion, and immediacy.

Photography was one of the important elements in steering public opinion away from support of the war in Indochina. The gritty realism of combat as seen on television and in the newspapers and magazines every day (more of it from civilian photojournalists) had a chilling effect on the nation.

War photography had lost some innocence of spirit. While military and government photographers covered all aspects of the war, both positive and negative, civilian photographers no longer felt compelled to portray war in a positive light to build morale on the homefront. The American public was demanding the truth, the whole truth, about the wars it had to fight.

## CONCLUSION

Over the last two centuries the portrayal of war in pictures has had certain characteristics that have remained the same and others that have changed greatly. The romanticizing of war in the paintings, prints, and drawings of early conflicts presents an abundance of gallant deeds, heroic deaths, and memorable victories.

With the invention of photography and its use in wartime, reality became inescapable. The public was fascinated with scenes of troops, ships, cannons, battlefields, ruined buildings, and dead soldiers. Looking back to the Civil War, this change seems drastic, but a large body of combat art provided a balance between the old and new iconography of war in the 1860s.

From its beginnings, photography seemed well suited for depicting war from the soldier's point of view. Both government and private photographers have always taken pictures of everything from the front lines to behind the lines, from men under fire to rest and relaxation, including all the subjects covered in this catalog — recruitment, training, supply, entertainment, religion, medical activities, and more.

Looking through the existing collections of war photos, one can see the unedited, unglamorous view of war. By examining a larger body of images, a clearer picture of life on the homefront and on the battlefront emerges. One of the advantages of still pictures is the ability to examine the subject slowly, closely, in detail. It is the look in a man's eyes, or the harsh details of a landing on a beach on a Pacific island that speak to us eloquently now. The viewer can imagine being in the shoes of the photographer to some extent and can better imagine what the war was like at that moment in time and history.

Such are the characteristics of still photography. Obviously, motion pictures of wartime convey much more of a sense of reality, in portraying both the happy moments and the more intense aspects of war. Additionally, in recent times, color photography has added another dimension, a true-to-life element, to the documentation of war. As historical records, photographs convey much information and feeling by themselves. But the written word is always necessary to ensure accuracy of interpretation and to bring to life the heightened emotions that always accompany the unnatural state of being at war.

Technological advances in photography and the other pictorial arts have also changed the ways in which we see war, from the static views of the Civil War to the action-packed photos of World War II, Korea, and Vietnam. This change is not so much in how photographers interpret war as in their ability to capture it.

Certain themes will always remain in pictures of war — patriotism, death and destruction, and the individual. It may not be so obvious at times, but an examination of such a large body of photographs, posters, and works of art among the holdings of the National Archives certainly confirms that the American people's outlook on war and experience of war both shape and are shaped by the pictures they see.

We hope that the images in *War & Conflict,* individually and as a group, will inspire, teach, and remind; cause laughter and tears; and help us to remember the past as we ponder our future.

1. *Soldiers of the American Revolution: A Sketchbook* (Washington, DC: Center of Military History, 1976), [p. 4].

2. Gus MacDonald, *Camera: Victorian Eyewitness. A History of Photography: 1826–1913* (New York: Viking Press, 1980), p. 80.

3. Tim N. Gidal, *Modern Photojournalism: Origin and Evolution, 1910–1933* (New York: MacMillan, 1972), p. 6.

4. Robert Taft, *Photography and the American Scene* (1938; reprint, New York: Dover Publications, 1964), pp. 223–225, 484–485.

5. Frances Fralin, *The Indelible Image: Photographs of War — 1846 to the Present* (New York: Harry N. Abrams, 1985), p. 12.

6. Jorge Lewinski, *The Camera at War: A History of War Photography from 1848 to the Present Day* (New York: Simon and Schuster, 1978), p. 37.

7. Taft, *Photography,* pp. 419–420.

8. George Alfred Townsend, "Still Taking Pictures. Brady, the Grand Old Man of American Photography," *The World* (New York), 12 April 1891, p. 23.

9. MacDonald, *Camera: Victorian Eyewitness,* p. 82.

10. Gidal, *Modern Photojournalism,* p. 7.

11. Townsend, "Still Taking Pictures," p. 23.

12. Francis Trevelyan Miller, *Original Photographs Taken on the Battlefields During the Civil War of the United States By Mathew B. Brady and Alexander Gardner* (Hartford, CT: Edward B. Eaton, 1907), pp. 7–9.

13. Gidal, *Modern Photojournalism,* p. 8.

14. Marcus M. Wilkerson, *Public Opinion and the Spanish-American War. A Study in War Propaganda* (Baton Rouge, LA: Louisiana State University Press, 1932), pp. 5–8.

15. William C. Darrah, *The World of Stereographs* (Gettysburg, PA: William C. Darrah, 1977), p. 190.

16. Frank Freidel, *The Splendid Little War* (Boston: Little, Brown & Co., 1958), p. 309.

17. Ibid., p. 308.

18. C. Tucker Beckett, "Military Photography in Mexico," *The Camera* (November 1916): 599.

19. Ibid., pp. 608–609.

20. Gidal, *Modern Photojournalism,* p. 11.

21. *War Department Annual Reports, 1919. Report of the Chief Signal Officer,* 66th Cong., 2d sess., H. Doc. 426, p. 1221.

22. Frank Freidel, *Over There: The Story of America's First Great Overseas Crusade* (Boston: Little, Brown & Co., 1964), p. 375.

23. War Department, *Catalogue of Official A.E.F. Photographs Taken by the Signal Corps, U.S.A.* (Washington, DC: U.S. Government Printing Office, 1919), p. 3.

24. *War Department Annual Reports, 1919,* p. 1226.

25. David E. Scherman, ed., *LIFE Goes to War: A Picture History of World War II* (New York: Pocket Books, 1977), p. 4.

26. Tom Maloney and Edward Steichen, eds., *U.S. Camera 1946 — Victory Volume* (New York: U.S. Camera, 1945), pp. 370, 429.

27. George R. Thompson and Dixie R. Harris, *United States Army in World War II — The Technical Services, The Signal Corps: The Outcome* (Washington, DC: Office of the Chief of Military History, 1966), p. 540.

28. Ibid., pp. 569–570.

29. Ibid., pp. 563–565.

30. Ibid., p. 579.

31. Christopher Phillips, *Steichen at War* (New York: Harry N. Abrams, 1981), pp. 43–45.

32. Ibid., p. 54.

33. Maloney and Steichen, eds., *U.S. Camera 1946,* p. 429.

34. S.Sgt. Dick Hannah, *Tarawa: The Toughest Battle in Marine Corps History* (New York: U.S. Camera, 1944), p. 97.

35. Ibid., p. 104.

36. Ibid., p. 110.

37. Malcolm F. Willoughby, *The U.S. Coast Guard in World War II* (Annapolis: U.S. Naval Institute, 1957), p. 32.

38. Ibid., pp. 32–33.

39. Ibid., p. 33.

40. Thompson and Harris, *U.S. Army in World War II,* p. 564.

41. Ibid., p. 565.

42. Maloney and Steichen, eds., *U.S. Camera 1946,* p. 370.

# CAPTIONS

Original captions are presented in this catalog in italics. Paraphrased captions, or those created when no original information was available, are in roman type. The captions for most of the pictures in *War & Conflict* were taken from the original prints or negatives in the National Archives Still Picture Branch. Further research was done to determine the artists and dates of the various works of art depicting wars fought prior to the invention or general use of photography.

In most cases, the original captions were relied upon for accuracy. However, the accuracy of all facts included in original caption information cannot be totally guaranteed. Indeed, sometimes almost identical photos are identified as being in different places. (See numbers 897 and 898, 1513 and 1514.) All dates were checked for accuracy. Photographer and artist credits were obtained from the original items, or from indexes, shelflists, or reliable published sources. Whenever possible, these identifications were based on primary source material. The staff of the Still Picture Branch generally does not undertake caption research for pictures, but leaves that task to the researcher. Many books have been published on Civil War photography, for example, which include dates, photographers, or locations that were not included in the branch's caption records.

Many captions had to be edited for length. Generally, names of individuals in groups were omitted, as were military divisions, companies, and battalions. Regiments were retained for identification of the units portrayed.

When names for a group have been included, they are listed left to right unless otherwise stated. Information in brackets has been added editorially to spell out abbreviations or to aid the reader in understanding the importance of the image. Occasional colloquial misspellings of words or places have been retained. Misspellings that were obvious errors have been corrected.

Determining the sources of some pictures required more research. Often photos that were originally taken by the armed forces were released by commercial photo agencies. Similarly, many prints among the records of civilian agencies also had a military origin. If this is the case, both sources have been given. For example, photos credited in this catalog to the Office of War Information (OWI) that were obtained from the military are annotated to that effect: "Army. (OWI).", and if the photographer is identified, "Pvt. John Smith, USN. (OWI)." Some other photos were obtained during or after the World Wars in exchanges with foreign governments. These are indicated as British, German, or Canadian Official.

Additional caption information accompanies the nonphotographic images. For posters, prints, drawings, and paintings, the artist is identified, as well as the printmaker, date of publication, and medium. If a poster is in color, that fact is so indicated. For photographs that were taken as stereo images, this is so stated in the caption.

# CAPTION FORMATS

## Artwork

1. Picture number
2. Title or caption (or both)
3. Location of event pictured (if not in original caption)
4. Date of event pictured (if not in original caption)
5. Medium of original
6. Artist or printmaker (or in some cases publisher)
7. Artist of original work from which a print was made
8. Date of original artwork or date of publication
9. Record group

*Example:*

**11.** *The Struggle at Concord Bridge.* April 1775. Copy of engraving by W. J. Edwards after Alonzo Chappel, ca. 1859. (Marine Corps)

## Posters

1. Picture number
2. Title
3. Date
4. Whether color original
5. Artist
6. Source
7. Record group

*Example:*

**429.** *Gee!! I Wish I Were A Man / I'd Join The Navy / Be a Man and Do It / United States Navy Recruiting Station.* 1917. Color poster by Howard Chandler Christy. Issued by Navy Publicity Bureau. (Office of Naval Records and Library)

## Photographs

1. Picture number
2. Title or caption (or both)
3. Location of event pictured (if not in original caption)
4. Date
5. Photographer
6. Record Group

*Example:*

**1179.** *Marines storm Tarawa. Gilbert Islands.* November 1943. WO Obie Newcomb, Jr. (Marine Corps.)

# HOW TO ORDER REPRODUCTIONS

Reproductions of the pictures in this catalog can be obtained from the National Archives. To the best of our knowledge, all of the images are in the public domain and there are no restrictions on their use. Extensive research was undertaken to determine the copyright status of all privately produced pictures, and Copyright Office records indicate that those reproduced here are no longer under copyright protection.

All requests for copies should be sent to the National Archives, Still Picture Branch (NNSP), Washington, DC 20408. Please cite the catalog, *War & Conflict,* and the picture number, 1 through 1522. Prints, negatives, or slides can be ordered in various sizes. All items are black and white, except that copies of some posters can be obtained in color as well. This latter option is indicated in the caption. Ordering instructions and price lists will be sent in response to each request. All orders must be prepaid.

# ABBREVIATIONS USED

| | | | | |
|---|---|---|---|---|
| AAA | Anti Aircraft Artillery | | Lt. Col. | Lieutenant Colonel |
| Adm. | Admiral | | Maj. | Major |
| (Army) | Army Signal Corps | | Maj. Gen. | Major General |
| Bn. | Battalion | | M.Sgt. | Master Sergeant |
| Brig. Gen. | Brigadier General | | OWI | Office of War Information |
| Btry. | Battery | | Pfc. | Private First Class |
| Capt. | Captain | | PH1. | Photographer's Mate, First Class |
| Cav. | Cavalry | | PhoM3c. | Photographer's Mate, Third (or other) Class |
| Co. | Company | | Pvt. | Private |
| Col. | Colonel | | Q.M.Sgt. | Quartermaster Sergeant |
| Comdr. | Commander | | Regt. | Regiment |
| CPhoM. | Chief Photographer's Mate | | S.A.T.C. | Students' Army Training Corps |
| Cpl. | Corporal | | Sfc. | Sergeant First Class |
| Div. | Division | | Sgt. | Sergeant |
| Engr. | Engineer | | SP/5 | Specialist, Fifth Class |
| Ens. | Ensign | | Sp3c. | Specialist, Third (or other) Class |
| F.A. | Field Artillery | | S.Sgt. | Staff Sergeant |
| 1st Lt. | First Lieutenant | | T4c. | Technician, Fourth (or other) Class |
| Gen. | General | | T.Sgt. | Technical Sergeant |
| IFS | International Film Service | | USA | U.S. Army |
| Inf. | Infantry | | USIA | U.S. Information Agency |
| INP | International News Photos | | USMC | U.S. Marine Corps |
| JUSPAO | Joint United States Public Affairs Office | | USN | U.S. Navy |
| Lt. | Lieutenant | | USNR | U.S. Navy Reserve |
| Lt. Gen. | Lieutenant General | | WO | Warrant Officer |
| Lt. Comdr. | Lieutenant Commander | | WRA | War Relocation Authority |

*GENERAL ORDERS*
*Headquarters, at the Gulph, December 17, 1777.*

*The Commander in Chief with the highest satisfaction expresses his thanks to the officers and soldiers for the fortitude and patience with which they have sustained the fatigues of the Campaign. Altho' in some instances we unfortunately failed, yet upon the whole Heaven hath smiled on our Arms and crowned them with signal success; and we may upon the best grounds conclude, that by a spirited continuance of the measures necessary for our defence we shall finally obtain the end of our Warfare, Independence, Liberty and Peace.*

GEN. GEORGE WASHINGTON

John C. Fitzpatrick, ed., *The Writings of George Washington* (Washington, DC: U.S. Government Printing Office, 1933), vol. 10, p. 167.

The origins of the American Revolution lie in the repressive measures taken by the British in the 1760s and 1770s in their American colonies. Although battles were fought before 1776, the signing of the Declaration of Independence is commemorated as the major step toward self-government. The armed struggle of 6 years ended with the British surrender at Yorktown in 1781, and its goal of independence from Britain reached a symbolic fulfillment in George Washington's triumphant entry into New York City in 1783, after the last foreign troops left the new United States of America.

*Opposite: Photo 10*

# BEGINNINGS

*Photographs 1–8*

**1.** *Patrick Henry Addressing the Virginia Assembly.* 1765. Engraving attributed to H. B. Hall after Alonzo Chappel, published 1867. (OWI)

**2.** *Boston Massacre, March 5, 1770.* Copy of chromolithograph by John Bufford after William L. Champney, ca. 1856. (Work Projects Administration)

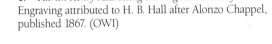

**3.** *The Destruction of Tea at Boston Harbor.* 1773. Copy of lithograph by Sarony & Major, 1846. (George Washington Bicentennial Commission)

**4.** *The Bostonians in Distress.* Copy of mezzotint attributed to Philip Dawe, 1774. (George Washington Bicentennial Commission)

**5.** *The Bostonian's Paying the Excise-Man, or Tarring & Feathering.* Copy of mezzotint attributed to Philip Dawe, 1774. (George Washington Bicentennial Commission)

**6.** *The able Doctor, or America Swallowing the Bitter Draught.* Illustrates the aftermath of the Boston Tea Party — the Boston Port Bill and the closing of the port. Copy of engraving by Paul Revere, June 1774. (OWI)

**7.** *First Prayer in Congress, September 1774, in Carpenters Hall, Philadelphia, Pa.* Copy of print by H. B. Hall after T. H. Matteson. (George Washington Bicentennial Commission)

**8.** *Paul Revere's Ride.* 1775. Copy of illustration by Modern Enterprises, ca. 1942. (OWI)

# FIGHT FOR A NEW NATION

*Photographs 9–42*

**9.** *The First Blow for Liberty.* Battle of Lexington, April 1775. Copy of print by A. H. Ritchie after F.O.C. Darley. (National Archives Gift Collection)

**10.** *Battle of Lexington.* April 19, 1775. Copy of print by John Baker, 1832. (George Washington Bicentennial Commission)

**11.** *The Struggle at Concord Bridge.* April 1775. Copy of engraving by W. J. Edwards after Alonzo Chappel, ca. 1859. (Marine Corps)

**12.** *Ethan Allen and Capt. de la Place.* May 1775. The capture of Fort Ticonderoga, NY. Copy of engraving after Alonzo Chappel. (Army)

**13.** *Genl. Putnam Leaving his Plow for the Defence of his Country.* 1775. Copy of lithograph. (George Washington Bicentennial Commission)

**14.** *The Battle of Bunker's Hill, near Boston.* June 1775. Copy of engraving by James Mitan after John Trumbull, published 1808. (George Washington Bicentennial Commission)

**15.** *View of The Attack on Bunker's Hill, with the Burning of Charles Town, June 17, 1775.* Copy of engraving by Lodge after Millar, ca. 1775–80. (George Washington Bicentennial Commission)

**16.** *Washington Taking Command of the American Army, at Cambridge, Mass. July 3rd, 1775.* Copy of lithograph by Currier & Ives, 1876. (George Washington Bicentennial Commission)

**17.** *The Death of General Montgomery at Quebec.* 1775. Copy of engraving by W. Ketterlinus after John Trumbull, published 1808. (George Washington Bicentennial Commission)

**18.** *Washington's First Successes at Boston.* 1776. Copy of lithograph by Turgis. (George Washington Bicentennial Commission)

**19.** *Drafting the Declaration of Independence. The Committee — Franklin, Jefferson, Adams, Livingston and Sherman.* 1776. Copy of engraving after Alonzo Chappel. (Bureau of Public Roads)

**20.** *The Declaration of Independence.* 1776. Copy of painting by John Trumbull, 1817–18. (George Washington Bicentennial Commission)

**21.** *Reading of the Declaration of Independence from the East balcony of the Old State House, Boston, Mass. July 18, 1776.* Copy of artwork. (George Washington Bicentennial Commission)

**22.** Betsy Ross making the first flag, 1776 (according to legend). Copy of painting attributed to Frank McKernan. (Army)

**23.** Raising the first flag at Independence Hall, Philadelphia, ca. 1776–77. Copy of painting by Clyde O. DeLand. (OWI)

**24.** *Spirit of '76.* Copy of painting by Archibald M. Willard, 1876. (George Washington Bicentennial Commission)

**25.** *Provincial Company, New York Artillery. Captain Alexander Hamilton 1776.* Watercolor by D.W.C. Falls, 1923. (U.S. Regular Army Mobile Units)

**26.** *Don't Tread On Me.* Believed to be the first flag of the Marines and of the Continental Navy. This coiled snake was painted on the drums of the early Marines. Copy of artwork. (Marine Corps)

**27.** *Washington and his Generals.* Copy of print by A. H. Ritchie, ca. 1870. (George Washington Bicentennial Commission)

**28.** *Washington's Retreat at Long Island.* August 1776. Copy of engraving by J. C. Armytage after Wageman, published ca. 1860. (George Washington Bicentennial Commission)

**29.** *Washington Crossing the Delaware.* December 1776. Copy from painting by Emanuel Leutze, 1851. (Commission of Fine Arts)

**30.** *Washington at the Battle of Trenton.* December 1776. Copy of engraving by Illman Brothers after E. L. Henry, ca. 1870. (George Washington Bicentennial Commission)

**31.** *Surrender of the Hessian Troops to General Washington, after The Battle of Trenton.* December 1776. Copy of lithograph, 1850. (George Washington Bicentennial Commission)

**32.** *Washington at Princeton Jany. 3rd, 1777.* Copy of lithograph by D. McLellan, 1853. (George Washington Bicentennial Commission)

**33.** *The Surrender of General Burgoyne at Saratoga.* October 1777. Copy of painting by John Trumbull, 1820–21. (Dept. of Agriculture)

**34.** *The Prayer at Valley Forge.* Gen. George Washington, winter 1777–78. Copy of engraving by John C. McRae after Henry Brueckner, published 1866. (George Washington Bicentennial Commission)

**35.** *General George Washington and a Committee of Congress at Valley Forge.* Winter 1777–78. Copy of engraving after W. H. Powell, published 1866. (George Washington Bicentennial Commission)

**36.** *Valley Forge — Washington & Lafayette.* Winter 1777–78. Copy of engraving by H. B. Hall after Alonzo Chappel. (George Washington Bicentennial Commission)

**37.** *Molly Pitcher at the Battle of Monmouth.* June 1778. Copy of engraving by J. C. Armytage after Alonzo Chappel. (George Washington Bicentennial Commission)

**38.** *Clark's march against Vincennes across the Wabash through wilderness and flood.* George Rogers Clark, February 1779. Copy of painting by Ezra Winter, ca. 1933–34. (Commission of Fine Arts)

**39.** *Clark's attack on Fort Sackville, Vincennes.* February 1779. Copy of painting by Ezra Winter, ca. 1933–34. (Commission of Fine Arts)

**40.** *The Unfortunate Death of Major Andre (Adjutant General to the English Army) at Head Quarters in New York, Octr. 1. 1780, who was found within the American Lines in the character of a Spy.* Copy of engraving by John Goldar after Hamilton, 1783. (OWI)

**41.** *Battle of Camden — Death of De Kalb.* August 1780. Copy of engraving after Alonzo Chappel. (George Washington Bicentennial Commission)

**42.** *Col.* [William Augustine] *Washington at the Battle of Cowpens.* January 1781. Copy of print by S. H. Gimber. (George Washington Bicentennial Commission)

# NAVY

*Photographs 43–49*

**43.** *U.S.S.* Alfred. *The first battleship ever owned by the United States of America, commissioned at Philadelphia, Pennsylvania, December 23, 1775, Lieutenant John Paul Jones commanding.* Copy of artwork by Harry W. Carpenter, 1920. (Bureau of Ships)

**44.** *Commodore Hopkins, Commander in Chief of the American Fleet.* Copy of mezzotint, 1776. (George Washington Bicentennial Commission)

**45.** *Paul Jones.* Portrait of John Paul Jones. Copy of mezzotint after C. J. Notté, ca. 1780s. (George Washington Bicentennial Commission)

**46.** *Paul Jones the Pirate.* Caricature of John Paul Jones. Copy of engraving, ca. 1779. (OWI)

**47.** The *Bonhomme Richard,* 1779. Copy of artwork by F. Muller. (Bureau of Ships)

**48.** *Action between the* Bon Homme Richard *and Serapis off Flamborough Head, England, on 23 September 1779.* Copy of painting attributed to William Strickland. (Marine Corps)

**49.** *The hand-to-hand fight on the deck of the* Serapis. From the battle of the American ship *Bonhomme Richard* with the British *Serapis,* September 1779. Copy of engraving. (Marine Corps)

# VICTORY

*Photographs 50–56*

**50.** *Surrender of Cornwallis.* October 1781. Copy of painting by John Trumbull, 1819–20. (Dept. of Agriculture)

**51.** *Surrender of Cornwallis at Yorktown, Virginia, October 19, 1781, by which over 7,000 British and Hessians became prisoners.* Copy of lithograph by James Baillie, ca. 1845. (George Washington Bicentennial Commission)

**52.** *The Peace Ball at Fredericksburg, Va. held at the Rising Sun Tavern after the surrender at Yorktown.* November 1781. Copy of painting by Jennie Brownscombe, ca. 1895–97. (George Washington Bicentennial Commission)

**53.** *Triumph of Patriotism.* George Washington entering New York, 1783. Copy of print by A. H. Ritchie after F.O.C. Darley. (George Washington Bicentennial Commission)

**54.** *Washington's Farewell to His Officers.* 1783. Copy of engraving by Phillibrown after Alonzo Chappel. (George Washington Bicentennial Commission)

# PERSONALITIES

*Photographs 57–69*

**55.** *Gen. Washington Resigning his Commission to Congress. Annapolis, Md. Dec. 23d, 1783.* Copy of painting by John Trumbull, 1822–24. (Dept. of Agriculture)

**56.** George Washington. Copy of painting by Gilbert Stuart. (George Washington Bicentennial Commission)

**57.** Portrait of Gen. Nathanael Greene. Copy of mezzotint by Valentine Green, executed by J. Brown after Charles Willson Peale, 1785. (George Washington Bicentennial Commission)

**58.** *Liberté. Conclusion de la Campagne de 1781 en Virginie. To his Excellency General George Washington this Likeness of his friend, the Marquess de la Fayette, is humbly dedicated.* Copy of engraving by Noël le Mire, 1780s. (Bureau of Ships)

**59.** Baron Frederick Wilhelm von Steuben. Copy of painting by Ralph Earl. (George Washington Bicentennial Commission)

**60.** *Thaddeus Kosciuszko.* Copy of engraving by H. B. Hall after Joseph Grassi. (George Washington Bicentennial Commission)

**61.** *Count Casimir Pulaski.* Copy of engraving by H. B. Hall, published 1871. (Army)

**62.** Benedict Arnold. Copy of engraving by H. B. Hall after John Trumbull, published 1879. (George Washington Bicentennial Commission)

**63.** Thomas Paine. Copy of engraving after George Romney. (Army)

**64.** Samuel Adams. Copy of engraving after Alonzo Chappel, published 1858. (George Washington Bicentennial Commission)

**65.** Benjamin Franklin. Copy of painting by Joseph Duplessis, ca. 1794–1802. (George Washington Bicentennial Commission)

**66.** Thomas Jefferson. Copy of painting by Rembrandt Peale, ca. 1805. (OWI)

**67.** John Hancock. Copy of painting by John Singleton Copley, ca. 1770–72. (George Washington Bicentennial Commission)

**68.** John Adams. Copy of painting by or after John Singleton Copley, ca. 1783. (George Washington Bicentennial Commission)

**69.** *Washington Receiving a Salute on the Field of Trenton.*
1776. Copy of print by William Holl after John Faed,
published ca. 1860s. (George Washington Bicentennial
Commission)

# AMERICA GROWS

*Under a brilliant sun, I entered the city at the head of the cavalry, cheered by Worth's division of regulars drawn up in the order of battle in the Alameda, and by Quitman's division of volunteers in the grand plaza between the National Palace and the Cathedral — all the bands playing, in succession, Hail Columbia, Washington's March, Yankee Doodle, Hail to the Chief, etc. Even the inhabitants catching the enthusiasm of the moment, filled the windows and lined the parapets, cheering the cavalcade as it passed at the gallop.*

GEN. WINFIELD SCOTT
Mexico City
September 1847

Winfield Scott, *Memoirs of Lieut.-General Scott, LL.D.* (New York: Sheldon & Co., 1864), vol. 2, p. 535.

Even as a young nation, the United States refused to be intimidated by foreign powers. The illegal seizure of American ships and citizens led to military confrontations with France, Tripoli, and again with Great Britain, all within three decades of gaining independence. Victories in these wars were factors in the rise of nationalism and the concept of Manifest Destiny that resulted in the Mexican War in the 1840s. That military success added Texas and California to the territory of the United States.

*Opposite: Photo 104*

# FRENCH NAVAL WAR

*Photographs 70–72*

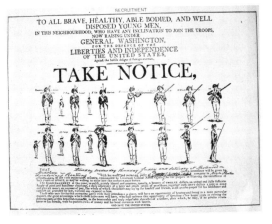

**70.** Army recruiting notice used during the period of threatened war with France, 1799. Copy of engraving by B. Jones. (OWI)

**71.** Battle between U.S. frigate *Constellation* and French frigate *L'Insurgente,* in the Naval War with France, February 1799. Copy of artwork by Hoff. (Bureau of Ships)

# TRIPOLITAN WAR

*Photographs 73–78*

**72.** *Capture of the French Privateer* Sandwich *by armed Marines on the Sloop* Sally, *from the U.S. Frigate* Constitution, *Puerto Plata Harbor, Santo Domingo, 11 May 1800.* Copy of painting by Philip Colprit, 1960. (Marine Corps)

**73.** *Decatur's Conflict with the Algerine at Tripoli. Reuben James Interposing His Head to Save the Life of His Commander.* August 1804. Copy of engraving after Alonzo Chappel. (Bureau of Public Roads)

**74.** *Blowing Up of the Fire Ship* Intrepid *commanded by Capt. Somers in the Harbour of Tripoli on the night of 4th Sepr. 1804. This . . . shows her blowing up with Somers and her entire crew.* Copy of engraving, ca. 1810. (OWI)

**75.** *Burning of the Frigate* Philadelphia *in the Harbour of Tripoli, 16th Feb. 1804, by 70 Gallant Tars of Columbia commanded by Lieut. Decatur.* Copy of aquatint by F. Kearny, ca. 1804–8. (OWI)

**76.** *Lieutenant Stephen Decatur and Midshipman Thomas Macdonough boarding a Tripolitan gun boat during attack on Tripoli by the squadron under Commodore Preble on August 3, 1804.* Copy of painting by Dennis Malone Carter. (OWI)

**77.** Enterprise *capturing Tripolitan Corsair.* 1801. Copy of artwork by Hoff. (Bureau of Ships)

**78.** *After a bombardment of Tripoli, a landing party with Lt. O'Bannon of the Marines in command hauled down the Tripolitan flag and hoisted Old Glory for the first time over a fort in the old world.* April 27, 1805. Copy of artwork by Capolino. (Marine Corps)

# WAR OF 1812

*Photographs 79–95*

**79.** *The Capture of H.B.M. Sloop of War* Frolic, *Capn. Whinyates, by the U.S. Sloop of War* Wasp, *Capn. Jab. Jones, on the 18th of Octr.* 1812. Copy of print by F. Kearny from sketch by Lt. Claxton. (George Washington Bicentennial Commission)

**80.** *Capture of the* Guerriere *by the* Constitution. August 1812. Copy of engraving by D. Kimberly after T. Birch. (Marine Corps)

**81.** *The* Java *in a Sinking state, set fire to, & Blowing up. The* Constitution *at a distance . . . repairing her Rigging &c. in the Evening of 29th Decr.* 1812. Copy of aquatint by N. Pocock, engraved by R. & D. Havell after sketch by Lt. Buchanan, 1814. (OWI)

**82.** *Perry's Victory on Lake Erie, Fought Sept. 10th, 1813.* Copy of lithograph by Napoleon Sarony after J. J. Barralet, published by N. Currier, ca. 1840s. (Army)

**83.** *Battle of Lake Erie.* September 1813. Oliver Hazard Perry, standing. Copy of engraving by Phillibrown after W. H. Powell, published 1858. (Marine Corps)

84. *Death of Captain Lawrence. "Don't Give Up the Ship."* June 1813. Copy of engraving by H. B. Hall after Alonzo Chappel, ca. 1856. (Army)

85. *Capture of Fort George. Col. Winfield Scott leading the attack.* July 1813. Copy of engraving after Alonzo Chappel, ca. 1850s. (Army)

86. *Col. Miller at the Battle of Chippewa.* July 1814. Copy of engraving by W. Ridgway after F.O.C. Darley, ca. 1860. (Army)

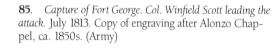

87. *Marines Aboard USS* Wasp *Engage HMS* Reindeer. June 1814. Copy of painting by Sgt. John Clymer. (Marine Corps)

88. *John Bull making a new Batch of Ships to send to the Lakes.* After Macdonough's victory over the British fleet on Lake Champlain, September 1814. Copy of cartoon engraving by William Charles, 1814. (Army)

89. *The Taking of the City of Washington . . . by the British Forces Under Major Genl. Ross on Aug. 24, 1814 . . . the public property destroyed amounted to thirty Million of Dollars.* Copy of engraving, 1814. (George Washington Bicentennial Commission)

90. *Ruins of the Capitol After the Fire.* 1814. Copy of print. (Commission of Fine Arts)

91. Battle of New Orleans, January 1815. Copy of lithograph by Kurz and Allison, published 1890. (Army)

92. *Bird's-Eye View of the Battle near New Orleans, January 8, 1815.* Copy of engraving from a sketch by Latour, Jackson's chief engineer. (Army)

93. *The Battle of New Orleans.* January 1815. Copy of engraving by H. B. Hall after W. Momberger. (Army)

94. *Gen. Andrew Jackson. The Hero of New Orleans.* 1815. Copy of lithograph by James Baillie, ca. 1840s. (OWI)

95. *The signing of the Treaty of Ghent with Great Britain, December 24, 1814.* Copy from painting by A. Forestier. (Army)

# MEXICAN WAR

*Photographs 96–108*

**96.** Bezaleel W. Armstrong. Graduated U.S. Military Academy and Bvt. 2d Lt., 1st Dragoons, 1845; 2d Lt., 2d Dragoons, 1846; served in Mexican War at Vera Cruz and Mexico City, 1847–48; died 1849, aged 26. Copy of daguerreotype, ca. 1846. (Army)

**97.** *U.S. Marines and Sailors Under the Command of Commander James B. Montgomery Landed at Yerba Buena and Raised the American Flag July 9, 1846.* Copy of painting by Capolino. (Marine Corps)

**98.** *Battle of Resaca de la Palma.* May 1846. Copy of lithograph by James Baillie, 1846. (Army)

**99.** *Genl. Taylor at the Battle of Resaca de la Palma. Capt. May receiving his orders to Charge the Mexican Batteries, May 9th, 1846.* Copy of lithograph by Nathaniel Currier, ca. 1846. (Army)

**100.** *Storming of Independence Hill at the Battle of Monterey.* September 1846. Copy of lithograph by Kelloggs & Thayer, ca. 1847. (Army)

**101.** *Storming of Monterey. Attack on the Bishop's Palace.* September 1846. Copy of lithograph by Kelloggs & Thayer, ca. 1847. (Army)

**102.** *Major General Winfield Scott at Vera Cruz.* March 25, 1847. Copy of lithograph by Nathaniel Currier, 1847. (Army)

**103.** *Battle of Churubusco — Capture of the Tête de Pont.* August 1847. Copy of engraving by Phillibrown after Alonzo Chappel, published 1859. (Army)

**104.** *Battle of Molino del Rey, Fought September 8th 1847. Blowing up the Foundry by the Victorious American Army under General Worth.* Copy of lithograph by James Baillie, 1848. (Army)

**105.** *Battle of Chapultepec.* September 1847. Copy of print by J. Duthie after H. Billings. (Army)

**106.** *General Quitman Entering Mexico City With Battalion of Marines.* September 1847. Copy of painting by Sgt. Tom Lovell. (Marine Corps)

**107.** *Scott's Triumphal Entry Into Mexico.* September 1847. Copy of engraving after Carl Nebel. (OWI)

**108.** President James K. Polk, ca. 1840s. Copy of engraving by H. W. Smith. (OWI)

# CIVIL WAR

*As mementoes of the fearful struggle through which the country has just passed, it is confidently hoped that the following pages will possess an enduring interest. Localities that would scarcely have been known, and probably never remembered, save in their immediate vicinity, have become celebrated, and will ever be held sacred as memorable fields, where thousands of brave men yielded up their lives a willing sacrifice for the cause they had espoused.*

*Verbal representations of such places, or scenes, may or may not have the merit of accuracy; but photographic presentments of them will be accepted by posterity with an undoubting faith. . . .*

ALEXANDER GARDNER
1866

Alexander Gardner, *Gardner's Photographic Sketch Book of the Civil War* (1866; reprint, New York: Dover Publications, 1978), unpaginated.

The Civil War represented a loss of innocence for the United States as the conflict tore apart the nation, its Constitution, states, and families. While remembrance of the War Between the States has been one of nostalgia and noble sentimental values, the realities were actually of great suffering and an enormous toll of death and destruction. As the last major conflict fought on American soil, the Civil War resulted in social upheaval, the beginnings of freedom for blacks, and eventual reaffirmation of the values stated by the Founding Fathers in the Constitution.

*Opposite: Photo 188*

# BACKGROUND: SLAVERY & ABOLITIONISM

*Photographs 109–116*

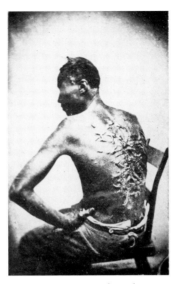

**109.** *Overseer Artayou Carrier whipped me. I was two months in bed sore from the whipping. My master come after I was whipped; he discharged the overseer. The very words of poor Peter, taken as he sat for his picture. Baton Rouge, La., April 2, 1863.* (War Dept.)

**110.** *Slave Pen of Price, Birch and Co. Alexandria, Va.* Capt. Andrew J. Russell. Mathew Brady Collection. (Army)

**111.** *Slave Pen — Interior.* Alexandria, VA. (Army)

**112.** *Contraband School, or Freedman's Village, Arlington, Va.* Mathew Brady Collection. (Army)

**113.** Frederick Douglass, ca. 1879. George K. Warren. (National Archives Gift Collection)

114.  *John Brown (before acquisition of beard which typifies him as the stormy prophet of emancipation).* Ca. 1850. Copy of daguerreotype. (Marine Corps)

115.  *The Tragic Prelude.* John Brown. Copy of mural by John Steuart Curry in the State Capitol in Topeka, KS, ca. 1937–42. (National Park Service)

116.  Harriet Beecher Stowe, ca. 1870s–80s. (OWI)

# LEADERS

*Photographs 117–134*

117.  President Abraham Lincoln, 1864. Mathew Brady Collection. (Army)

118.  Maj. Allan Pinkerton, President Lincoln, and Gen. John A. McClernand, Antietam, MD, October 1862. Alexander Gardner. Mathew Brady Collection. (Army)

**119.** *President Lincoln on the Battle-Field of Antietam.* October 1862. Alexander Gardner. (War Dept.)

**120.** Crowd at Gettysburg, November 19, 1863. Mathew Brady Collection. (Army)

**121.** Crowd at Gettysburg, November 19, 1863. Lincoln in center. Mathew Brady Collection. (Army)

**122.** *Gen. Ulysses S. Grant at Cold Harbor, Va.* 1864. Mathew Brady. Mathew Brady Collection. (Army)

**123.** General Grant's Council of War near Massaponax Church, VA, May 21, 1864. Grant is bending over the bench looking over General Meade's shoulder at a map. Timothy O'Sullivan. Stereo. (National Archives Gift Collection)

**124.** Gen. Philip H. Sheridan, ca. 1864. Mathew Brady Collection. (Army)

**125.** Gen. William T. Sherman, ca. 1864–65. Mathew Brady Collection. (Army)

**126.** *Maj. Gen. William T. Sherman, Commanding Military Division of the Mississippi, and his generals.* Ca. 1865. Mathew Brady Collection. (Army)

**127.** Gen. George B. McClellan, ca. 1863. Mathew Brady Collection. (Army)

**128.** Gen. Ambrose E. Burnside, ca. 1861. Mathew Brady Collection. (Army)

**129.** Adm. John A. Dahlgren and officers. Mathew Brady Collection. (Army)

**130.** Adm. David G. Farragut, ca. 1863. Mathew Brady Collection. (War Dept.)

**131.** Jefferson Davis, President of the Confederacy, ca. 1860. Mathew Brady Collection. (Army)

**132.** Gen. Robert E. Lee, C.S.A., 1865. Mathew Brady Collection. (Army)

**133.** Gen. "Stonewall" Jackson, C.S.A., 1863. George W. Minnes. Mathew Brady Collection. (Army)

**134.** Gen. "Jeb" Stuart, C.S.A., 1863. George S. Cook. (National Archives)

# TROOPS & OFFICERS

*Photographs 135–158*

**135.** *Cassius M. Clay Battalion Defending White House, April 1861.* Washington, DC. (National Archives)

**136.** *Edmund Ruffin. Fired the 1st shot in the Late War. Killed himself at close of War.* Ca. 1861. (Army)

**137.** *Recruiting in the New York City Hall Park in 1864.* Illustration from a sketch by George Law, published in *Frank Leslie's Illustrated Newspaper,* March 19, 1864. (OWI)

**138.** *Private of Fourth Michigan Infantry in his hickory shirt.* Mathew Brady Collection. (Army)

**139.** *Taylor — Drummer Boy, 78th Regt. U.S.C.I.* U.S. Colored Infantry. (War Dept.)

**140.** *Band, Fourth Michigan Infantry.* Mathew Brady Collection. (Army)

**141.** *Wounded Zouave.* Mathew Brady Collection. (Army)

**142.** *Soldiers' Winter Quarters.* "Pine Cottage." Mathew Brady Collection. (Army)

**143.** *Engineer Camp, 8th New York State Militia.* Mathew Brady Collection. (Army)

**144.** *A Fancy Group, Army of the Potomac.* Petersburg, VA, August 1864. David Knox. (War Dept.)

**145.** *In the trenches before Petersburg.* Mathew Brady Collection. (Army)

**146.** *Officers of 69th New York Infantry at Fort Corcoran, Va.* Mathew Brady Collection. (Army)

**147.** *Group of officers at headquarters.* Mathew Brady Collection. (Army)

**148.** *Infantry company on parade.* Mathew Brady Collection. (Army)

**149.** *Group of soldiers.* Mathew Brady Collection. (Army)

**150.** Flag of the Eighth Pennsylvania Infantry. Mathew Brady Collection. (Army)

**151.** *Infantry company on parade.* Mathew Brady Collection. (Army)

**152.** Soldiers of a New York Zouave regiment. Mathew Brady Collection. (Army)

**153.** Gen. Edward Ferrero and staff. (War Dept.)

**154.** Group of officers. Mathew Brady Collection. (Army)

**155.** *Twenty-sixth United States Colored Volunteer Infantry, massed. Camp William Penn, Pennsylvania.* (War Dept.)

**156.** *Infantry regiment in camp.* Probably 96th Pennsylvania Infantry at Camp Northumberland near Washington, DC, ca. 1861. Mathew Brady Collection. (Army)

**157.** *Grand Review, Washington, D.C., showing reviewing stand with General Grant, and President Johnson, and Cabinet. 1865.* Mathew Brady Collection. (Army)

**158.** *Parade, Pennsylvania Avenue, Lincoln's Time.* Washington, DC, ca. 1865. (Commission of Fine Arts)

# ARTILLERY, FORTS, FORTIFICATIONS

*Photographs 159–171*

**159.** *Interior view of Fort Sumter on the 14th April 1861, after its evacuation by Maj. Robert Anderson, 1st Arty. U.S.A. Comdg.* (Public Buildings Service)

**160.** *Making gabions, lines of investment, Petersburg, Va. 1865. Mathew Brady Collection.* (Army)

**161.** *Interior of Fort Sedgewick ("Fort Hell") near Petersburg.* Capt. Andrew J. Russell. April 1865. (National Archives)

**162.** *Inside of the Confederate lines, Petersburg, Va. 1865.* Mathew Brady Collection. (Army)

**163.** *Officers of Fifty-fifth Infantry at Fort Gaines, near Tenley, D.C.* Mathew Brady Collection. (Army)

**164.** *Rebel Fort (Now Federal No. 7 of new lines) Atlanta; looking towards Chattanooga R.R. (North). Battery M. 5th U.S. Artil'y with Gen. Sherman in background.* 1864. George N. Barnard. (War Dept.)

**165.** *The Siege of Yorktown, Va. Immense batteries of enormous guns and mortars were planted all along the line by the First Connecticut Heavy Artillery. This is a battery of 13-inch sea-coast mortars.* April 1862. Stereo. (National Archives Gift Collection)

**166.** *Railroad Mortar at Petersburg, Va., July 25, 1864. "The Dictator."* Capt. Andrew J. Russell. (National Archives)

**167.** *Rebel Battery, Pensacola.* Ca. 1861. Attributed to J. D. Edwards. (Corps of Engineers)

**168.** *Rebel Works in Front of Atlanta, Ga., No. 1. Confederate lines near Chattanooga Railroad, showing Potter's House.* 1864. George N. Barnard. (War Dept.)

**169.** *Barricades at Alexandria. Stockade built by Gen. Haupt, for the Protection of Government Property, enclosing Machine Shops and Yard of Orange & Alexandria Railroad.* Capt. Andrew J. Russell. Mathew Brady Collection. (Army)

170.  *Park of captured guns, Richmond, Virginia.* May 1865. Capt. Andrew J. Russell. Mathew Brady Collection. (Army)

171.  *View of Barracks No. 1.* or *View of Citadel Looking South-West.* Fort Morgan, AL, 1864. Moses & Piffet. (Corps of Engineers)

# BATTLE AREAS

*Photographs 172–179*

172.  *Refugees Leaving the Old Homestead. Union families persecuted by the Rebels would hastily gather up a little furniture, pile it on to an old wagon, and take up their march northward toward the land of freedom.* Stereo. (National Archives Gift Collection)

173.  *Antietam Bridge, Maryland.* September 1862. Alexander Gardner. (War Dept.)

**174.** *The John Ross House.* Ca. 1863–64. George N. Barnard. (War Dept.)

**175.** *Fredericksburg, from the river. Showing Confederate troops and bridge. Taken at a distance of one mile.* Ca. 1863. Mathew Brady Collection. (Army)

**176.** *Barlows' Knoll after first day's battle, Gettysburg, Pa., northwest of town. July 1, 1863.* (National Archives Gift Collection)

**177.** *View of a portion of the Gettysburg Battlefield.* Ca. 1863. Mathew Brady Collection. (Army)

**178.** *Part of the Gettysburg Battlefield.* Ca. 1863. Mathew Brady in center of photograph. Mathew Brady Collection. (Army)

**179.** *Breaking Camp.* Brandy Station, VA, May 1864. James Gardner. (War Dept.)

# Navy

*Photographs 180–199*

**180**.   Confederate naval recruiting poster, issued at New Berne, NC, 1863. (Naval Records Collection)

**181**.   *Battle between the* Monitor *and* Merrimac, *Hampton Roads, Va., March 9, 1862.* Copy of engraving by Evans after J. O. Davidson. (Army)

**182**.   *Naval Engagement in Hampton Roads.* Merrimac *and* Monitor. *March 1862.* Copy of print by J. Davies after C. Parsons, 1863. (National Archives)

**183**.   *The Original* Monitor *after her Fight with the Mer-rimac. Near the port-hole can be seen the dents made by the heavy steel-pointed shot from the guns of the Merrimac.* Hampton Roads, VA, July 1862. Stereo. (National Archives Gift Collection)

**184**.   *The Sinking of the* Cumberland *by the Iron Clad* Merrimac, *off Newport News, Va., March 8th, 1862.* Cumberland *went down with all her Flags flying: destroyed but not conquered.* Copy of lithograph by Currier & Ives, 1862. (Bureau of Ships)

**185.** Battle between the *Sassacus* and the *Albemarle,* May 1864. Copy of painting. (Bureau of Ships)

**186.** *First ironclad gunboat built in America. The Saint Louis,* ca. 1862. (War Dept.)

**187.** *Monitor: Gun squad on deck.* Probably the gunboat *Hunchback.* Mathew Brady Collection. (Army)

**188.** Deck of the gunboat *Hunchback* on the James River. Mathew Brady Collection. (Army)

**189.** Between decks on a transport. Mathew Brady Collection. (Army)

**190.** Officers of the *Kearsarge* on deck, ca. 1864. Mathew Brady Collection. (Army)

**191.** Crew of the monitor *Saugus* on the James River. Mathew Brady Collection. (Army)

**192.** Crew of the gunboat *Hunchback* on the James River. Mathew Brady Collection. (Army)

**193.** *Gunboat, altered from a ferryboat, on Pamunkey River.* Probably the *Commodore Perry*, ca. 1864–65. Mathew Brady Collection. (Army)

**194.** Gunboat *Commodore Barney.* Mathew Brady Collection. (Army)

**195.** Gunboat *Mendota* on James River, August 1864. Mathew Brady Collection. (Army)

**196.** *Arago*, June 28, 1864. (War Dept.)

**197.** *Torpedo Boat.* Charleston, 1865. Selmar Rush Seibert. (War Dept.)

**198.** *Deck of Monitor on James River.* 1864. Double-turreted monitor *Onondaga.* Mathew Brady Collection. (Army)

**199.** *U.S. Frigate* Pensacola, *off Alexandria, Va., in June, 1861.* Stereo. (National Archives Gift Collection)

# SUPPLY & SUPPORT

*Photographs 200–222*

**200.** *Magazine wharf, City Point, Virginia.* Mathew Brady Collection. (Army)

**201.** *City Point, view in 1864.* Mathew Brady Collection. (Army)

**202.** *Group of Negro laborers.* Mathew Brady Collection. (Army)

**203.** *U.S. Army Transport* Chattanooga, *built at Bridgeport, Alabama, by Captain Arthur Edwards, Quartermaster Dept., for service with the Army of the Cumberland.* Ca. 1863. (War Dept.)

**204.** Transport steamer *Missionary* on Tennessee River, ca. 1863. (War Dept.)

**205.** *Artillery, Gunners and Twenty Infantry, Crossing on Raft.* 1863. Capt. Andrew J. Russell. (Corps of Engineers)

**206.** *Expedients for Crossing Streams. A pair of small pontoons, designed to facilitate scouting operations. A boat can be made of these by running a pole through the loops, and then placing sticks across.* Ca. 1863. Capt. Andrew J. Russell. (Corps of Engineers)

**207.** *Lower pontoon bridge. Deep Bottom, James River.* Attributed to Capt. Andrew J. Russell. (War Dept.)

**208.** U.S. Military Railroad engine "W. H. Whiton." Mathew Brady Collection. (Army)

**209.** *Orange and Alexandria Railroad: Cars and military bridge.* Mathew Brady Collection. (Army)

**210.** *Roundhouse, Chattanooga Railroad, Atlanta.* 1864. George N. Barnard. (War Dept.)

**211.** *Post Corral, Chattanooga.* Ca. 1864. (War Dept.)

**212.** *Wagon Park.* Brandy Station, VA, May 1863. Timothy O'Sullivan. (War Dept.)

**213.** *Sutler's row, Chattanooga.* Ca. 1864. Mathew Brady Collection. (Army)

**214.** Mary Tippee or Tebe. Vivandere with Collis Zouaves, Gettysburg, ca. 1863. Attributed to Charles J. and Isaac G. Tyson. Tipton Collection. (National Park Service)

**215.** *Miss Clara Barton.* Mathew Brady Collection. (Army)

**216.** *Dr. Mary Walker.* Wearing Medal of Honor, ca. 1866. Mathew Brady Collection. (Army)

**217.** *Surgeons of Harewood Hospital, Washington, D.C.* Mathew Brady Collection. (Army)

**218.** *Hospital No. 15. Beaufort, S.C.* December 1864. (War Dept.)

**219.** *Hospital, interior view.* Probably Carver Hospital, near Washington, DC. Mathew Brady Collection. (Army)

**220.** *Amputation scene, general Hospital.* 1863. Attributed to Charles J. and Isaac C. Tyson. Tipton Collection. (National Park Service)

**221.** *Religious services in camp, Catholic.* Probably 69th New York State Militia. Mathew Brady Collection. (War Dept.)

# COMMUNICATIONS

*Photographs 223–231*

**222.** *Bomb-proof Restaurant on the Petersburg Line.* Who but a "Yank" would think of starting a "store" or restaurant on the line of battle where shot and shell are constantly falling? Ca. 1864–65. Stereo. (National Archives Gift Collection)

**223.** *Long Bridge, Lincoln's Time.* Washington, DC. Union troops guarding a bridge over the Potomac River to Virginia to prevent infiltration by Confederate spies. (Commission of Fine Arts)

**224.** *Cutting telegraph wire and connecting the ends, so that the point at which the connection is broken cannot be seen from the ground.* Ca. 1862–63. Capt. Andrew J. Russell. (Corps of Engineers)

**225.** *Signal Tower on Cobbs Hill, Appomattox River, Va.* (War Dept.)

**226.** *Signal Tower, Elk Mountain, overlooking Battle-field of Antietam.* September 1862. Timothy O'Sullivan. (War Dept.)

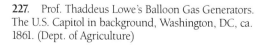

**227.** Prof. Thaddeus Lowe's Balloon Gas Generators. The U.S. Capitol in background, Washington, DC, ca. 1861. (Dept. of Agriculture)

**228.** *View of balloon ascension.* Ca. 1862. Mathew Brady Collection. (Army)

**229.** *View of balloon ascension.* Prof. Thaddeus Lowe observing the Battle of Seven Pines or Fair Oaks from his balloon "Intrepid" on the north side of the Chickahominy, 1862. Mathew Brady Collection. (Army)

**230**. *New York Herald wagon in the field.* Mathew Brady Collection. (Army)

**231**. *Army Picture Gallery.* Mathew Brady Collection. (Army)

# PRISONS & PRISONERS

*Photographs 232–238*

**232**. *Three "Johnnie Reb" prisoners captured at Gettysburg. There were hardly two suits alike in a whole regiment; however, "a man is a man for a' that." These "Johnnies" were royal good fighters.* 1863. Stereo. (National Archives Gift Collection)

**233.** *Camp scene — Confederate prisoners under guard.* Mathew Brady Collection. (Army)

**234.** *Drawing rations; view from main gate.* Andersonville Prison, GA, August 17, 1864. A. J. Riddle. (War Dept.)

**235.** *How they buried them.* Andersonville Prison, GA, August 17, 1864. A. J. Riddle. (War Dept)

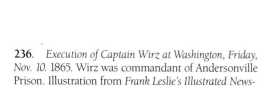

**236.** *Execution of Captain Wirz at Washington, Friday, Nov. 10.* 1865. Wirz was commandant of Andersonville Prison. Illustration from *Frank Leslie's Illustrated Newspaper,* Nov. 25, 1865. (National Archives)

**237.** *Military Prison, Jacksonville, Fla.* Photographed Dec. *11th, 1864.* (War Dept.)

**238.** Libby Prison, Richmond, May 1865. (War Dept)

# DEATH & DESTRUCTION

*Photographs 239–258*

**239.** *Mills House, Charleston.* 1865. Selmar Rush
Seibert. (War Dept.)

**240.** *Destruction of Hood's Ordnance Train.* Near Atlanta, 1864. George N. Barnard. (War Dept)

**241.** *Ruins of Atlanta.* 1864. George N. Barnard. (Army)

**242.** *The Potter House, Atlanta.* 1864. George N. Barnard. (War Dept.)

**243.** *Interior view of ruins of Catholic Cathedral, Charleston.* 1865. Selmar Rush Seibert. (War Dept)

**244.** *Ruins of Northwestern depot, Charleston.* 1865. Selmar Rush Seibert. (War Dept.)

**245.** *Ruins in Charleston, South Carolina.* 1865. Mathew Brady Collection. (Army)

**246.** *Ruins in Columbia, S.C. No. 2.* 1865. George N. Barnard. (War Dept.)

**247.** *Ruins of Norfolk Navy Yard.* December 1864. James Gardner. (War Dept.)

**248.** *Ruins of Richmond and Petersburg Railroad Bridge, Across the James.* Richmond, April 1865. Alexander Gardner. (War Dept.)

**249.** *Ruins of Arsenal, Richmond.* April 1865. Alexander Gardner. (War Dept.)

**250.** *Ruins of the Galligo Mills, Richmond.* April 1865. Mathew Brady Collection. (Army)

**251.** *Ruins of Haxall's Mills, Richmond.* April 1865. Mathew Brady Collection. (Army)

**252.** *Ruins of Richmond.* April 1865. Capt. Andrew J. Russell. Mathew Brady Collection. (Army)

**253.** *A Harvest of Death.* Gettysburg, July 1863. Timothy O'Sullivan. (War Dept.)

**254.** *The Home of a Rebel Sharpshooter, Gettysburg.* July 1863. Alexander Gardner. (War Dept.)

**255.** *A Sharpshooter's Last Sleep.* Gettysburg, July 1863. Alexander Gardner. (War Dept.)

**256.** *Dead Confederate Soldier in the Trenches. This photograph was taken April [3], 1865, in the Rebel trenches at Petersburg just after their capture by Union troops.* Attributed to Thomas C. Roche. Mathew Brady Collection. (Army)

**257.** *"Havoc," effects of a 32-pound shell from gun of Second Massachusetts Heavy Artillery. Confederate caisson and eight horses destroyed.* Fredericksburg, May 3, 1863. Capt. Andrew J. Russell. Mathew Brady Collection. (Army)

**258.** *A Burial Party on the Battle-Field of Cold Harbor.* Virginia, April 1865. John Reekie. (War Dept.)

# Surrender

*Photograph 259*

**259.** *McLean's House, Appomattox Court-House.* Virginia, April 1865. Site of Lee's surrender to Grant. Timothy O'Sullivan. (War Dept.)

# Lincoln's Assassination

*Photographs 260–264*

**260.** *Ford's Theatre in Lincoln's time.* Washington, DC. (Commission of Fine Arts)

**261.** *This is the private box in Ford's Theater, Washington, where President Lincoln was assassinated by John Wilkes Booth, on the night of April 14, 1865.* Stereo. (National Archives Gift Collection)

**262.** John Wilkes Booth, ca. 1862. Charles DeForest Fredericks. (National Archives)

**263.** *Payne, Alias Wood, Alias Hall. Arrested as an associate of Booth in the conspiracy.* 1865. Lewis Payne, the conspirator who attacked Secretary of State Seward. (Army)

**264.** Execution of the four persons condemned as conspirators: Mary Surratt, Lewis Powell, David Herold, and George Atzerodt, July 7, 1865. Alexander Gardner. (Army)

# America and World Affairs

*On the edges of empire, where tomorrow is in the making, there is no guaranteed security, and your camera, like your rifle, must not only be fool-proof, it must be nerve- and terror-proof. Many of the big events of life are unheralded, swift and full of shattering excitement. Surely nothing is more worthy of perpetuation than these fleeting moments bursting with action and death and life. The study of such pictures in days of quiet might give a little more insight into the book of mysteries.*

CPL. C. TUCKER BECKETT

C. Tucker Beckett, "Military Photography in Mexico," *The Camera* (November 1916): 611.

In the latter part of the 19th century, a more mature United States began to take its place among world powers. Not immune to the influences of imperialism, America used its naval and fighting forces to protect its interests and citizens around the globe. U.S. Marines and U.S. Navy ships saw victory in the little-known Korean Punitive Expedition in 1870. In the Spanish-American War of 1898, modernized American forces defeated an Old World power in fields of battle on opposite sides of the world. Protectionism and other motives, including the reaffirmation of the Monroe Doctrine, resulted in further American military interventions in the Philippines, 1899–1900; China, 1900; Mexico, 1916–17; and Central America and the Caribbean, 1910s–30s. America's role as peacemaker played more of a part in the military incursions in Lebanon and the Dominican Republic in the 1950s and 1960s, and America's long struggle in Vietnam in more recent times was a culmination of international military involvement.

*Opposite: Photo 369*

# KOREAN PUNITIVE EXPEDITION

*Photographs 265–269*

**265.** *Council of war on board the U.S. Flagship after the treacherous attack of the Coreans on 1 June 1871. U.S.S. Colorado.* (National Archives Gift Collection)

**266.** *The Monocacy towing the boats on their return to the fleet with trophies of victory.* June 1871. (National Archives Gift Collection)

**267.** *Officers & Crew of the U.S.S.* Monocacy. June 1871. (National Archives Gift Collection)

**268.** *Interior of Fort McKee.* June 1871. (National Archives Gift Collection)

**269.** *A Corean official bearing the first despatches on board the* Colorado. June 1871. (National Archives Gift Collection)

# SPANISH-AMERICAN WAR

## BEGINNINGS

*Photographs 270–277*

**270.** *The* Maine *entering Harbor of Havana.* January 1898. Scribners Collection. (Army)

**271.** Wreck of the U.S.S. *Maine*, 1898. (Bureau of Ships)

**272.** Wreck of the U.S.S. *Maine*, 1898. (Bureau of Ships)

**273.** *Your Country Calls You.* Cover of *Leslie's Weekly* magazine, June 30, 1898, by R. M. Wright. (War Dept.)

**274.** *Review of troops by Secretary of War.* Camp Wikoff, New York, 1898. (Army)

**275.** *71st N.Y. Volunteers boarding transport. U.S.A.T. Vigilancia, 1898. Scribners Collection. (Army)*

**276.** *Loaded transports moving out into Tampa Bay. Ca. 1898. Capt. A. L. Parmerter. (Army)*

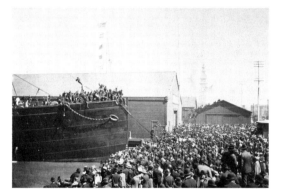

**277.** *Camp Merritt, Cal. Transport* Indiana *receiving troops and freight at Pacific Mail Docks on eve of departure. Crowd bidding farewell. June 27, 1898. (Army)*

# SPANISH-AMERICAN WAR

## THE PHILIPPINES
*Photographs 278–286*

**278.** *Battle of Manila. 1898. Copy of lithograph published by Butler, Thomas & Co., 1899. (Marine Corps)*

**279.** *Spanish warship* Reina Christina, *Admiral Montojo's flagship — completely destroyed by Dewey, Cavite, May 1st, 1898. Greely Collection. (Army)*

**280.** *General Merritt* [seated, center], *Staff and Line Officers on board S/S* Newport. Ca. 1898. Greely Collection. (Army)

**281.** *Maj. Genl. Arthur MacArthur* [2d from left] *and Staff.* Ca. 1898. Greely Collection. (Army)

**282.** *Manila. Advance on Left of American lines. Signal Corps extending telegraph lines from trenches. Flags displayed to indicate to the Navy progress of the advance.* *August 13, 1898.* (Army)

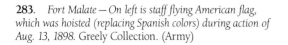

**283.** *Fort Malate — On left is staff flying American flag, which was hoisted (replacing Spanish colors) during action of Aug. 13, 1898.* Greely Collection. (Army)

**284.** *Re-modeled Spanish bronze cannon, overlooking Luneta. <Breech-block removed.>* Ca. 1898. Greely Collection. (Army)

**285.** *Staff and Line Officers, 2nd Regt. Oregon Vol. Infty.* Ca. 1898. Greely Collection. (Army)

# Spanish-American War

## Cuba & Puerto Rico

*Photographs 287–306*

**286.** *Spanish prisoners, at noon-day meal, Manila.* Ca. 1898. Greely Collection. (Army)

**287.** *Destruction of Adml. Cervera's Spanish Fleet off Santiago de Cuba.* 1898. Copy of lithograph published by Kurz & Allison, 1898. (Marine Corps)

**288.** *Wreck of the Spanish* Reina Mercedes, *Santiago, Cuba.* Ca. 1898. (Army)

**289.** *Harbor and Principal Wharf, U.S. Transports. Ponce, Porto Rico.* 1899. (Army)

**290.** *Showing the manner our Army was landed at Baguiri, Cuba.* Ca. 1898. Scribners Collection. (Army)

**291.** *Group of Colored Soldiers. Camp Wikoff, Montauk Point, NY. Ca. 1898.* (Army)

**292.** Third Cavalry colors, Cuba, ca. 1898. Scribners Collection. (Army)

**293.** Cavalry bugler, Cuba, ca. 1898. Scribners Collection. (Army)

**294.** *The burned locomotives at Daiquiri. Cuba, ca. 1898. Col. Lee, British Army.* (Army)

**295.** *Battery B, 4th Artillery, shelling the blockhouse at Coamo, Porto Rico.* August 9, 1898. (Army)

**296.** *Spanish troops leaving Mayagues, Porto Rico, to engage the American forces at Hormiguero, P.R. August 10, 1898.* (War Dept.)

**297.** *Col. Theodore Roosevelt, 1st Cavalry, U.S.V.* Ca. 1898. Rockwood. (Army)

**298.** *Teddy's Rough Riders.* 1898. Chromolithograph by Stoopendaal. Published in *Truth*, July 27, 1898. (War Dept.)

**299.** *"Teddy's colts," at the top of the hill which they captured in the battle of San Juan.* Col. Theodore Roosevelt and his Rough Riders, 1898. William Dinwiddie. (USIA)

**300.** *Wounded Spanish prisoners at Brigade hospital on San Juan Hill, Cuba, July 3, 1898.* (War Dept.)

**301.** *Camp Thomas, Chickamauga Park, Ga. Sternberg Hospital, Third Army Corps. Nurses and convalescent patients.* Ca. 1898. (Army)

**302.** *25th Company, Alphonso Guards, Spanish Army, Porto Rico.* Ca. 1898. Scribners Collection. (Army)

**303.** *Santiago — The dead line at the arsenal. Cuba, ca. 1899.* E. C. Rost. (Army)

**304.** *Receiving the news of the surrender of Santiago, Cuba.* 1898. Scribners Collection. (Army)

**305.** *American graves. Cuba, ca. 1898.* Scribners Collection. (Army)

**306.** *Burial services of sailors recovered from the Battleship* Maine, *held at the south end of the State, War, and Navy Dept. Building, March 23, 1912.* Washington, DC. (Office of Public Buildings and Grounds)

# PHILIPPINE INSURRECTION

*Photographs 307–323*

**307.** *Staff and Assistants of Major General E. S. Otis in their quarters, Manila.* 1899. (Army)

**308.** *Embarkation of Nebraska Volunteers, June 23rd 1899. Pasig, Manila, 1899.* J. D. Saulsbury. (Army)

**309.** *17th Infantry going to the front.* Ca. 1899–1900. B. W. Kilburn. Stereo. (War Dept.)

**310.** *Transportation of Army supplies by "Caraboo" (Water ox cart) and rear of Signal corps quarters, Manila.* Ca. 1899. (Army)

**311.** *Pasig. Oregon Volunteer Infantry on firing line, March 14, 1899.* (Army)

**312.** *Bigaa. Kansas Volunteer Infantry in action. Insurgent entrenchments just beyond firing line and across river.* March 1899. (Army)

**313.** *Our Boys entrenched against the Filipinos.* Ca. 1899–1900. B. W. Kilburn. Stereo. (War Dept.)

**314.** *"Fire!" Utah Battery on McCloud Hill, Sunday morning, Feby. 5, 1899. This shot did great execution among the Insurgents on San Juan Bridge. A soldier was killed near this gun a few minutes after this shot.* Greely Collection. (Army)

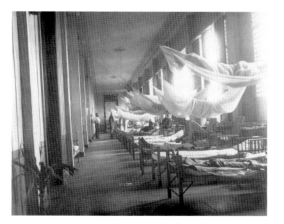

**315.** *Ward, 2nd Reserve Hospital.* Ca. 1899. Greely Collection. (Army)

**316.** *Dressing wounds of natives, Filipino Ward, Division Hospital, Asst. Surgeon J. L. Conant in charge.* Ca. 1899. Greely Collection. (Army)

**317.** *A group of wounded Filipinos.* Ca. 1899. Greely Collection. (Army)

**318.** *Insurgent dead just as they fell in the trench near Santa Ana, February 5th. The trench was circular, and the picture shows but a small portion.* 1899. Greely Collection. (Army)

**319.** *Aguinaldo [seated 3d from right] and other Insurgent leaders.* (U.S. Regular Army Mobile Units)

**320.** *Native Moros, Taluk Samgay, Zamboanga Province, Mindanao. Gov. Capt. Finley in the center.* 1900. (Army)

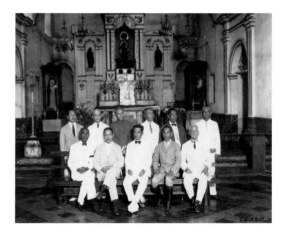

**321.** *Datto Piang, King of Mindanao, and American Officers.* Ca. 1899–1900. B. W. Kilburn. Stereo. (War Dept.)

**322.** *Prayer Before the Surrender. Philippine Insurgents.* Ca. 1900. (U.S. Army Overseas Operations and Commands)

**323.** *General Aguinaldo [seated, center] and ten of the delegates to the first Assembly of Representatives that passed the Constitución Política de la República Filipina on Jan. 21st, 1899, in the Barasoain Church, Malolos, Dec. 8, 1929.* (Army)

# Boxer Rebellion: China Relief Expedition

*Photographs 324–334*

**324.** *Troop L, 6th U.S. Cavalry, at the Great Wall of China, near the Ming Tombs. East of Nan-Kow Pass. Ca. 1900. Capt. C. F. O'Keefe. (Army)*

**325.** *Avenue of Statues, on road to the Ming Tombs, near Peking, China. Members of the 6th U.S. Cavalry in foreground. 1900. Capt. C. F. O'Keefe. (Corps of Engineers)*

**326.** *Brig. Gen. J. H. Wilson, U.S.V., and Lieutenant Turner, 10th Infantry, Aide de Camp. Temple of Agriculture, Peking. 1900. Capt. C. F. O'Keefe. (Army)*

**327.** *Marines in relief party, Peiping, China. 1900. Anna Graham Woodward. (Marine Corps)*

**328.** *Group of Signal men in China. Ca. 1900. (Army)*

**329.** *Typical sleeping quarters of an officer in China. Photo of Lieut. (now Captain) Stamford after the battle of Yang Sing. Ca. 1900. (Army)*

**330.** *Italian mounted infantry. 1900. (War Dept.)*

**331.** *Chinese "Boxer." 1900. (Army)*

**332.** *Marines fight rebellious Boxers outside Peking Legation, 1900. Copy of painting by Sgt. John Clymer. (Marine Corps)*

**333.** *Near the United States Legation looking north-west from Fort Myer on the Tartar Wall, Peking, China. Ca. 1900. Capt. C. F. O'Keefe. (Corps of Engineers)*

**334.** *Within historic grounds of the Forbidden City in Pekin, China, on November 28 celebrated the victory of the Allies. Ca. 1900. (Marine Corps)*

# Mexican Punitive Expedition

*Photographs 335–353*

**335.** *Central sectional view of the great camp at Ft. Bliss, Texas. Picket Lines and Battery Parks.* September 26, 1915. C. Tucker Beckett. (War Dept.)

**336.** *In Camp near San Antonio, Mexico, with the 6th Infantry, April 27, 1916 — United States and Carranzista soldiers.* William Fox. (Adjutant General)

**337.** *In Camp near San Antonio, Mexico, with the 6th Infantry. Carranzistas and United States troops. Carranzistas went through here on their way to different points along the railroad in search of Villa and his men.* 1916. William Fox. (Adjutant General)

**338.** *Headquarters of the American forces in Colonia Dublan, Mexico. General Pershing with his aide Lt. Collins.* 1916. William Fox. (Adjutant General)

**339.** *Brigade Headquarters near Casas Grandes, Mexico. General Pershing.* Ca. 1916. William Fox. (Adjutant General)

**340.** *Pvts. Daly, Ball, and Baldwin, Co. A, 16th Infty., testing out the burro. This burro came to camp one day and ever afterward persisted in hanging around. Sept. 29, 1916.* C. Tucker Beckett. (War Dept.)

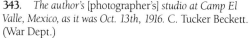

**341.** *The Studio, Camp of 16th Infantry, El Paso, Texas.* [The photographer Beckett] *in corporal's uniform beside his studio camera, a* 6½ x 8½ *combination plate or film, revolving back, cycle Graflex, November 3rd, 1916. Pvt. Willie Wynn. (War Dept.)*

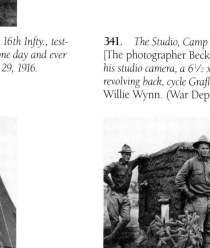

**342.** *Pvt. Browne, Co. M, 16th Infty., Camp El Valle, Mex., Sept. 29th, 1916.* C. Tucker Beckett. (War Dept.)

**343.** *The author's* [photographer's] *studio at Camp El Valle, Mexico, as it was Oct. 13th, 1916.* C. Tucker Beckett. (War Dept.)

**344.** *Major Charles Young of the 10th Cavalry who will be made Lieut. Colonel shortly. 1916.* William Fox. (Adjutant General)

**345.** *Inspecting packs, Co. M, 16th Infty., El Valle, Mexico, Sept. 16, 1916. Orderly-room and bulletin board, in foreground.* C. Tucker Beckett. (War Dept.)

**346.** *Around the camp-fire, men of Co. A, 16th Infty., San Geronimo, Mexico, May 27th, 1916. This photo was obtained by flashlight powder.* C. Tucker Beckett. (War Dept.)

**347.** *En route with the American Field Headquarters from El Valle to Las Cruces, Mexico, April 10, 1916. Company A, 6th Infantry, in emergency trench which has been prepared at its camp for attack by Mexicans.* William Fox. (Adjutant General)

**348.** *Column of 6th and 16th Infty. en route to the States, between Corralitos Rancho and Ojo Federico, Jan. 29th, 1917. Co. A, 16th Infty. in foreground. This was the longest hike of the return march, 28 miles.* C. Tucker Beckett. (War Dept.)

**349.** *Army airplane No. 75, Camp El Valle, Mexico, Sept. 28th, 1916. Pvt. Smith, Co. A, 16th Infty., standing as a measure.* C. Tucker Beckett. (War Dept.)

**350.** *Gen. Villa, Mexican bandit. 1. Gen. Fierro. 2. Gen. Villa. 3. Gen. Ortega. 4. Col. Mediña. Ca. 1913.* W. H. Horne Co. (War Dept.)

Mexican Rurales.

**351.** *Villa bandits who raided Columbus, N.M., caught by American soldiers in the mountains of Mexico and held, in camp near Namiquipa, April 27, 1916. William Fox. (War Dept.)*

**352.** *Mexican Rurales. W. H. Horne Co. (War Dept.)*

**353.** *A triple execution at Juarez, Mexico, about the time of the Columbus affair. Ca. 1916. W. H. Horne Co. (War Dept.)*

# SIBERIA & NORTH RUSSIA

*Photographs 354–366*

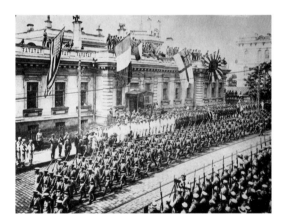

**354.** *American troops in Vladivostok parading before the building occupied by the staff of the Czecho-Slovaks. Japanese marines are standing at attention as they march by. Siberia, August 1918. Underwood and Underwood. (War Dept.)*

**355.** *Vladivostok, Russia. Soldiers and sailors from many countries are lined up in front of the Allies Headquarters Building. The United States is represented. September 1918. Underwood and Underwood. (War Dept.)*

**356.** *Scene at American transport docks on arrival of a transport from the States.* Ca. 1918–19. (U.S. Army Overseas Operations and Commands)

**357.** *Major General William S. Graves* [Commanding General Allied Expeditionary Force — Siberia; seated, center] *and Staff, Vladivostok, November 23rd, 1918.* (U.S. Army Overseas Operations and Commands)

**358.** *Maj. Gen. Graves, U.S.A., Gen. Otani, Japanese Army, and Staff, Vladivostok, Siberia.* Ca. 1918–19. Khosita. (War Dept.)

**359.** *Quartermaster supplies in warehouse at base, Vladivostok, Siberia.* Ca. 1918–19. (U.S. Army Overseas Operations and Commands)

**360.** *31st Inf. on practice hike. Officers of Co. "A" at mess. New rolling kitchens being tested. Vladivostok, Sib., Dec. 3, 1918.* (U.S. Army Overseas Operations and Commands)

**361.** *Dinner served in a box car on the Vologia railroad carrying the Red Cross gifts to Americans at the front. The thermometer registered 10 degrees below zero at this time.* Bakharitza, December 17, 1918. Sgt. Grier M. Shotwell. (Army)

**362.** *Russia in Asia. Lazian Militia. Ca. 1918–19.* (War Dept.)

**363.** *Colonel Geo. E. Stewart, commanding American forces in Northern Russia, passing by convoy through village of Chamova on his return from Dwina River front at Toulgas to Archangel. December 31, 1918. Sgt. Grier M. Shotwell.* (Army)

**364.** *American officers frequently employed reindeer teams in crossing the Dwina River and in going about Archangel. Here are two officers with a team they have just engaged. A Russian young lady is also a passenger. March 7, 1919. Sgt. Grier M. Shotwell.* (Army)

**365.** *Signal Corps Photographic Unit with A.E.F. North Russia. Lieut. Chas. I. Reid at the left; Master Signal Electrician Grier M. Shotwell at the right. In the background is the Monastery Church of Archangel. June 25, 1919.* (Army)

**366.** *American troops in Russian port about to leave that country. They are here cheering and displaying the stars and stripes as the tender was coming for them. Ca. 1919–20.* Central News Photo Service. (War Dept.)

# U.S. FORCES IN CENTRAL AMERICA & THE CARIBBEAN

*Photographs 367–376*

**367.** *Marines landing under fire at Santo Domingo. Ca.* 1916. Copy of illustration by Dickson. (Marine Corps)

**368.** *U.S. Marine Corps patrol boats on the Ozoma River, Santo Domingo City.* 1919. (Marine Corps)

**369.** *Cuba, Guantanamo Sentry beneath palms.* 1919. (Marine Corps)

**370.** *U.S. Marines and guide in search of bandits.* Haiti, ca. 1919. (Marine Corps)

**371.** *Gen. Sandino [center] and Staff enroute to Mexico.* June 1929. Siglo XX. (Marine Corps)

**372.** American Marines in Nicaragua, 1927. (Marine Corps)

**373.** *Chinandega, Nicaragua. Marines and Bluejackets who returned with ballot box from Somotillo. They started out with Bullock cart and horses and mules. About 30 miles from Chinandega the muddy roads became impassable.* 1928. (Marine Corps)

**374.** *Prisoners in Nicaragua.* November 1928. Palmer. (Marine Corps)

**375.** *One of our speed cars mounted with Heavy Browning Machine Gun to offset any possibility of rioting during the 1932 Presidential Elections in Nicaragua.* Capt. Charles Davis. (Marine Corps)

**376.** *Sandino's Flag.* Nicaragua, 1932. (Marine Corps)

# LEBANON

*Photograph 377*

# DOMINICAN REPUBLIC

*Photographs 378–381*

**377.** James Thaber, born in Lebanon, of Mount Clemens, MI, listens to President Eisenhower's broadcast of his decision to send troops to Lebanon. His son, a recent high school graduate, is in the U.S. Army. July 15, 1958. Bert Emanuel. (USIA)

**378.** *Humanitarian G.I.'s. Firefight where G.I. pushes little kid under jeep for protection, Santo Domingo, May 5. 1965.* Jack Lartz. (USIA)

**379.** *Honduran soldiers, first troops of Inter-American peace force, arrive to assume peace-keeping duties and to render emergency aid in revolt-torn country. 1965.* Jack Lartz. (USIA)

**380.** *G.I.'s playing baseball with Dominican kids. Santo Domingo, May 5. 1965.* Jack Lartz. (USIA)

**381.** *Food distribution in front of "Yankees come back" sign, Santo Domingo, May 9. 1965.* Jack Lartz. (USIA)

# VIETNAM

## BACKGROUND

*Photographs 382–386*

**382.** *A French Foreign Legionnaire goes to war along the dry rib of a rice paddy, during a recent sweep through communist-held areas in the Red River Delta, between Haiphong and Hanoi. Behind the Legionnaire is a U.S. gifted tank. Ca. 1954. Pix. (USIA)*

**383.** *The French Foreign Legion is playing the major combat role in the war against the Vietminh. Here a red-suspect has been found hiding in the jungle and is now being questioned by the advance patrol, who caught him. Ca. 1954. Pix. (USIA)*

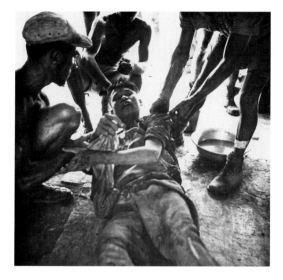

**384.** *A wounded Vietminh prisoner is given first aid by Franco Vietnamese medicals after hot fire fight near Hung Yen, south of Hanoi. Ca. 1954. (USIA)*

**385.** *Catholics escaping communist territory in the dead of night smile as they pull alongside French landing craft that will take them to freedom. Ca. 1954. (USIA)*

**386.** *Vietnam refugees. USS* Montague *lowers a ladder over the side to French LSM to take refugees aboard. Haiphong, August 1954. PH1 H. S. Hemphill. (Navy)*

# VIETNAM

## AMERICAN INVOLVEMENT

*Photographs 387–427*

**387.** *General Creighton W. Abrams, U.S. commander in South Vietnam, discusses the military situation in Vietnam with President Johnson and his advisors October 29 at the White House in Washington. 1968. White House. (USIA)*

**388.** *Chairman Nguyen Van Thieu, President Lyndon B. Johnson and Prime Minister Nguyen Cau Ky salute during the playing of the U.S. and Vietnamese National Anthems during welcoming ceremonies at Guam's International Airport. Agana, March 20, 1967. (USIA)*

**389.** *Pausing for refreshments during their visit to Huu Thanh, a recently pacified village, three U.S. Senators on President Nixon's fact-finding committee drink from local coconuts.* Thomas J. McIntyre, Howard Cannon, and George Murphy. *Ca. 1970.* (USIA)

**390.** *Hollywood comedian Bob Hope joins dancers Harold and Fayard Nicholas in a dance step aboard the U.S. aircraft carrier* Ticonderoga. *December 1965. Viet Nam Photo Service.* (USIA)

**391.** *Watusi, Frug, Shimmy, Twist! On a carrier? — It's swinging time on board* Ticonderoga *as Miss Joey Heatherton rocks out with a "Tico Tiger" during the Bob Hope Show.* December 27, 1965. PH1 Jean C. Cote, USN. (USIA)

**392.** *Twenty-one year old James R. Gould is the envy of 3,000 crewmembers as television actress Kathleen Nolan singles him out for a song. The young sailor and* Bon Homme Richard *both celebrated their "coming of age" on November 26. 1965. Navy.* (USIA)

**393.** *A contingent of the Royal Australian Air Force arrives at Tan Son Nhut Airport, Saigon, to work with the South Vietnamese and U.S. Air Forces in transporting soldiers and supplies to combat areas in South Viet-nam.* August 10, 1964. Army. (USIA)

**394.** President Lyndon B. Johnson greets American troops in Vietnam, 1966. (USIA)

**395.** President Lyndon B. Johnson greets American troops in Vietnam, 1966. (USIA)

**396.** South Vietnamese soldier, 1966. (USIA)

**397.** *These young men, from all of South Vietnam's 44 provinces, will return to their native villages after 13 weeks' training at the National Training Center. Their job: To help villagers help themselves. Ca. 1970.* (USIA)

**398.** *Girl volunteers of the People's Self-Defense Force of Kien Dien, a hamlet of Ben Cat district 50 kilometers north of Saigon, patrol the hamlet's perimeter to discourage Viet Cong infiltration.* (USIA)

**399.** *Ontos on Chu Lai beach search for a defensive position shortly after descending from the landing crafts aboard the USS* Thomaston. *June 1965. Navy.* (USIA)

**400.** *One of the unique pieces of equipment brought to Vietnam by the 1st Cavalry Division (Airmobile), U.S. Army, is the huge Sky Crane CH-54A helicopter which can lift tremendous loads. Viet Nam Photo Service.* (USIA)

**401.** *Moments before the U.S. flag was replaced by the Vietnamese flag, Vietnamese Air Force crewmen line up before one of the 62 UH-1 "Huey" helicopters turned over to them November 4, 1970, along with command of the Soc Trang airfield.* (USIA)

**402.** *Vietnam: helicopter and soldier approaching target.* Ca. 1965. Viet Nam Photo Service. (USIA)

**403.** *Crack troops of the Vietnamese Army in combat operations against the Communist Viet Cong guerrillas. Marshy terrain of the delta country makes their job of rooting out terrorists hazardous and extremely difficult.* 1961. (USIA)

**404.** *A young American lieutenant, his leg burned by an exploding Viet Cong white phosphorus booby trap, is treated by a medic.* 1966. JUSPAO. (USIA)

**405.** *This bridge over the Perfume River in Hue was still standing as these refugees fled across it to escape Tet fighting, but it soon was dropped into the river by the communists.* 1968. (USIA)

**406.** *The old and the young flee Tet offensive fighting in Hue, managing to reach the south shore of the Perfume River despite this blown bridge.* 1968. (USIA)

**407.** *Stunned by the viciousness of a Viet Cong attack on their village, Vietnam war refugees ride an Air Force helicopter to a safe area near Saigon.* March 1966. Air Force. (USIA)

**408.** *The strain shows clearly on the face of this Vietnamese farmer, one of 4,500 who recently fled their homes to escape Vietcong harassment. The refugees left hamlets which had been family homes for generations. Ca. 1966. (USIA)*

**409.** *A new market for "Tinh Thuong." Children gather before the market which was built with assistance from the government of Vietnam and USAID. (USIA)*

**410.** South Vietnamese children. (USIA)

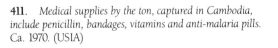

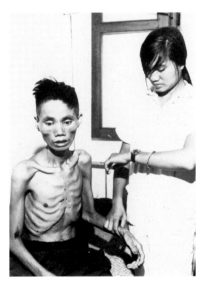

**411.** *Medical supplies by the ton, captured in Cambodia, include penicillin, bandages, vitamins and anti-malaria pills. Ca. 1970. (USIA)*

**412.** *It doesn't hurt, but it tickles. A U.S. Navy hospital corpsman, member of a USAID military health team, inoculates a flood refugee against cholera at the refugee center on Nui Sam mountain, Chau Doc province. 1966. JUSPAO. (USIA)*

**413.** *The effects of just one month spent in a Viet Cong prison camp show on 23-year-old Le Van Than, who had defected from the Communist forces and joined the Government side, was recaptured by the Viet Cong and deliberately starved. Ca. 1966. (USIA)*

**414.** *Youthful hard-core Viet Cong, heavily guarded, awaits interrogation following capture in the attacks on the capital city during the festive Tet holiday period. 1968. (USIA)*

**415.** *Operation Starlight, a U.S. Marine Corps search and destroy operation south of Chu Lai. VC casualties stood at 599 killed and six captured. Viet Cong prisoners await being carried by helicopter to rear area. August 1965. JUSPAO. (USIA)*

**416.** *Three Air Force F-105 Thunderchief pilots enroute to bomb military target in Vietnam pull up to a flying Air Force "gas station." The refueling aircraft is an Air Force KC-135 Stratotanker. January 1966. Air Force. (USIA)*

**417.** *Flying under radar control with a B-66 Destroyer, Air Force F-105 Thunderchief pilots bomb a military target through low clouds over the southern panhandle of North Viet Nam. June 14, 1966. Lt. Col. Cecil J. Poss, USAF. (USIA)*

**418.** *Black smoke covers areas of the capital city and fire trucks rush to the scenes of fires set during attacks by the Viet Cong during the festive Tet holiday period. Saigon, 1968. (USIA)*

**419.** *Tank from 1st Bn., 69th Armor, 25th Inf. Div., moves through Saigon shortly after disembarking from LST at Saigon Harbor. March 12, 1966. SP/5 Park, USA. (USIA)*

**420.** *Four Vietnamese and three Americans were killed, and dozens of Vietnamese buildings were heavily damaged during a Viet Cong bomb attack against a multi-story U.S. officers billet in Saigon. April 1, 1966. JUSPAO. (USIA)*

**421.** *Three Vietnamese women move back into the Cholon area after VC attack that left a two-block area leveled, in hopes of salvaging meager belongings. Saigon, January 31, 1968. (USIA)*

**422.** *A girl, holding a small child, stands in the ruins of their home after a Viet Cong attack. Saigon, January 31, 1968. JUSPAO. (USIA)*

**423.** *With fear and apprehension showing on their faces, and at the urging of South Vietnamese troops, women and children loaded down with salvaged possessions scurry past the bodies of three Viet Cong killed in the fighting. May 1968. (USIA)*

**424.** *One of 48 persons wounded by a Viet Cong explosion which killed 14 persons in Saigon awaits treatment in the Cong Hoa Hospital. Blast was set off on a busy street corner and the victims included women and children. February 1966. JUSPAO. (USIA)*

**425.** *Two battalions of Viet Cong systematically killed 252 civilians in a "vengeance" attack on the small hamlet of Dak Son. Tears are streaming down the face of little three-year-old Dieu Do, now homeless, and fatherless. December 6, 1967. (USIA)*

**426.** *Tuy Hoa: Fifteen civilians were killed in the explosion of a homemade Viet Cong mine on a country road. Most of the victims were riding in a Lambretta Tricycle which struck the mine and was ripped apart by the blast. Ca. 1966.* JUSPAO. (USIA)

**427.** *Almost 400 men, women and children massacred by the Viet Cong during "Tet 1968" were mourned at a common-grave burial on October 14. This young widow, carrying a photograph of her missing husband, mourns at the mass funeral service. Hue, 1968. (USIA)*

# WORLD WAR I 1914–1918

*On the Chemin-des-Dames we tried to specialize in shell bursts. The modern war maker did not consider the photographer. Brady in the Civil War was handicapped in apparatus and had his subjects more concentrated. The present long range gun has enlarged the fighting area and trench warfare is very hard to picture. It is more like hunting game. If you're lucky you find it, and the Boche simply would not put down shells where we wanted them.*

CAPT. EDWIN H. COOPER
U.S. Signal Corps

Albert E. George, and Capt. Edwin H. Cooper, *Pictorial History of the Twenty-Sixth Division* (Boston: Ball Publishing Co., 1920), p. 52.

A seemingly unstoppable series of events in the early 20th century led to the outbreak of global conflict in 1914. Involving nations on five continents, World War I was the first war to employ modern scientific technology on a huge scale. Homefront activities saw the massive use of photographs and motion pictures. Advanced technology in military equipment, weapons, transportation, and communication was pioneered on the battlefronts. America was drawn into war as an equal world power coming to the aid of freedom and democracy in the Old World. European nations, however, suffered the worst toll of death, injury, and destruction. American troops, during the last year of war, helped to turn the tide of stalemate in the muddy trenches of France and Belgium. Allied victory was reached at the 11th hour of the 11th day of the 11th month of 1918.

*Opposite: Photo 595*

# BEGINNING

*Photograph 428*

**428.** *President Wilson before Congress, announcing the break in the official relations with Germany.* February 3, 1917. Harris & Ewing. (War Dept.)

# RECRUITMENT & TRAINING

*Photographs 429–459*

**429.** *Gee!! I Wish I Were A Man / I'd Join The Navy / Be a Man and Do It / United States Navy Recruiting Station.* 1917. Color poster by Howard Chandler Christy. Issued by Navy Publicity Bureau. (Office of Naval Records and Library)

**430.** *If You Want To Fight! Join The Marines.* Color poster by Howard Chandler Christy. (Food Administration)

**431.** *Treat 'Em Rough! Join the Tanks / United States Tank Corps.* Ca. 1917–18. Color poster by August Hutaf. (Food Administration)

**432.** *James Montgomery Flagg, appointed "official artist" in New York State by Governor Whitman. 1917. Arnold Genthe. (War Dept.)*

**433.** *Second Draft. The first number drawn was 246, and was picked from the urn by Secretary of War Baker. Photo shows Sec'y Baker picking the first capsule out of the bowl. June 1918. IFS. (War Dept.)*

**434.** *Naval Reserves from Washington, D.C. in New York City. Ca. 1917–18. (Bureau of Ships)*

**435.** *Recruits for U.S. Marine Corps being sworn in at recruiting station, New York City. Ca. 1918. New York Herald. (War Dept.)*

**436.** *San Francisco Yeomanettes attached to the Naval Reserve, Twelfth District. June 1918. San Francisco Bulletin. (War Dept.)*

**437.** *Mother escorting her son to train, who is bound for camp. Newark, New Jersey.* Ca. 1918. Mayor's Office, Newark. (War Dept.)

**438.** *Platte County, Neb., draft group to Camp Grant, Ill.* September 5, 1918. Fennel. (War Dept.)

**439.** *"Are We Downhearted?" You don't have to hear their answer to know these men on their way to Camp Upton are not. These men from New York are radiating their joy at getting into the nation's service.* September 19, 1917. Underwood & Underwood. (War Dept.)

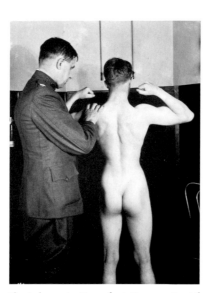

**440.** *Physical examinations of aviation recruits at the Episcopal Hospital, Washington, D.C. Muscular development.* April 1918. Lt. Reid. (Army)

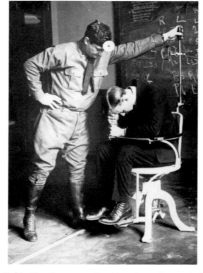

**441.** *Subjecting the prospective American airman to the falling test. The sixth sense — that of equilibrium — is the function of the labyrinth of the internal ear.* March 19, 1918. Underwood & Underwood. (War Dept.)

**442.** *Ambulance Training Corps, Allentown, Pa. Uncle Sam is training his ambulance drivers for the business of administering to battered humanity. Photo shows the men being "iodined" preparatory to getting an inoculation.* Ca. 1917. IFS. (War Dept.)

**443.** *Drafted men reporting for service. Camp Travis, San Antonio, Texas. Ca. 1917–18. San Antonio Chamber of Commerce. (War Dept.)*

**444.** *Vocational training for S.A.T.C. in University of Michigan, Ann Arbor. Class in Pole-Climbing in the course for telephone electricians, with some of their instructors. Ca. 1918. University of Michigan. (War Dept.)*

**445.** *Government preparing men for radio work under direction of Federal Vocational Board. Student transmitting a message to four of his classmates in the class room at the Stuyvesant Evening High School, N.Y. April 1918. Western Newspaper Union. (War Dept.)*

**446.** *Inspection of quarters in Great Hall, Signal Corps School of Radio and Multiplex Telegraphy, College of the City of New York. Ca. 1918. (War Dept.)*

**447.** *Lecture at the S.A.T.C. Tuskegee Normal and Industrial Institute, Tuskegee, Ala. Ca. 1918. Photographic Division, Tuskegee Institute. (War Dept.)*

**448.** *Wall scaling at Camp Wadsworth, S.C. Ca. 1918. Paul Thompson. (War Dept.)*

**449.** *Training Camp Activities. Bayonet fighting instruction by an English Sgt. Major, Camp Dick, Tex. Ca. 1917–18.* (War Dept.)

**450.** *Bayonet practice. Camp Bowie, Fort Worth, Texas. Ca. 1918.* (War Dept.)

**451.** *Boxing instructions, main barracks, Naval Training Station, San Francisco, Cal. Ca. 1918. Metzgar.* (War Dept.)

**452.** *Exercises, Naval Militia Camp, Somersville, N.Y. Ca. 1917–18.* Committee on Public Information. (War Dept.)

**453.** *Mess formation, detention barracks, Naval Training Station, San Francisco, Cal. Ca. 1918. Metzgar.* (War Dept.)

**454.** *Soldiers trying out their gas masks in every possible way. Putting the respirator to good use while peeling onions. 40th Div., Camp Kearny, San Diego, Calif. March 1918. Lt. E. N. Jackson.* (Army)

**455.** *"Getting em up" at U.S.N.T. Camp, Seattle, Wash.* Ca. 1917–18. Webster & Stevens. (War Dept.)

**456.** *Activity in the ranks of University of California unit. Photo shows California students inspection drill on the University Campus at Berkeley, Calif.* Ca. 1917–18. IFS. (War Dept.)

**457.** *Headquarters Troop of the 27th Division, New York National Guard, silhouetted against the gathering dusk as they march to the training camp.* September 5, 1917. Underwood & Underwood. (War Dept.)

**458.** *These guns will soon be spouting the fire of victory. Right now they are being placed into position for review at Camp Hancock.* Georgia, 1918. Underwood & Underwood. (Food Administration)

**459.** *Night attack with phosphorus bombs in maneuvers. First Corps School. Gondrecourt, France.* August 15, 1918. Sfc. J. J. Marshall. (Army)

# TROOPS

*Photographs 460–476*

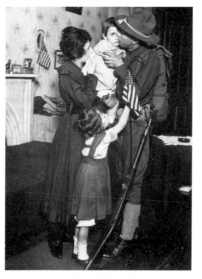

**460.** *Private T. P. Loughlin of the 69th Regiment, N.Y.N.G., (165th Infantry) bidding his family farewell.* 1917. IFS. (War Dept.)

**461.** *A soldier boy of the 71st Regiment Infantry, New York National Guard, saying good bye to his sweetheart as his regiment leaves for Camp Wadsworth, Spartanburg, S.C., where the New York Division trained for service.* 1917. IFS. (War Dept.)

**462.** *Embarked for France.* 1917. Western Newspaper Union. (War Dept.)

**463.** *Soldiers aboard U.S. Transport* Hancock *about to sail for France.* 1917. IFS. (War Dept.)

**464.** *Garde-Kürassier Regiment in Berlin leaving for the front.* Ca. August 1914. (Army)

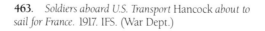

**465.** *American troops on way to the front march thru London amid the plaudits of the multitudes, crossing Westminster Bridge.* September 5, 1917. Underwood & Underwood. (Army)

**466.** American troops entering Perth, Scotland, 1918. (Army)

**467.** *Yankees sleep in London law courts.* Ca. 1917–18. Underwood & Underwood. (War Dept.)

**468.** *"First to Fight." A group of U.S. Marines.* 1918. USMC Recruiting Publicity Bureau. (War Dept.)

**469.** *"Gobs" and Guns. A scene aboard the U.S.S. Texas, just back from foreign waters, showing the "gobs" enjoying a little fun on the big guns.* Ca. 1918. Underwood & Underwood. (War Dept.)

**470.** *On board an American destroyer. A five inch gun and its crew.* Ca. 1918. Central News Photo Service. (War Dept.)

**471.** *Personnel, 3d Motor Mechanics — 1st Air Depot. Colombey, France, ca. 1918. Air Service Photographic Section.* (Army Air Forces)

**472.** *1st Army Post Band (Colored) — Souilly. France, 1918. Air Service Photographic Section.* (Army Air Forces)

**473.** Officers of the Morristown, NJ, Infantry Battalion, July 1918. Parker Studio. (War Dept.)

**474.** *Co. "B" — 113th Infantry — A.E.F. — France.* April 1919. Richards Film Service. (War Dept.)

**475.** *Officers of the "Buffalos," 367th Infantry, 77th Division in France.* Ca. 1918. IFS. (War Dept.)

**476.** *Negro troops in France. Picture shows a part of the 15th Regt. Inf. N.Y.N.G. organized by Col. Haywood, which has been under fire.* Ca. 1918. IFS. (War Dept.)

# NAVY

*Photographs 477–489*

**477.** *The leader* Arizona *passing 96th St. Pier in great naval review at N.Y. City.* Ca. 1918. Paul Thompson. (War Dept.)

**478.** *U.S. battleship* New Jersey *in camouflage coat.* Ca. 1918. Navy Dept. (War Dept.)

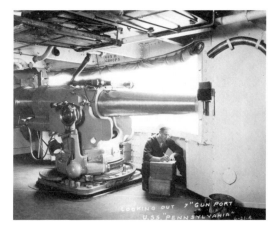

**479.** U.S.S. *Arkansas*, ca. 1918. Enrique Muller. (War Dept.)

**480.** *Looking out 7″ gun port, U.S.S.* Pennsylvania. Ca. 1918. Navy Bureau of Construction & Repair. (War Dept.)

**481.** *Anti-aircraft gun practice. Photo taken on one of the converted yachts now being used in the Naval Reserve.* Ca. 1918. Edwin Levick. (War Dept.)

**482.** *Recovering Torpedo.* Ca. 1918. Enrique Muller. (War Dept.)

**483.** U.S.S. *Michigan*, ca. 1918. Enrique Muller. (War Dept.)

**484.** *USS* Allen *convoying USS* Leviathan. Ca. 1917–18. Copy of painting by Burnell Poole. (Bureau of Ships)

**485.** *S.M.S.* Kaiser *Parade vor S.M. dem Kaiser.* The German battleship *Kaiser* on parade for Kaiser Wilhelm II at Kiel, Germany, ca. 1911–14. K. Koch. (War Dept.)

**486.** *1. und 2. Geschwader und kleine Kreuzer im Kieler Hafen.* First and second battleship squadrons and small cruiser of the German navy, in Kiel Harbor, Germany, ca. 1911–14. K. Koch. (War Dept.)

**487.** *Das 2. Geschwader fährt nach der Nordsee.* The second battleship squadron of the German navy sailing to the North Sea, ca. 1911–14. K. Koch. (War Dept.)

**488.** *German Submarine in rough seas.* F. Schensky. (Bureau of Ships)

**489.** Engine room of an oil-burning German submarine. German Official. (War Dept.)

# PERSONALITIES

*Photographs 490–502*

**490.** *General John J. Pershing. General Headquarters, Chaumont, France.* October 19, 1918. 2d Lt. L. J. Rode. (Army)

**491.** German General Headquarters. General von Hindenburg, Kaiser Wilhelm, General Ludendorff, January 1917. German Official. (War Dept.)

**492.** *Brig. Gen. Douglas MacArthur cleaned up after the Germans left and restored what he could of the original splendor. He is seated in the original chair of the old lord of the chateau. St. Benoit Château, France.* September 19, 1918. Lt. Ralph Estep. (Army)

**493.** *Lillian Russell shown as a U.S. Marine Corps Woman Reserve, with Privates O'Keefe, Kelly and Spike.* Ca. 1917–18. (Marine Corps)

**494.** *Helen Keller Christens a United States Emergency Fleet ship launched in the Los Angeles harbor. The newly completed ship was the twelfth boat launched by the Los Angeles Shipbuilding & Dry Dock Company.* Ca. 1918. Central News Photo Service. (War Dept.)

**495.** Hazel Carter of Douglas, AZ, donned an Army uniform to stay with her soldier husband. She stowed away on the ship to France, was discovered and sent home. She died while her husband, Cpl. John Carter, was still overseas. Ca. 1918. IFS. (War Dept.)

**496.** *Capt. Edward Rickenbacker, America's premier "Ace" officially credited with 22 enemy planes and the proud wearer of the French War Cross as he appeared upon his arrival on board the* Adriatic. *Ca. 1919. Underwood & Underwood. (War Dept.)*

**497.** *Freiherr Rittmeister von Richtofen.* Baron Captain Manfred von Richtofen, ca. 1917. (Foreign Records Seized)

**498.** *Sergt. Alvin C. York, 328th Infantry, who with aid of 17 men, captured 132 German prisoners; shows hill on which raid took place* [October 8, 1918]. *Argonne Forest, near Cornay, France.* February 7, 1919. Pfc. F. C. Phillips. (Army)

**499.** Officers, 129th Field Artillery, at regimental headquarters at Château le Chanay near Courcemont, France, March 1919. Capt. Harry Truman, second row, third from right. M. Le Chanoine E. Valleé. (Army)

**500.** German soldiers. Adolf Hitler at left. (OWI)

**501.** *Secretary of the Treasury William G. McAdoo and his son William, Jr., who is in the aviation branch of the Navy.* September 1918. Underwood & Underwood. (War Dept.)

**502.** *Dr. Stephen S. Wise, Rabbi of the Free Synagogue, has become a laborer in the shipbuilding yards of the Luder Marine Construction Co., at Stanford, Conn., together with his eighteen year old son.* July 1918. Underwood & Underwood. (War Dept.)

# Patriotism

*Photographs 503–533*

**503.** *Ike Sims of Atlanta, Georgia, 87 years old, has eleven sons in the service.* Ca. 1918. Underwood & Underwood. (War Dept.)

**504.** *Patriotic old women make flags.* Born in Hungary, Galicia, Russia, Germany, Rumania. Their flag-making instructor, Rose Radin, is standing. Ca. 1918. Underwood & Underwood. (War Dept.)

**505.** *Nebraska State Council of Defense.* Ca. 1918. Townsend Studio. (War Dept.)

**506.** *"Victory" spelled by men in training at Great Lakes Naval Training Station, Great Lakes, Ill.* Ca. 1917–18. Committee on Public Information. (Army)

**507.** *Pelham Bay sailors celebrate Independence Day. Secretary of the Navy Daniels making a patriotic speech to the officers and men of the Pelham Bay Naval Training Station on July 4, 1918.* New York. Underwood & Underwood. (War Dept.)

**508.** *Human Statue of Liberty. 18,000 Officers and Men at Camp Dodge, Des Moines, Ia. Col. Wm. Newman, Commanding. Col. Rush S. Wells, Directing. September 1918. Mole & Thomas. (War Dept.)*

**509.** *Save Her From Hun — Buy Liberty Bonds. From a photograph posed for by Miss Francis Fairchild, a 1918 debutante of New York, in behalf of the Fourth Liberty Loan. August 1918. Underwood & Underwood. (War Dept.)*

**510.** *Chinese Day in the Fourth Liberty Loan Campaign was appropriately celebrated. One of the features of the Chinese Parade is shown. China, Liberty, and Uncle Sam united. October 1, 1918. Underwood & Underwood. (War Dept.)*

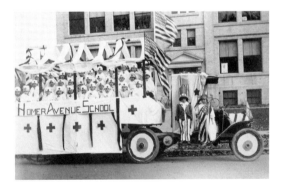

**511.** *Second Liberty Loan Parade, Homer Ave. School float, at Cortland, N.Y. Ca. 1917. (War Dept.)*

**512.** *Sailors from Pelham Bay Naval Training Station marching down Fifth Avenue in the Fourth Liberty Loan Parade, New York City. 1918. Paul Thompson. (War Dept.)*

**513.** *Bell ringers on Seattle, Wash., streets during 4th Liberty Loan. Bells were afterwards muffled, as a reproach, subscriptions coming too slow. 1918. Webster & Stevens. (War Dept.)*

**514.** *Members of the "Liberty Loan Choir" singing on the steps of City Hall, New York City, in the third Liberty Loan campaign. At the right is Bishop William Wilkinson, who led the choir. April 1918. Paul Thompson.* (Army)

**515.** *Douglas Fairbanks, movie star, speaking in front of the Sub-Treasury building, New York City, to aid the third Liberty Loan. April 1918. Paul Thompson.* (Army)

**516.** *Charlie Chaplin, comedy star of the "movies," making his first speech for the third Liberty Loan in front of the State, War and Navy Bldg., Washington, D.C., on first anniversary of U.S. entry into war. April 6, 1918. Lt. Edmond deBerri.* (Army)

**517.** *James Montgomery Flagg has given the public an opportunity to see him in action. He produced a life size picture of poster "Tell it to the Marines" in the N.Y. Public Library, to stimulate recruiting. July 1918. Underwood & Underwood.* (War Dept.)

**518.** *Albert Sterner painting war posters for the Government. Ca. 1918. IFS.* (War Dept.)

**519.** *Second Liberty Loan, Oct. 1917. Fattie Arbuckle, the movie star, putting up a Liberty Loan poster at Times Square, New York. Paul Thompson.* (War Dept.)

**520.** *Henry Reuterdahl (Lieut. U.S.N.R.) and N.C. Wyeth, noted artists, putting the last touches on the giant battle picture before the Sub-Treasury building, New York City, in the Third Liberty Loan campaign.* April 1918. Paul Thompson. (War Dept.)

**521.** *The "Human Squirrel" who did many daring "stunts" in climbing for benefit of War Relief Funds in New York City. He is shown here at a dizzy height in Times Square.* Ca. 1918. Times Photo Service. (War Dept.)

**522.** *Traffic policeman using 4th Liberty Loan fans for signals.* St. Louis, 1918. The Schreiber Co. (Bureau of Public Debt)

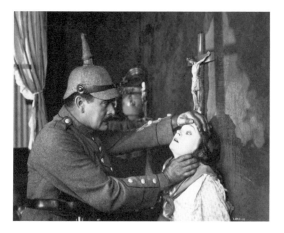

**523.** *Repairing front line trench after bomb explosion fifty yards from enemy trenches. D. W. Griffith in civilian clothing.* During filming of the motion picture *Hearts of the World* in France, 1917. (War Dept.)

**524.** *The Motion Picture — A Win-The-War Factor. Dorothy Gish in* The Greatest Thing in Life, *a D. W. Griffith Artcraft picture released by Famous Players–Lasky Corp.* 1918. (War Dept.)

**525.** *Mae Marsh, as a Belgian girl, and A. C. Gibbons as a German soldier, in Goldwyn's all-star Liberty Loan picture,* Stake Uncle Sam to Play Your Hand. 1918. (Bureau of Public Debt)

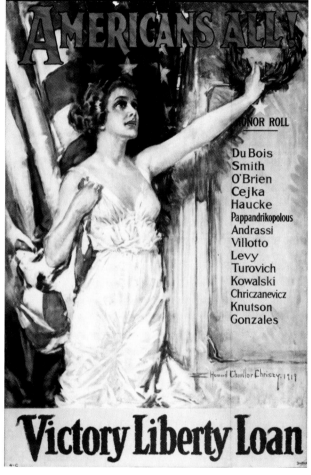

**526.** *Americans All! Victory Liberty Loan.* Ca. 1919. Color poster by Howard Chandler Christy. (Bureau of Public Debt)

**527.** *U*S*A Bonds / Third Liberty Loan Campaign / Boy Scouts of America / Weapons for Liberty.* 1918. Color poster by Joseph Christian Leyendecker. (Bureau of Public Debt)

**528.** *Beat back the Hun with Liberty Bonds.* Ca. 1918. Color poster by Frederick Strothmann. (Food Administration)

**529.** *Buy Your Victory Bonds.* Ca. 1917. Color poster. Issued by Victory Bond Committee, Ottawa, Canada. (Office of Naval Records and Library)

**530.** *On les aura! 2e Emprunt de la Défense Nationale / Souscrivez.* We will beat them! 2d National Defense Loan. Subscribe. 1916. Color poster by Jules Abel Faivre. (Office of Naval Records and Library)

**531.** *Clear The Way!! Buy Bonds / Fourth Liberty Loan.* Ca. 1918. Color poster by Howard Chandler Christy. (Food Administration)

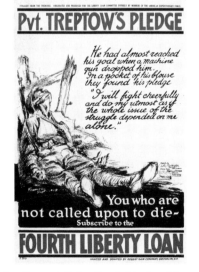

**532.** *Pvt. Treptow's Pledge.* "I will fight cheerfully and do my utmost as if the whole issue of the struggle depended on me alone." You who are not called upon to die — Subscribe to the Fourth Liberty Loan. 1918. Poster by Pvt. C. LeRoy Baldridge. (Food Administration)

**533.** *That Liberty Shall Not Perish From The Earth / Buy Liberty Bonds / Fourth Liberty Loan.* Ca. 1918. Color poster by Joseph Pennell. (Bureau of Public Debt)

# WAR WORK & PRODUCTION

*Photographs 534–558*

**534.** *Riveter at work at Hog Island Shipyard.* Pennsylvania, 1918. Kadel & Herbert. (War Dept.)

**535.** *Charles Knight (left) who won the prize offered by the London Mail for expert rivet driving. He drove 4,875 rivets in nine hours in a Government shipyard.* Ca. 1918. IFS. (War Dept.)

**536.** *Women electric welders at Hog Island shipyard. These are the first women to be engaged in actual ship construction, in the United States.* Ca. 1918. Paul Thompson. (War Dept.)

**537.** *Twenty five Indians from the Carlisle Indian College, Pa., are learning to build ships in the greatest shipyard in the world at Hog Island.* September 4, 1918. Western Newspaper Union. (War Dept.)

**538.** *Women Rivet Heaters and Passers on, Ship Construction Work. Navy Yard, Puget Sound, Washington.* May 29, 1919. (Women's Bureau)

**539.** *Building 100-foot concrete water tank boats for the Government. Inside of stern showing progress of construction. Manufactured by Great Northern Concrete Shipbuilding Co., Vancouver, Wash.* Ca. 1918. Gordon Stuart. (War Dept.)

**540.** *Building ships for the U.S. Navy at Hog Island, Pa. Group No. 1 from tower.* April 29, 1918. U.S. Shipping Board. (War Dept.)

**541.** *Launching the* Quistconck, *first completed at Hog Island shipyards. The President and Mrs. Wilson are standing on the platform on opposite sides of the flagpole. Mrs. Wilson christened the vessel.* Ca. 1918. Carl Thoner. (War Dept.)

**542.** Wooden ship built for United States Shipping Board Emergency Fleet Corp., by Pacific American Fisheries, Bellingham, WA, 1918. Grosart Studio. (War Dept.)

**543.** *Women taking place of men on Great Northern Railway at Great Falls.* Montana, ca. 1918. Great Falls Commercial Club. (War Dept.)

**544.** *Acetylene welding on cylinder water jacket.* 1918. (Army)

**545.** *Women workers in ordnance shops, Midvale Steel and Ordnance Co., Nicetown, Pa. Hand chipping with pneumatic hammers. 1918. Lt. Lubbe. (Army)*

**546.** *Some of the employees. All wear bloomers. Ca. 1918. Hope Webbing Co. (War Dept.)*

**547.** *English women in munition factory. Women and men working in storage shed for large shells. In most of the munition centers the Y.W.C.A. has established cafeterias and shampoo parlors. Ca. 1918–19. (Women's Bureau)*

**548.** *Hats manufactured for American soldiers by John B. Stetson Co., Phila., Pa. Pressing Army service hats. Ca. 1917–18. John B. Stetson Co. (War Dept.)*

**549.** *Manufacturing helmets. Large power press for shaping helmets in the plant of Hale & Kilburn Corp., Phila., Pa. Ca. 1918. Hale & Kilburn Corp. (War Dept.)*

**550.** *Stage Women's War Relief. Peggy O'Neil has supplied hundreds of American children with yarn and knitting needles to knit garments for destitute children of France and Belgium. January 28, 1919. Paul Thompson. (War Dept.)*

**551.** *Manufacturing heavy wool socks for the Government at Chipman Knitting Mills, Easton, Pa. The finished product, a pile of 84 needle heavy wool socks. Ca. 1918. Chipman Knitting Mills. (War Dept.)*

**552.** *Manufacturing barbed wire. Wire rods. Raw material from which steel wire is drawn. Pittsburgh Steel Co., Monessen, Pa. Ca. 1918. Pittsburgh Steel Co. (War Dept.)*

**553.** *Team Work Wins! Your work here makes their work over there possible / With your help they are invincible / Without it they are helpless. Ca. 1917–18. Color poster by Roy Hull Still. Issued by Army Ordnance Dept. (Food Administration)*

**554.** *Manufacturing steel ingots for the Government. Layout of Plant #1. Sullers Steel Co., St. Louis, Mo. Ca. 1918. W. C. Persons. (War Dept.)*

**555.** *Shop No. 2 annex. 6″ guns with their mounts in foreground; immediately iin the rear, slides or cradles for 10″, 12″, and 14″ guns. Bethlehem Steel Co. Ca. 1918. Bethlehem Steel Co. (War Dept.)*

**556.** *Interior view of projectile shop #1, machining 3″ shells. Bethlehem Steel Company, Bethlehem, Pa. Ca. 1918. Bethlehem Steel Co. (War Dept.)*

**557.** *Warning! Consider the Possible Consequences if You Are Careless in Your Work!* Ca. 1917–18. Color poster by L. N. Britton. Issued by Navy Publicity Bureau. (Office of Naval Records and Library)

**558.** *Manufacturing airplanes for the government by Dayton-Wright Airplane Company. Completed plane on exhibition. Plant-1. Operation No. 4.* July 25, 1918. Dayton-Wright Airplane Co. (War Dept.)

# FOOD CONSERVATION

*Photographs 559–573*

**559.** *W. A. McGirt, President of New Hanover Food Conservation Commission. Under his able leadership this Commission has led the state in methods, plans and accomplishments for food production and conservation.* Ca. 1917. Hodges. (Food Administration)

**560.** *School No. 26, Indianapolis, Indiana. Mrs. Hattye Gaillard, Instructor. Making preserves,* ca. 1917–18. (Food Administration)

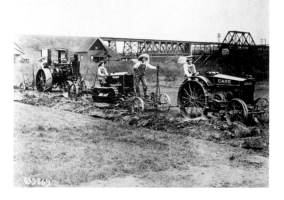

**561.** *Mrs. Mina C. van Winkle of Newark, N.J., in uniform of Food Administration. She was president of Woman's Political Union of New Jersey 8 years and is now head of Lecture Bureau of Food Administration.* Ca. 1917–18. (Food Administration)

**562.** *School children holding one of the large heads of cabbage raised in the War garden of P.S. 88, Borough of Queens, N.Y. City. The garden covers a tract of 1½ acres and yielded over $500 worth of produce.* Ca. 1918. J. H. Rohrbach. (War Dept.)

**563.** *Farmerettes guiding tractors.* Ca. 1917–18. (Army)

**564.** *Newton Square Unit of the Women's Land Army under command of National Defense.* Pennsylvania, 1918. Philadelphia Public Ledger. (War Dept.)

**565.** *Heroic Women of France. Hitched to the plough, cultivating the soil. All agriculture rests upon their shoulders. Uncomplaining, with an attitude that amounts almost to religious exultation, the woman of France bears the burden.* (Food Administration)

**566.** *Tacking up U.S. Food Administration posters at Mobile, Alabama.* Ca. 1918. Erik Overbey. (War Dept.)

**567.** *Foreign Legion, 4th Liberty Loan Drive, New Orleans, La.* October 2, 1918. Charles L. Franck. (War Dept.)

**568.** U.S. Food Administration sign, Baltimore, MD, ca. 1917–18. A. Jackson Co. (Food Administration)

**569.** *Food for France Fund booth at Connecticut State Fair, Hartford, Conn., week of Sept. 3, Housewives' Army, Hartford, Conn.* Ca. 1917. (Food Administration)

**570.** *Women of Boston are lending a helping hand in the drive for peach stones, which are being used by the Government in the production of gas masks. This Tableau was arranged to help in the campaign.* September 23, 1918. Underwood & Underwood. (War Dept.)

**571.** *Conserving food. Combing the wilds of Northern Michigan for wild game is one method of conservation employed in that section of the country.* Ca. 1918. Young. (War Dept.)

**572.** *Eat more corn, oats and rye products — fish and poultry — fruits, vegetables and potatoes / Baked, boiled and broiled foods / Eat less wheat, meat, sugar and fats to save for the Army and our allies.* 1917. Color poster by L. N. Britton. (Food Administration)

**FEED a FIGHTER**
Eat only what you need —
*Waste nothing* —
That he and his family
may have enough

# SUPPLY & SUPPORT

*Photographs 574–589*

**573.** *Feed a Fighter / Eat only what you need — Waste nothing — That he and his family may have enough. Ca. 1918.* Poster by Wallace Morgan. (Food Administration)

**574.** *Mighty battalion of Mack war trucks, all for the Engrs. Corps. Manufactured by the International Motor Co., Allentown, Pa. Ca. 1918.* G. W. King. (War Dept.)

**575.** *Thirty 45 H.P. "Caterpillar" Tractors comprising motorized equipment, 9th Field Artillery, Schofield Barracks, Hawaii, 1917. (First motorized artillery regiment in U.S. Army.)* Holt Manufacturing Co. (War Dept.)

**576.** *Mobile anti-aircraft searchlight, used by Engineer Corps. Night view of illumination from 24″ searchlights. Washington Barracks, D.C. April 17, 1918. Lt. William C. Fox.* (Army)

**577.** *Front view of the two-man tank manufactured by the Ford Motor Co., Detroit, Mich. Ca. 1918. Ford Motor Co.* (War Dept.)

**578.** *Three 5,000 cubic feet Nurse Balloons in Hangar. Fort Sill, OK, May 1, 1918.* (War Dept.)

**579.** *American telephone girls on arrival for "hello" duty in France. They all can speak both English and French.* March 1918. Q.M. Sgt. Leon H. Caverly. (Army)

**580.** *Attaching a message to a Signal Corps carrier pigeon, ca. 1917–18.* (Food Administration)

**581.** *Chain screens on steel helmet to protect soldiers' eyes from fragments of shell, rock, etc.; manufactured by E. J. Codd Co., Baltimore, Md. Ca. 1918. E. J. Codd Co.* (War Dept.)

**582.** *Soldier in black and white uniform to conceal him while climbing trees. He stands in front of a house camouflaged to represent a fence and trees. Co. F, 24th Engnrs. American University, D.C. November 14, 1917. Army Engineer Corps. (Army)*

**583.** *Recruits with their mattresses tied to them to serve as life preservers. Photo taken at Newport Naval Training Station, Rhode Island. April 1917. Underwood & Underwood. (War Dept.)*

**584.** *Result of Ordnance Department body armor test at Fort de la Peigney, Langres, France. Exhibit of body armor, heavy weight, showing effect of pistol, rifle and machine gun fire. Ca. 1918. Army Ordnance Dept. (Army)*

**585.** Private Shook trying to move mules hauling an American ammunition wagon stuck in the road, holding up the advance of the whole column. St. Baussant, east of St. Mihiel, France, September 13, 1918. Sgt. J. A. Marshall. (Army)

**586.** *The congestion of traffic on roads back of the American lines in the Argonne is, at certain places, so great that the streams of vehicles are not able to move faster than two miles an hour. This scene, in the ruins of Esnes, is typical. France, 1918. (Army)*

**587.** *View of Mudros showing French wine store. In the background is the French hospital. Lemnos Island, Aegean Sea. Dardanelles Campaign, ca. 1915. British Official. (War Dept.)*

**588.** *A pile of 85,000 solid tires for A.E.F. motor vehicles is one of the treasures of Langres, France. Shows men of Motor Transport Corps, assisted by German prisoners, building up wall of rubber to greater height.* January 6, 1919. (Army)

**589.** *Small portions of the Christmas mail that is being sorted at Pier 86, North River, N.Y.C., for the American Expeditionary Forces. The mail comes from every part of the country.* November 20, 1918. Lt. George Lyon. (Army)

# AVIATION, PHOTOGRAPHY, OBSERVATION

*Photographs 590–612*

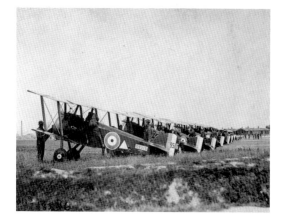

**590.** *Twenty-six aeroplanes in line for inspection, aviation field, Issoudon, France.* April 1918. (Army)

**591.** *148th American Aero Squadron field. Making preparations for a daylight raid on German trenches and cities. The machines are lined up and the pilots and mechanics test their planes. Petite Sythe, France.* August 6, 1918. Lt. Edward O. Harrs. (Army)

**592.** *First Lieut. E. V. [Eddie] Rickenbacker, 94th Aero Squadron, American ace, standing up in his Spad plane. Near Rembercourt, France.* October 18, 1918. Sgt. Gideon J. Eikleberry. (Army)

**593.** *2nd Lieut. Lawrence S. Churchill.* Rockwell Field, San Diego, CA, 1915. (War Dept.)

**594.** *Lt. Earl Carroll, prominent composer, is now a full-fledged aviator in the U.S. Service. He is shown beside his fast scout machine. Ca.* 1918. IFS. (War Dept.)

**595.** American pilot, 91st Aero Squadron, France, February 1919. Air Service Photographic Section. (Army Air Forces)

**596.** *1st Lt. Joseph E. Carberry, S.C.* Rockwell Field, San Diego, CA, 1914. (War Dept.)

**597.** *Marjorie Stinson, only woman to whom a pilot's license has been granted by Army & Navy Committee of Aeronautics.* Harris & Ewing. (War Dept.)

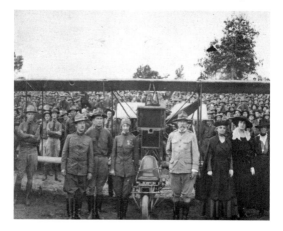

**598.** Ruth Law, the only woman permitted to wear the government aviation uniform in France for nonmilitary purposes, with members of the 29th Division, Camp McClellan, AL, ca. 1918. (National Archives Gift Collection)

**599.** *Lt. Frank Luke, who is running Lt. Eddie Ricken-backer a spirited race for the honor of being called the "ACE" of the American fliers overseas. Lt. Luke brought down three German observation balloons in thirty five minutes. 1918.* (Army)

**600.** *German plane C.L. 111 A 3892/18 brought down in the Argonne by American machine gunners, between Mont-faucon and Cierges, France, showing Red Cross painted on wings and fuselage of planes.* October 4, 1918. Pvt. J. E. Gibbon. (Army)

**601.** *First Air Depot — Process of repairing damaged planes.* Colombey, France, ca. 1918. Air Service Photographic Section. (Army Air Forces)

**602.** German aviator dropping a bomb somewhere on the western front. German Official. (War Dept.)

**603.** *Aeroplane Graflex camera in action.* Ca. 1917–18. (Army)

**605.** *14th Photo Section, 1st Army, "The Balloonatic Section." Capt. A. W. Stevens (center, front row) and personnel.* Ca. 1918. Air Service Photographic Section. (Army Air Forces)

**606.** *Major Steichen and Base Photo Section at Headquarters, Air Service, Paris, France.* Ca. 1918–19. Air Service Photographic Section. (Army Air Forces)

**604.** *Second Lieut. George E. Stone, Signal Corps, United States Army, in charge Fourth Army Corps Photo Unit. Cochem, Germany.* January 9, 1919. Sgt. Charles E. Mace. (Army)

**607.** *Second Lieut. Paul Weir Cloud, still operator, photographic unit with 89th Division. Near Kyllburg, Germany.* January 16, 1919. (Army)

**608.** *British balloon observer ready to make an ascension in Mesopotamia. Practically all the members of this crew are Indian troops.* Ca. 1915–17. Kadel & Herbert. (War Dept.)

**609.** *Camp de Meucon. Balloon ascending.* France, ca. 1918. Air Service Photographic Section. (Army Air Forces)

**610.** *Close-up view of an American major in the basket of an observation balloon flying over territory near front lines.* June 1918. (Army)

**611.** *Lieut. Kirk Booth of the U.S. Signal Corps being lifted skyward by the giant Perkins man-carrying kite at Camp Devens, Ayer, Mass.* Ca. 1918. IFS. (War Dept.)

**612.** *Returning from a U-Boat scouting party. Aerial naval observer coming down from a "Blimp" type balloon after a scouting tour somewhere on the Atlantic Coast.* Ca. 1918. Central News Photo Service. (War Dept.)

# THE FRONT

*Photographs 613–646*

**613.** *Fresh troops moving up to advanced position, France. Yorkshire regiment advancing at dusk.* IFS. (Army)

**614.** *Troops ready to hold the railway line. Merville, France. Ypres Salient and area.* April 11, 1918. British Official. (War Dept.)

**615.** *American snipers of the 166th Infantry (formerly 4th Inf., Ohio National Guard), in nest picking off Germans on the outer edge of town. Villers sur Fère, France.* July 30, 1918. Cpl. R. H. Ingleston. (Army)

**616.** *Sharpshooters have good view of enemy from shelter behind old brick wall. 28th Infantry, Bonvillers, France.* May 22, 1918. Pvt. Robert Longacre. (Army)

**617.** *Lieut. Col. R. D. Garrett, chief signal officer, 42nd Division, testing a telephone left behind by the Germans in the hasty retreat from the salient of St. Mihiel. Essey, France.* September 19, 1918. Cpl. R. H. Ingleston. (Army)

**618.** *Roof of Crown Prince's observatory, showing holes made by German shells. Americans using observation instruments left behind by the Germans in their hasty retreat from the Marne.* Montfaucon, France, October 17, 1918. Lt. Richard W. Sears. (Army)

**619.** *French troopers under General Gouraud, with their machine guns amongst the ruins of a cathedral near the Marne, driving back the Germans.* 1918. Central News Photo Service. (War Dept.)

**620.** *Gun crew from Regimental Headquarters Company, 23rd Infantry, firing 37mm gun during an advance against German entrenched positions.* 1918. (Army)

**621.** *French "37" in firing position on parapet in second-line trench. This gun has a maximum range of a mile and a half, is more accurate than a rifle, and is capable of firing 28 rounds a minute. Dieffmatten, Germany.* June 26, 1918. Cpl. Allen H. Hanson. (Army)

**622.** *Anti-aircraft machine gun of 101st Field Artillery (formerly 1st Massachusetts F.A., New England Coast Artillery), firing on a German observation plane at Plateau Chemin des Dames, France.* March 5, 1918. Lt. Edwin H. Cooper. (Army)

**623.** *Battery C, 6th Field Artillery, fired the first shot for America on the Lorraine front. A shell case flying through the air and a new shell sliding into the breech in the same fraction of a second. Beaumont, France.* September 12, 1918. Sgt. J. A. Marshall. (Army)

**624.** *Types of ordnance. British guns — elevated position mobile mount at the front.* Engineer Division Ordnance Dept. (War Dept.)

**625.** *14-inch gun talks for U.S. Men of the 35th Coast Artillery loading a mobile railroad gun, 13.9 inches calibre, on the Argonne front. Baleycourt, France.* September 26, 1918. Lt. Richard W. Sears. (Army)

**626.** *Greatest French gun [320mm] at moment of firing during a night bombardment. The belch of smoke from the explosion of the charge is a flash of light at night and makes a most unusual sight.* Underwood & Underwood. (War Dept.)

**627.** *Discharge of a huge French cannon caught by the camera just as the projectile left for the German lines. The gunners have stuffed their fingers into their ears to protect them from noise of explosion.* Ca. 1918. Underwood & Underwood. (War Dept.)

**628.** *Men entering a novel billet with their packs. Near Riencourt, France.* 1918. British Official. (War Dept.)

**629.** *W. Beach. It was a terrible place to live on. Shells would fall all through the night. British troops in bombproof shelter, Dardanelles Campaign.* Ca. 1915. British Official. (War Dept.)

**630.** *American troops going forward to the battle line in the Forest of Argonne.* France, September 26, 1918. Attributed to Lt. Adrian C. Duff. (Army)

**631.** *With the Americans northwest of Verdun. The skipper and gunner of a "whippet" tank, with the hatches open.* France, 1918. (Army)

**632.** *Machine gun set up in railroad shop. Company A, Ninth Machine Gun Battalion. Château Thierry, France.* June 7, 1918. Pvt. J. E. Gibbon. (Army)

**633.** *Germans in their well protected trenches on the Belgian frontier showing the men in the act of aiming at their enemy.* Underwood & Underwood. (War Dept.)

**634.** *American soldiers on the Piave front hurling a shower of hand grenades into the Austrian trenches. Varage, Italy.* September 16, 1918. Sgt. A. Marcioni. (Army)

**635.** *Canadian troops going "over the top" during training near St. Pol, France, October 1916.* Lt. Ivor Castle. Canadian Official. (Army)

**636.** *Scene just before the evacuation at Anzac. Australian troops charging near a Turkish trench. When they got there the Turks had flown.* Dardanelles Campaign, ca. 1915. British Official. (War Dept.)

**637.** *German infantry on the battlefield.* August 7. 1914. Underwood & Underwood. (War Dept.)

**638.** *A French assault on German positions. Champagne, France.* 1917. (Army)

**639.** *Picture posed in France, near front line trenches, by Major Evarts Tracey, Engineer Corps, U.S.A., to illustrate effects of phosgene gas.* 1918. (Army)

**640.** Gas masks for man and horse demonstrated by American soldier, ca. 1917–18. (Bureau of Medicine and Surgery)

**641.** *French soldiers using liquid fire to good advantage in front line trenches in France.* (Bureau of Medicine and Surgery)

**642.** *French soldiers making a gas and flame attack on German trenches in Flanders.* Belgium. (Army)

**643.** *At a height of 150 meters above the fighting line, the daring French photographer was able to get this rare photograph of French troops on the Somme Front, launching an attack on the Germans.* Ca. 1916–18. French Pictorial Service. (War Dept.)

**644.** *Eighteenth Infantry, Machine Gun Battalion passing through St. Baussant in advance upon St. Mihiel Front.* September 13, 1918. Attributed to Sgt. J. A. Marshall. (Army)

**645.** *These Tommies are in the trenches at St. Quentin getting their provisions which were brought up in limbers at night.* 1918. British Official. (Food Administration)

**646.** *French soldier resting after battle.* Underwood & Underwood. (War Dept.)

# AID & COMFORT

*Photographs 647–674*

**647.** *Visitors Day at the Naval Training Station. Boys of the Training Station shown taking their friends and relatives to the Hostess House, Great Lakes Naval Training Station, Chicago, Illinois.* Ca. 1918. (War Dept.)

**648.** *Cutting hair at the camp. 166th Field Hospital, Baccarat, France. May 15, 1918. Sfc. Charles H. White. (Army)*

**649.** *Thanksgiving cheer distributed for men in service. New York City turned host to the boys in service today and cared for every man in uniform. Ca. 1918. Underwood & Underwood. (War Dept.)*

**650.** *The "First Passover Sedar Dinner" given by Jewish Welfare Board to men of Jewish Faith in the A.E.F. in order that they may observe the Passover Holidays. Paris, France. April 1919. Pvt. L. Cohen. (Army)*

**651.** *The "Second Passover Sedar Dinner" given by Jewish Welfare Board, to the men of Jewish Faith in the A.E.F. Shows them singing "The Star Spangled Banner." Paris, France. April 1919. Pvt. L. Cohen. (Army)*

**652.** *Members of the 101st Field Signal Battalion (formerly 1st Massachusetts F.S.B.) at outdoor church services in the ruins of a church destroyed by shell fire. Verdun, France. October 18, 1918. Cpl. A. Klein. (Army)*

**653.** *Squad of American soldiers listening to one of their comrades playing the organ in the half-wrecked old church in Exermont, in the Argonne. France, October 11, 1918. Sgt. J. A. Marshall. (Army)*

**654.** *William Simmons, Marie Tiffany and A. W. Kramer, rendering a musical program at Camp Upton, Long Island, N.Y. Ca. 1918. C. Curtis. (War Dept.)*

**655.** *A very popular part of the Casino, the former restaurant. American boys are always ready for a song. Here are a few Y.M.C.A. girls rounding out the chorus. Aix-le-Bains, France. August 27, 1918. Lt. Duthewich. (Army)*

**656.** *Honoring men about to leave for camps. Colored women open a club to care for their men in the service, Newark, NJ. Ca. 1918. Mayor's Office, Newark, NJ. (War Dept.)*

**657.** *Wounded officers and Mrs. W. E. Corey, wife of the American steel magnate, who has given her home to wounded American officers. A game of bridge in progress on the veranda. Château de Villegenis at Palaiseau, France. September 18, 1918. Sgt. R. Sullivan. (Army)*

**658.** *Scene at A.R.C. Canteen at the station of Bordeaux, France, where soldiers of the Allied Armies get lunches, tobacco, etc. October 1918. American Red Cross. (War Dept.)*

**659.** *Time to open the A.R.C. hut at American Military Hospital No. 5, Auteuil, France. September 1918. American Red Cross. (War Dept.)*

**660.** *American Red Cross in Great Britain. One unit of the famous "Flying Squadron" priding themselves on being able to get under way within three minutes of the time a call is received. Ca. 1918. American Red Cross. (War Dept.)*

**661.** *American Red Cross Parade, Birmingham, Alabama. May 21, 1918. Birmingham View Co. (War Dept.)*

**662.** *Group of Polish nurses who were recruited through the efforts of the president of the Polish White Cross, Mme. Helena Paderewski. These 37 nurses will be the first unit of Polish nurses to go overseas. June 1918. Underwood & Underwood. (War Dept.)*

**663.** *Working personnel of Field Medical Supply Depot. Washington, DC, March 22, 1919. Cpl. Steiniger. (War Dept.)*

**664.** *The irrepressible Australians at Anzac. An Australian bringing in a wounded comrade to hospital. Dardanelles Campaign, ca. 1915. British Official. (War Dept.)*

**665.** *Members of the Medical Corps removing the wounded from Vaux, France. July 22, 1918. Sgt. Adrian C. Duff. (Army)*

**666.** *Marine receiving first aid before being sent to hospital in rear of trenches. Toulon Sector, France. March 22, 1918. Sgt. Leon H. Caverly, USMC. (Army)*

**667.** *This shattered church in the ruins of Neuvilly furnished a temporary shelter for American wounded being treated by the 110th Sanitary Train, 4th Ambulance Corps. France, September 20, 1918. Sgt. J. A. Marshall. (Army)*

**668.** *Salvation Army worker writing a letter to the home folks for the wounded soldier. Ca. 1917–18. Salvation Army. (War Dept.)*

**669.** *Soldier of Company K, 110th Regt. Infantry (formerly 3rd and 10th Inf., Pennsylvania National Guard), just wounded, receiving first-aid treatment from a comrade. Varennes-en-Argonne, France. September 26, 1918. Lt. Adrian C. Duff. (Army)*

**670.** *On the British Western Front during Battle of Menin Road. Scottish territorials being examined in a dressing station.* Belgium, 1914. British Bureau of Information. (War Dept.)

**671.** *Treatment room for gassed patients at American Evacuation Hospital No. 2, Baccarat, France.* June 8, 1918. Lt. J. S. Brown. (Army)

**672.** *Re-educating wounded. Blind French soldiers learning to make baskets.* American Red Cross. (War Dept.)

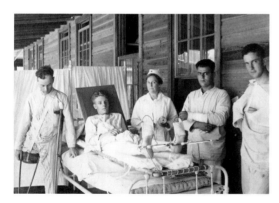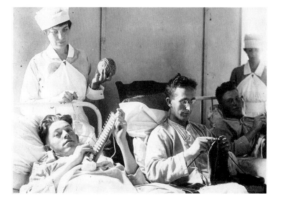

**673.** *Surgical patients. Base hospital, Camp Joseph E. Johnston, Florida.* Ca. 1918. (War Dept.)

**674.** *Bed-ridden wounded, knitting. Walter Reed Hospital, Washington, D.C.* Ca. 1918–19. Harris & Ewing. (War Dept.)

# CIVILIANS & REFUGEES

*Photographs 675–683*

**675.** *Avez Vous Place Dans Votre Coeur Pour Nous? Have you room in your heart for us.* Ca. 1918. Color poster by Walter de Maris. Issued by the Fatherless Children of France, Inc. (Office of Naval Records and Library)

**676.** *A Christmas street fiddler, Belgrade.* Serbia (Yugoslavia), December 1918. American Red Cross. (War Dept.)

**677.** *French Refugee Children. While waiting for train, children were fed with bread and milk from A.R.C. soldiers canteen.* American Red Cross. (War Dept.)

**678.** *Refugee children at Grand Val, near Paris, France, where a home has been established for them by the A.R.C.* Ca. 1918–19. American Red Cross. (War Dept.)

**679.** *An American Red Cross outing center on the coast near Dieppe, Belgium, where Belgian school children are able to spend the few happy moments they know.* Ca. 1917–18. IFS. (War Dept.)

**680.** *Refugees of Serbia entering Uskut showing the disheartened men, women and children as they streamed in.* Ca. 1917–19. American Red Cross. (War Dept.)

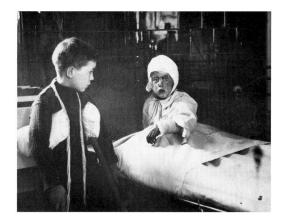

**681.** *The Great Air Raid on London. Some of the wounded schoolchildren in a hospital.* Ca. 1915. British Official. (War Dept.)

**682.** *Marcel Dupuy, young Belgian whose father was killed while fighting for his country, was a stowaway aboard the* Matsonia, *which brought California troops home from France.* January 3, 1919. IFS. (War Dept.)

**683.** *An old French couple, M. and Mme. Baloux of Brieulles-sur-Bar, France, under German occupation for four years, greeting soldiers of the 308th and 166th Infantries upon their arrival during the American advance.* November 6, 1918. Lt. Adrian C. Duff. (Army)

# PRISONERS & DETAINEES

*Photographs 684–690*

**684.** *Columns of German prisoners taken by the Americans in the first day of the assault on the St. Mihiel salient, marching in the rain toward the prison pens prepared for them at Ansauville, France.* September 25, 1918. Cpl. R. H. Ingleston. (Army)

**685.** *Turkish prisoners behind their own barbed wire at Seddul Bahr.* Ca. 1915. Dardanelles Campaign. British Official. (War Dept.)

**686.** *Wounded German prisoners receiving medical attention at first-aid station of 103rd and 104th Ambulance Companies. German second-line trench.* September 12, 1918. Pvt. J. M. Liles. (Army)

**687.** *German prisoners in a French prison camp.* French Pictorial Service. (War Dept.)

**688.** *Officers and crew of the German submarine U.58, captured by the U.S.S.* Fanning, *entering the War Prison Camp at Ft. McPherson, Ga.* April 1918. Mathewson & Winn. (War Dept.)

**689.** *Dr. Ernst Kunwald, former conductor of the Cincinnati Symphony Orchestra, entering the Federal Building, Cincinnati, Ohio, as a prisoner of war in charge of two U.S. deputy marshals.* 1917. J. R. Schmidt. (War Dept.)

**690.** *Woman anarchist leader and aid in draft war. Emma Goldman and Alexander Berkman convicted of conspiracy against draft law and sentenced to two years in penitentiary and fined $10,000 each, July 9, 1917.* IFS. (War Dept.)

# Death & Destruction

*Photographs 691–709*

**691.** *Austria's Atrocities. Blindfolded and in a kneeling position, patriotic Jugo-Slavs in Serbia near the Austrian lines were arranged in a semi-circle and ruthlessly shot at a command.* Underwood & Underwood. (War Dept.)

**692.** *German machine-gun nest and dead gunner. Villers Devy Dun Sassey, France.* November 4, 1918. Lt. M. S. Lentz. (Army)

**693.** *Sinking of the German Cruiser* Bluecher, *in the naval engagement between German and British dreadnoughts in the North Sea, on Jan. 24, 1915. This photo was taken from the deck of the British Cruiser* Arethusia. IFS. (War Dept.)

**694.** *Last minute escape from vessel torpedoed by German sub. The vessel has already sunk its bow into the waves, and her stern is slowly lifting out of the water. Men can be seen sliding down ropes as the last boat is pulling away. Ca. 1917.* Underwood & Underwood. (Army)

**695.** *Rescued passengers from the French Liner* Sontay, *which was torpedoed and sunk by a German submarine on April 10, 1918 while enroute from Marseilles to Salonika, climbing up the sides of a French gunboat which came to the rescue.* IFS. (War Dept.)

**696.** Ruins of St. Martin's Church in Ypres, Belgium, ca. 1918. (War Dept.)

**697.** *American advance northwest of Verdun. The ruined church on the crest of the captured height of Montfaucon. This was the condition of the site after the Americans finally drove the Germans out from it. France, 1918.* (Army)

**698.** *Town of Varennes, France, view due west across the River Aire. September 27, 1918. Lt. Stone.* (Army)

**699.** *View of ruins in front of the Cathedral of St. Quentin. France, October 14, 1918. Lt. Edward O. Harrs.* (Army)

**700.** *Ruins of Cathedral of St. Quentin. France, October 18, 1918. Pfc. William B. Gunshor.* (Army)

**701.** *Home Again. An old French couple visiting their former house in the devastated region, vacated by the Germans, find a mass of stone and debris, representing what was once home to them. Ca. 1916. Halftone from* Le Monde Illustre. (War Dept.)

**702.** *Street corner in Poelcapelle, Belgium.* December 19, 1918. Lt. Ira H. Morgan. (Army)

**703.** *A view of the ruins of Avocourt, situated just behind the American trenches before the Allied drive of September 26, 1918. Avocourt is now a pile of stones, scarcely a wall is standing.* France, October 6, 1918. Sgt. Gideon J. Eikleberry. (Army)

**704.** Aerial view of ruins of Vaux, France, 1918. Attributed to Edward Steichen. (Army Air Forces)

**705.** Combres Hill, France, ca. 1918–19. Air Service Photographic Section. (Army Air Forces)

**706.** *Aisne-Marne American Cemetery, Belleau, France. View of Block B, showing marble crosses. The crosses follow the conformity of the hillside at Aisne-Marne and produce a pleasing effect.* 1928. (American Battle Monuments Commission)

**707.** *St. Mihiel American Cemetery, near Thiaucourt, France. Soldier Monument and Chapel.* Ca. 1925–35. (American Battle Monuments Commission)

**708.** *President Harding placing wreath of flowers on casket of Unknown Soldier in rotunda of the Capitol.* November 9, 1921. (Army)

# PEACE

*Photographs 710–727*

**709.** *A most remarkable post-war incident was the washing up on the rocks at Falmouth, England, of two German U-boats. They were cast up but a few feet apart; both had been sunk during the war. 1921. INP. (OWI)*

**710.** *Peace rumor, New York. Crowd at Times Square holding up Extras telling about the signing of the Armistice. The Government report that the news was not true did not stop the celebration.* November 7, 1918. Western Newspaper Union. (War Dept.)

**711.** *President Wilson reading the Armistice terms to Congress.* November 11, 1918. Sgt. Vincent J. Palumbo. (Army)

**712.** *One of the guns of Battery D, 105th Field Artillery, showing American flag which was hoisted after the last shot had been fired when the armistice took effect. Etraye, France.* November 11, 1918. Sfc. Morris Fineberg. (Army)

**713.** *Armistice celebration. Yanks and Tommies.* November 1918. (Army)

**714.**   *Luxembourg girls greeting American Army of Occupation. 1918.* (Army)

**715.**   *The announcing of the armistice on Nov. 11, 1918, was the occasion for a monster celebration in Phila., Pa. Thousands massed on all sides of the replica of the Statue of Liberty on Broad Street, and cheered unceasingly. Philadelphia Public Ledger.* (War Dept.)

**716.**   *Home Again. Returning soldiers on the* Agamemnon. *Hoboken, N.J. Troops arriving from France, ca. 1919.* (Army)

**717.**   *The famous 369th arrive in N.Y. City. Members of the 369th Colored Inf., formerly 15th N.Y. regulars. "Back to little old New York." 1919. Paul Thompson.* (War Dept.)

**718.**   *Part of Squadron "A" 351st Field Artillery, colored troops who returned on the Transport* Louisville. *These men are mostly from Pennsylvania. February 17, 1919. Western Newspaper Union.* (War Dept.)

**719.**   *The Past is Behind Us, The Future is Ahead / Let us all strive to make the future better and brighter than the past ever was. 1918. Color poster by Gerrit A. Beneker. Issued by Dept. of Labor.* (U.S. Government Publications)

**720.** *Overseas men welcomed home. Parade in honor of returned fighters passing the Public Library, N.Y. City. 1919.*
Paul Thompson. (War Dept.)

**721.** *Col. Donovan and staff of 165th Inf., passing under
the Victory Arch, N.Y.C. 1919.* Paul Thompson. (War Dept.)

**722.** *Council of Four of the Peace Conference. Mr. Lloyd George; Signor Orlando; M. Clemenceau; President Woodrow Wilson. Hotel Crillon, Paris, France.* May 27, 1919. Capt. Jackson. (Army)

**723.** *Interior of the Galerie des Glaces showing the arrangement of tables for the signing of Peace Terms, Versailles, France.* June 27, 1919. Lt. M. S. Lentz. (Army)

**724.** *Interior of the Palace des Glaces during the signing of the Peace Terms. Versailles, France.* June 28, 1919. Lt. M. S. Lentz. (Army)

**725.** *This old castle perched on a hilltop above the Moselle River and the town of Cochem, Germany, is headquarters of the U.S. Fourth Army Corps. In foreground is Cpl. James C. Sulzer, Fourth Army Corps, Photo Unit.* January 9, 1919. Sgt. Charles E. Mace. (Army)

**726.** *A Merry Christmas *Peace* Your Gift to the Nation.* Ca. 1918. Color poster. (Food Administration)

**727.** *Soldiers being mustered out at Camp Dix.* New Jersey, 1918. Underwood & Underwood. (War Dept.)

*12:30. From the port side of the bridge we are watching the* Yorktown *land her planes. . . . "What's that?" . . . Strings of smoke-puffs just above the horizon, the distant rumble and boom of exploding shells, indicate that low flying enemy planes must be moving in for another attack. The skipper points his binoculars in the direction of the firing and I point my camera, begin taking pictures. It's too far away to see clearly what is going on; I find myself wishing they would head this way, want to get a close-up of a Jap plane coming in head-on . . . then develop a sickish feeling in the pit of the stomach as I realize with sudden clarity what it is I am wishing for. . . .*

COMDR. EDWARD STEICHEN

Edward Steichen, *The Blue Ghost — A Photographic Log and Personal Narrative of the Aircraft Carrier U.S.S. Lexington* in *Combat Operation*. (New York: Harcourt, Brace & Co., 1947), p. 101.

The Second World War was an inevitable result of the ascendance of Nazi fanaticism in Germany and the decades-long growth of nationalistic fervor in Japan. During the initial stages of the war in Europe, neutral America started building up its own defenses. The surprise attack on Pearl Harbor by the Japanese brought America into the war in 1941. After conquests in Southeast Asia, China, and the Pacific, the Japanese were gradually driven back, island by island, by the determined troops of the United States and its allies. The Germans were similarly pushed back, from North Africa, then from Italy, France, and the rest of Europe. Final victory was achieved on both fronts in 1945. The excesses of suffering, death, and destruction were immeasurable. The deprivations and atrocities levelled on civilian populations, the horrors of the concentration camps, and the devastation wrought by millions of tons of bombs can hardly be imagined by looking only at the following pictures.

*Opposite: Photo 1047*

# RECRUITMENT & TRAINING

*Photographs 728–742*

**728.** *I Want You for the U.S. Army / Enlist Now.* Color poster by James Montgomery Flagg. (Office of Government Reports)

**729.** *Man the Guns / Join the Navy.* 1942. Color poster by McClelland Barclay. (Office of Government Reports)

**730.** *For your country's sake today — For your own sake tomorrow / Go to the nearest recruiting station of the armed service of your choice.* 1944. Color poster by Steele Savage. (Office of Government Reports)

**731.** *The 93rd Infantry Division reactivated May 15, 1942, was the first all-Negro division to be formed during World War II. 2nd Lt. Arthur Bates waits for zero hour to give the command to attack. Fort Huachuca, AZ, 1942. Carl Gaston. (Army)*

**732.** *Students studying in diesel lab at submarine training school, New London, Conn. August 1943. (Navy)*

**733.** *Aviation cadets check flight boards for last minute instructions at NATC, Corpus Christi, Texas.* November 1942. Lt. Comdr. Charles Fenno Jacobs. (Navy)

**734.** *Aviation cadets await hops in ready room at Kingsville Field, NATC, Corpus Christi, Tex.* November 1942. Lt. Comdr. Charles Fenno Jacobs. (Navy)

**735.** *Crew members who man the 20 MM guns of a Coast Guard fighting ship have won an enviable reputation for gunnery results, due primarily to incessant practice in assembly and operation. As expressed by the intent faces in this picture, these men play for keeps.* (Coast Guard)

**736.** *Two Jeds scale brick wall in training exercises.* Milton Hall, England, ca. 1944. (OSS)

**737.** *Jeds on high bars in obstacle course.* Milton Hall, England, ca. 1944. (OSS)

**738.** *Audience in demolition class.* Milton Hall, England, ca. 1944. (OSS)

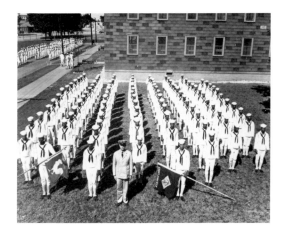

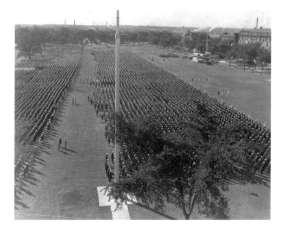

**739.** *Group of recently appointed Negro officers. Eleven of these men were recently appointed to the temporary rank of Ensign D-V(S), and one to Warrant Officer, USNR. February 1944.* (Navy)

**740.** *A Company of Negro recruits which has been entered in the "Hall of Fame" at the Great Lakes, Ill. Naval Training Station. The "hall" is to honor crack recruits. August 1943.* (Navy)

**741.** *Ceremony at Navtrasta, Great Lakes, as seen from roof of main administration building. 1942.* (Navy)

# PERSONALITIES

*Photographs 743–760*

**742.** *The Negro Seabees, members of Naval Construction Battalions, whose training center is at Camp Allen and Camp Bradford, near Norfolk, Virginia, are trained in landing tactics as well as in general military drill. Ca. 1942. Navy.* (OWI)

**743.** President Franklin D. Roosevelt signing the declaration of war against Japan, December 8, 1941. (National Park Service)

**744.** *General MacArthur surveys the beachhead on Leyte Island, soon after American forces swept ashore from a gigantic liberation armada into the central Philippines, at the historic moment when the General made good his promise "I shall return."* 1944. (Coast Guard)

**745.** *General Dwight D. Eisenhower, Supreme Allied Commander, at his headquarters in the European theater of operations. He wears the five-star cluster of the newly-created rank of General of the Army.* February 1, 1945. T4c. Messerlin. (Army)

**746.** *Führer und Duce in München.* Hitler and Mussolini in Munich, Germany, ca. June 1940. Eva Braun Collection. (Foreign Records Seized)

**747.** *Generalissimo and Madame Chiang Kai Shek and Lt. Gen. Joseph W. Stilwell, Commanding General, China Exped. Forces, on the day following Japanese bombing attack* [Doolittle Raid]. Maymyo, Burma. April 19, 1942. Capt. Fred L. Eldridge. (Army)

**748.** *Allies grand-strategy conference in N. Africa. Adm. E. J. King; Mr. Churchill; President Roosevelt; Standing, Maj. Gen. Sir Hastings Ismay; Lord Louis Mountbatten; and Field Marshal Sir John Dill.* 1943. New York Times Paris Bureau Collection. (USIA)

**749.** *Pres. F. D. Roosevelt in conference with Gen. D. MacArthur, Adm. Chester Nimitz, and Adm. W. D. Leahy, while on tour in Hawaiian Islands.* 1944. (Navy)

**750.** *Conference of the Big Three at Yalta makes final plans for the defeat of Germany. Here the "Big Three" sit on the patio together, Prime Minister Winston S. Churchill, President Franklin D. Roosevelt, and Premier Josef Stalin. February 1945. (Army)*

**751.** *"This is the brass that did it. Seated are Simpson, Patton (as if you didn't know), Spaatz, Ike himself, Bradley, Hodges and Gerow. Standing are Stearley, Vandenberg, Smith, Weyland and Nugent." Ca. 1945. Army. (OWI)*

**752.** *General of the Army Douglas MacArthur and Lt. Gen. Jonathan Wainwright greet each other at the New Grand Hotel, Yokohama, Japan, August 31, 1945, in their first meeting since they parted on Corregidor more than three years before. (Army)*

**753.** General George S. Patton acknowledging the cheers of the welcoming crowds in Los Angeles, CA, during his visit on June 9, 1945. Acme. (OWI)

**754.** *Faithful friend mourns American hero. Along with the many millions to mourn the passing of American hero, General George S. Patton, Jr., is his dog "Willie," the late general's pet bull terrier. Bad Nauheim, Germany. January 1946. INP. (OWI)*

**755.** *Brig. Gen. Benjamin O. Davis watches a Signal Corps crew erecting poles, somewhere in France. August 8, 1944. Cunningham. (Army)*

**756.** *Betty Hutton visits chow halls with sailors and Marines in the Marshall Islands. Peering over the screen star's shoulder is Virginia Carrol, dancer with the Hutton troupe.* December 1944. (Navy)

**757.** *Lieut. (j.g.) Robert Taylor, USNR, standing beside a Navy trainer at a West Coast Naval Air Station.* 1944. (Navy)

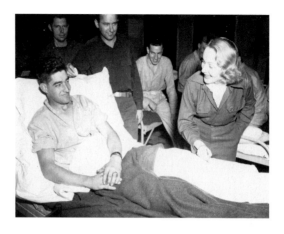

**758.** *Marlene Dietrich, motion picture actress, autographs the cast on the leg of Tec 4 Earl E. McFarland of Cavider, Texas, at a United States hospital in Belgium, where she has been entertaining the GIs.* November 24, 1944. Tuttle. (Army)

**759.** *Edward J. Steichen, photographic expert, on island platform, studies his surroundings for one of his outstanding photographs of life aboard an aircraft carrier. Steichen held the rank of Comdr. at this time. Ca.* 1943. Attributed to Lt. Victor Jorgensen. (Navy)

**760.** The five Sullivan brothers, all of whom were lost in the sinking of the U.S.S. *Juneau,* November 13, 1942. Acme. (OWI)

# The Home Front

## Patriotism & Propaganda

*Photographs 761–771*

**761.** *. . . we here highly resolve that these dead shall not have died in vain. . . Remember Dec. 7th!* 1942. Color poster by Allen Saalberg. (Office of Government Reports)

**762.** *This is Nazi brutality.* The Lidice Massacre, Czechoslovakia, 1942. Color poster by Ben Shahn. (Office of Government Reports)

**763.** *The five Sullivan brothers "missing in action" off the Solomons / They did their part.* 1943. Color poster. (Office of Government Reports)

**764.** *The Sowers.* Ca. 1942. Color poster by Thomas Hart Benton. (Office of Government Reports)

**765.** *We French workers warn you. . . defeat means slavery, starvation, death.* 1942. Color poster by Ben Shahn. (Office of Government Reports)

**766.** *The Fighting Filipinos / We will always fight for FREEDOM! Ca. 1943. Color poster by Isip. (War Production Board)*

**767.** *Buy War Bonds. 1942. Color poster. (Office of Government Reports)*

**768.** *Buy bonds at your nearest Skouras theatre! What d'ya mean — you ain't gonna buy no bonds! Owen Murphy Jr., at 7 months is super salesman for Uncle Sam. (Office of Government Reports)*

**769.** *Hasten the Homecoming / Buy Victory Bonds. Color poster by Norman Rockwell. (Office of Government Reports)*

**770.** *Forming a U.S. Coast Guard shield, high school students at Long Beach, Calif. make a striking appeal for the support of the current 7th War Loan drive, in which every purchase of a war bond helps to land that knockout blow against the Japs. Ca. 1945. (Coast Guard)*

**771.** *To prove that every working man in America is heart and soul behind this country's all-out war effort, the Wholesale and Warehouse Workers Union in New York City met for this imposing Victory rally in the city's famous Madison Square Garden. (OWI)*

# The Home Front

## Relocation

*Photographs 772–786*

**772.** *Following evacuation orders, this store was closed. The owner, a University of California graduate of Japanese descent, placed the "I AM AN AMERICAN" sign on the store front the day after Pearl Harbor. Oakland, CA, April 1942. Dorothea Lange. (WRA)*

**773.** *John W. Abbott, investigator for the Tolan Congressional Defense Committee on Migration, is shown speaking to a young celery grower who has just completed arrangements for leasing his farm during evacuation. San Jose, CA, March 27, 1942. Dorothea Lange. (WRA)*

**774.** *Field laborers of Japanese ancestry from a large delta ranch have assembled at WCCA Control Station to receive instructions for evacuation in three days under Civilian Exclusion Order No. 24. Byron, CA, April 28, 1942. Dorothea Lange. (WRA)*

**775.** *Dressed in uniform marking service in the first World War, this veteran enters Santa Anita Park assembly center for persons of Japanese ancestry evacuated from the West Coast. Arcadia, CA, April 5, 1942. Dorothea Lange. (WRA)*

**776.** *Members of the Mochida family awaiting evacuation bus. Identification tags are used to aid in keeping the family unit intact during all phases of evacuation. Hayward, CA, May 8, 1942. Dorothea Lange. (WRA)*

**777.** *These young evacuees of Japanese ancestry are awaiting their turn for baggage inspection upon arrival at this Assembly Center. Turlock, CA, May 2, 1942. Dorothea Lange. (WRA)*

**778.** *A young evacuee of Japanese ancestry waits with the family baggage before leaving by bus for an assembly center in the spring of 1942. California, April 1942. Clem Albers. (WRA)*

**779.** *A young evacuee of Japanese ancestry identifies her baggage at this assembly center prior to transfer to a War Relocation Authority center. Salinas Assembly Center, Salinas, California. March 31, 1942. Clem Albers. (WRA)*

**780.** *Persons of Japanese ancestry arrive at the Santa Anita Assembly Center from San Pedro. Evacuees lived at this center at the former Santa Anita race track before being moved inland to relocation centers. Arcadia, CA, April 5, 1942. Clem Albers. (WRA)*

**781.** *Trucks were jammed high with suitcases, blankets, household equipment, as well as children, all bearing registration tags, as the last Redondo Beach residents of Japanese ancestry were moved to assembly center at Arcadia. April 5, 1942. Clem Albers. (WRA)*

**782.** *These two girls peer out of a window in their quarters just after their arrival at Turlock assembly center. California, May 2, 1942. Dorothea Lange. (WRA)*

**783.** The Hirano family, left to right: George, Hisa, and Yasbei. Colorado River Relocation Center, Poston, AZ. (WRA)

**784.** *This assembly center has been open for two days. Only one mess hall was operating today. Photograph shows line-up of newly arrived evacuees outside this mess hall at noon. Tanforan Assembly Center.* San Bruno, CA, April 29, 1942. Dorothea Lange. (WRA)

**785.** *A close-up of an entrance of a family apartment (converted horse stall). Five people occupy two small rooms, the inner one of which is without outside door or windows. Tanforan Assembly Center.* San Bruno, CA, June 16, 1942. Dorothea Lange. (WRA)

**786.** *Dust storm at this War Relocation Authority center where evacuees of Japanese ancestry are spending the duration. Manzanar, California.* July 3, 1942. Dorothea Lange. (WRA)

# THE HOME FRONT

## RATIONING & CONSERVATION

*Photographs 787–797*

**787.** *SCRAP.* 1942. Color poster by Roy Schatt. (Office of Government Reports)

**788.** *Harvesting bumper crop for Uncle Sam. Movie star Rita Hayworth sacrificed her bumpers for the duration. Besides setting an example by turning in unessential metal car parts, Miss Hayworth has been active in selling war bonds.* 1942. Wide World. (OWI)

**789.** *As this big pile of used auto tires indicates, the United States with its many passenger cars has in discarded tires a large source of reclaimed rubber for use in the war effort.* (OWI)

**790.** Rationed tires. (Office of Price Administration)

**791.** Sugar rationing. (OWI)

**792.** *An eager school boy gets his first experience in using War Ration Book Two. With many parents engaged in war work, children are being taught the facts of point rationing for helping out in family marketing. February 1943. Alfred Palmer.* (OWI)

**793.** *If the points are cut, so must the price be. Slashed points without slashed prices are one of the surest clues to black-market meats. 1943. Ann Rosener.* (OWI)

**794.** *We're just MADE for each other. . . I water his victory garden, and he stakes my tomato plants. Cartoon drawing by Hilda Terry.* (OWI)

**795.** *I'm conserving wool, this bathing suit's painted on.* Cartoon drawing by Charles Shows. (OWI)

**796.** *You're the man, Jones, who said car pooling wouldn't work!* Cartoon drawing by Alain. (OWI)

**797.** *Don't travel unless essential.* Cartoon drawing by O. Soglow. (OWI)

# The Home Front

## War Work & Production

*Photographs 798–826*

**798.** *We Can Do It.* Color poster by J. Howard Miller. (War Production Board)

**799.** *Production aids — Ruby Reed and Merle Judd of Grumman Aircraft Eng. Corp.* Al Gould. (OWI)

**800.** *Women workers install fixtures and assemblies to a tail fuselage section of a B-17F bomber [the "Flying Fortress"] at the Long Beach, Calif., plant of Douglas Aircraft Company.* October 1942. Alfred Palmer. (OWI)

**801.** *Secretaries, housewives, waitresses, women from all over central Florida are getting into vocational schools to learn war work. Typical are these in the Daytona Beach branch of the Volusia county vocational school.* April 1942. Howard R. Hollem. (OWI)

**802.** *Stars over Berlin and Tokyo will soon replace these factory lights reflected in the noses of planes at Douglas Aircraft's Long Beach, Calif., plant. Women workers groom lines of transparent noses for deadly A-20 attack bombers. October 1942. Alfred Palmer. (OWI)*

**803.** *Construction of aircraft at the Glenn L. Martin plant at Baltimore, Md. Machine gun turrets are completely assembled and operated before installed in the carcass of PBM. February 1943. Lt. Comdr. Charles Fenno Jacobs. (Navy)*

**804.** *Riveter at Lockheed Aircraft Corp., Burbank, CA. (Women's Bureau)*

**805.** *Workmen at the Vega aircraft plant, Burbank, Calif. Two women employees working through the bombardier's hatch. August 1943. Attributed to Lt. Comdr. Charles Fenno Jacobs. (Navy)*

**806.** *Mary Josephine Farley, who at 20 is considered a top notch mechanic, working on a Wright Whirlwind airplane motor which she rebuilt at a Naval Air Base. Girls like Miss Farley are helping to keep our fighting ships flying. October 1942. Howard R. Hollem. (OWI)*

**807.** *Kaiser shipyards, Richmond, Calif. Miss Eastine Cowner, a former waitress, is helping in her job as a scaler to construct the Liberty Ship SS George Washington Carver launched on May 7, 1943. E. F. Joseph. (OWI)*

**808.** *Checking finished PV-1 at the Vega aircraft plant, Burbank, Calif. Workmen spin propeller.* August 1943. Lt. Comdr. Charles Fenno Jacobs. (Navy)

**809.** *Line up of some of women welders including the women's welding champion of Ingalls.* Ingalls Shipbuilding Corp., Pascagoula, MS, 1943. Spencer Beebe. (Women's Bureau)

**810.** Trackwomen, 1943. B & O Railroad. (Women's Bureau)

**811.** Mechanical helper, B & O Railroad. (Women's Bureau)

**812.** *Like girls from Mars are these "top women" at U.S. Steel's Gary, Indiana, Works. Their job is to clean up at regular intervals around the tops of twelve blast furnaces. As a safety precaution, the girls wear oxygen masks.* U.S. Steel Corp. (Women's Bureau)

**813.** *Chippers.* 1942. Marinship Corp. (Women's Bureau)

**814.** *Safety garb for women workers. The uniform at the left, complete with the plastic "bra" on the right, will prevent future occupational accidents among feminine war workers.* Los Angeles, CA, 1943. Acme. (Women's Bureau)

**815.** *Welders work on hull of new submarine at Electric Boat Co., Groton, Conn.* August 1943. Lt. Comdr. Charles Fenno Jacobs. (Navy)

**816.** *Steel under giant rolls being shaped for submarine construction at Electric Boat Co., Groton, Conn.* August 1943. Lt. Comdr. Charles Fenno Jacobs. (Navy)

**817.** *A woman war worker checks over 1,000-pound bomb cases before they are filled with deadly charges of explosives and shipped off to Allied bases and battlefronts all over the world. Firestone Tire and Rubber Co.* Omaha, NE, ca. May 1944. Acme. (OWI)

**818.** *Lunch time at the Vega aircraft plant, Burbank, Calif. A quartet of girl workers.* August 1943. Photograph attributed to Lt. Comdr. Charles Fenno Jacobs. (Navy)

**819.** *Workers eat lunch against PBY wing panels at Consolidated Vultee aircraft plant, San Diego, Cal.* August 1943. Lt. Comdr. Charles Fenno Jacobs. (Navy)

**820.** *Man working on hull of U.S. submarine at Electric Boat Co., Groton, Conn.* August 1943. Lt. Comdr. Charles Fenno Jacobs. (Navy)

**821.** *Launching of USS* ROBALO *9 May 1943, at Manitowoc Shipbuilding Co., Manitowoc, Wis.* (Navy)

**822.** *Give us LUMBER for more PT's.* 1943. Color poster. (Office of Government Reports)

**823.** *Save them this fate / don't stay home from work! Back up our battleskies!* Color poster. (War Production Board)

**824.** *Jap. . . You're Next!* 1944. Color poster by James Montgomery Flagg. (Office of Government Reports)

**825.** *They're watching us. . . PLENTY! The stuff "on order" doesn't count. . . but real production hurts them! Put ALL your power in the job!* Color poster. (War Production Board)

826. *Night view of the final assembly section at the Vultee Aircraft Corporation plant.* Assembling the "Vengeance" bomber, Nashville, TN, August 1942. Jack Delano. (OWI)

# THE HOME FRONT

## SECURITY

*Photographs 827–832*

827. *Someone talked!* 1942. Color poster by Siebel. (Office of Government Reports)

828. *Silence means security.* 1944. Color poster by Schlaikjer. (Office of Government Reports)

**829.** *Don't be a sucker! Keep your mouth shut.* 1944. Color poster. (Office of Government Reports)

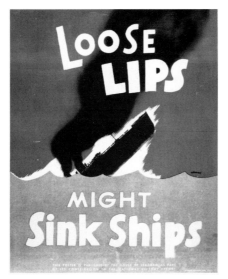

**830.** *Loose lips might sink ships.* Color poster by Ess-argee. (Office of Government Reports)

**831.** *Eyes of the Home Skies / Civil Air Patrol of the U.S. Office of Civilian Defense.* 1943. Color poster by Kenney. (Office of Government Reports)

**832.** *Accident or Sabotage? Prevent it by vigilance.* Color poster. (War Production Board)

# Supply & Support

*Photographs 833–871*

**833.** Machine for deciphering Japanese "Purple" diplomatic code, ca. 1940–41. (National Archives)

**834.** *Radar scope. Ca. 1944–45.* (Navy)

**835.** *Installing a bearing ring on a 5″ gun aboard a submarine at an advanced base.* May 1945. Lt. Comdr. Horace Bristol. (Navy)

**836.** *Mechanics check engine of SNJ at Kingsville Field, NATC, Corpus Christi, Texas.* November 1942. Lt. Comdr. Charles Fenno Jacobs. (Navy)

**837.** *Sailor adjusts aerial of plane in front of control tower at NATC, Corpus Christi, Texas.* November 1942. Lt. Comdr. Charles Fenno Jacobs. (Navy)

**838.** *Ordnancemen loading belted cartridges into SBD-3 at NAS Norfolk, Va.* September 1942. (Navy)

**839.** *Five-inch rockets being loaded under the wing of an F4U of MAG-33. Just before take-offs, the safety pins are removed and the rockets are ready for charging.* Okinawa, June 1945. Lt. David D. Duncan. (Marine Corps)

**840.** *Aviation machinists mates at Navy pier, Chicago, Illinois. Students working on a complex aircraft engine.* July 1942. (Navy)

**841.** *Torpedomen relaxing beneath rows of deadly torpedoes in torpedo shop.* May 1945. Lt. Comdr. Horace Bristol. (Navy)

**842.** *Integral wing tanks on plane at ARU [Aircraft Repair Unit] Guadalcanal.* September 1944. (Navy)

**843.** *PBM is hosed down after it was hauled up ramp at NAS Banana River, Fla.* March 1943. Lt. Comdr. Charles Kerlee. (Navy)

**844.** *Beaching crew clings to bow line of PBM at NAS Banana River, Fla.* March 1943. Lt. Comdr. Charles Kerlee. (Navy)

**845.** *Enlisted men repair and check instruments aboard a submarine just returned to Pearl Harbor.* Hawaii. May 1945. Lt. Comdr. Horace Bristol. (Navy)

**846.** *Balloons safely tucked away in the hangar for the night. W.A.A.F. balloon operators report for inspection before going off duty after a strenuous day of training on the balloon site.* England. New York Times Paris Bureau Collection. (USIA)

**847.** *Lower Away. Down goes a jeep from the deck of a Coast Guard-manned assault transport into a landing craft, during amphibious maneuvers of Coast Guard and infantry units in the European war theatre.* Shelby Smith. (Coast Guard)

**848.** *Group 4. Torpedo room.* England, ca. 1944. (OSS)

**849.** *Group 4. Checking pipe.* England, ca. 1944. (OSS)

**850.** *Red Cross field men preparing to ship gift boxes to servicemen fighting on Leyte and other islands in the Philippines. Efforts are being made to assure each man a gift package on Christmas Day.* New Guinea, November 20, 1944. American Red Cross. (OWI)

**851.** *Group 4. Looking over guns in guard room.* England, ca. 1944. (OSS)

**852.** *Bomb handling at an advanced Pacific base.* Ca. 1944. Marine Corps. (Navy)

**853.** *Corporal Charles H. Johnson of the 783rd Military Police Battalion, waves on a "Red Ball Express" motor convoy rushing priority materiel to the forward areas, near Alençon, France.* September 5, 1944. Bowen. (Army)

**854.** *Victory cargo ships are lined up at a U.S. west coast shipyard for final outfitting before they are loaded with supplies for Navy depots and advance bases in the Pacific. Ca. 1944. (OWI)*

**855.** *Invasion of Cape Gloucester, New Britain, 24 Dec. 1943. Crammed with men and material for the invasion, this Coast Guard-manned LST nears the Japanese held shore. Troops shown in the picture are Marines. PhoM1c. Don C. Hansen. (Coast Guard)*

**856.** *Out of the gaping mouths of Coast Guard and Navy Landing Craft, rose the great flow of invasion supplies to the blackened sands of Iwo Jima, a few hours after the Marines had wrested their foothold on the vital island. 1945. PhoM2c. Paul Queenan. (Coast Guard)*

**857.** *Hundreds of drums of gasoline rolling up on the sands of Luzon from Coast Guard-manned landing craft tell graphically why the home front motorists carry gas ration books and why occasionally the fuel pumps run dry. Ca. 1945. (Coast Guard)*

**858.** *"Water Buffalo" [amphibious tanks] line up for invasion of Cape Sansapor at the western end of Dutch New Guinea. In silhouette, Coast Guardsman Robert Campbell stands guard. Ca. 1944. (Coast Guard)*

**859.** *Kwajalein Atoll. Pfc. N. E. Carling stands beside the medium tank "Killer" on which is mounted a dead Japanese light tank. February 2, 1944. Tennelly. (Marine Corps)*

**860.** *Giant seawall under construction by Seabees of the 76th Construction Battalion at Apra Harbor, Guam. A 30-ton boulder is hauled to dumping spot. 1945. Lt. Comdr. Charles Fenno Jacobs. (Navy)*

**861.** *"Don't tell me there's anything the engineers can't do. We built bridges where bridges couldn't be built. We built them with or without material. Mostly, though, we laid Baileys." Army. (OWI)*

**862.** *Looking up from Taiping River as cables are attached to suspension clamps of stiffening girder section from west bank, in order to raise or lower it to level of section from opposite bank. Bailey bridge. 209th Engr. Combat Bn. China, February 4, 1945. Metzger. (Army)*

**863.** *The war over, German soldiers here are crossing a pontoon bridge from Branau, Austria to Simbach, Germany. Soldiers of 245th Engineers who made the bridge watch the trucks go by. May 11, 1945. Pvt. T. R. Romero. (Army)*

**864.** *Installing cross beams on a 10,000 bbl. gasoline tank, being built by the 775th P.D.L. Co. at Myitkyina, Burma. September 28, 1944. T4c. Zimmerman. (Army)*

**865.** *T/3 Clifford Wright, of Culver City, Calif., a U.S. Army Signal Corps Photographer, shoots motion pictures of supplies being dropped by aircraft to Chinese Forces in the interior of China. June 17, 1944. T4c. Clayton. (Army)*

**866.** *T/3 James Ellis, Ehrenfeld, Pa., laying out the photographs to check their sequence. 660th Engineers, Kew Gardens, England.* January 11, 1943. Ham. (Army)

**867.** *S/Sgt. Blake Ellis, Sheel Creek, Tenn., inking in the pencil tracings. Culture, Hydrography, and Contours are shown. England,* January 11, 1943. Ham. (Army)

**868.** *Sgt. Carl Weinke and Pfc. Ernest Marjoram, Signal Corps cameramen, wading through stream while following infantry troops in forward area during invasion at a beach in New Guinea. Red Beach 2, Tanahmerah.* April 22, 1944. T4c. Ernani D'Emidio. (Army)

**869.** *Canines of the QM War Dog Platoon were used on Biak Island, off the coast of New Guinea, to track down Japanese hidden in caves and jungle fastness. One of these dogs is seen here, at the order to attack, straining at the leash.* July 18, 1944. (Army)

**870.** *U.S. Marine "Raiders" and their dogs, which are used for scouting and running messages, starting off for the jungle front lines on Bougainville.* Ca. November/December 1943. T.Sgt. J. Sarno. (Marine Corps)

**871.** *Pfc. Angelo B. Reina, of Utica, N.Y., Co. A, 391st Inf. Regt., guards a lonely Oahu beach position. Kahuku, Oahu. Hawaii,* March 1945. Rosenberg. (Army)

# Rest & Relaxation

*Photographs 872–900*

**872.** *Life beneath the seas on a U.S. submarine. A submariner reading his favorite comic-strip. The submarine mascot pants in the shade of the conning tower.* (Navy)

**873.** *Marines pause at Agat during lull in battle for recapture of Guam.* July 1944. Lt. Paul Dorsey. (Navy)

**874.** *Marine Pfc. Douglas Lightheart (right) cradles his 30-cal. machine gun in his lap, while he and his buddy Pfc. Gerald Churchby take time out for a cigarette, while mopping up the enemy on Peleliu Is.* September 14, 1944. Cpl. H. H. Clements. (Marine Corps)

**875.** *Using an unexploded 16-inch naval shell for a resting place, Marine Pfc. Raymond Hubert, shakes a three-day accumulation of sand from his boondocker.* Saipan, July 4, 1944. S.Sgt. A. B. Knight. (Marine Corps)

**876.** *Crewman of a PT covering himself with soap prior to dive over side of ship in the Philippines.* December 1944. Lt. Wayne Miller. (Navy)

**877.** *Marines of VMF-222 on Bougainville relaxing in between strikes.* April 1944. Lt. Comdr. Charles Fenno Jacobs. (Navy)

**878.** *Sailor reading in his bunk aboard USS* CAPELIN *at submarine base New London, Conn.* August 1943. Lt. Comdr. Charles Fenno Jacobs. (Navy)

**879.** Soldiers in bunks on Army transport SS *Pennant*, San Francisco Port of Embarkation, November 1, 1942. (Army)

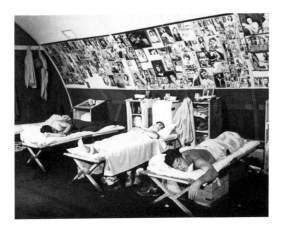

**880.** *Sailors of ARU-145, Guadalcanal, during their free time. Sack time a favorite past time.* August 1944. (Navy)

**881.** *Marine Corporal Earl Brunitt (left) and Private Genare Nuzzi share a foxhole and a couple of ponchos on Okinawa with a war orphan.* April 1945. Sgt. W. A. McBride or Sgt. Howard S. England. (Marine Corps)

**882.** *Pfc. Rez P. Hester, 7th War Dog Platoon, 25th Regt., takes a nap while Butch, his war dog, stands guard. Iwo Jima,* February 1945. S.Sgt. M. Kauffman. (Marine Corps)

**883.** *Blanket-bouncing time out west. Marines in the Pacific have their own ways and means of "touching the sky." Pictured in the spread-eagle pose is Marine Pvt. John Serdula, being tossed in the air by a group of his fellow Marines. Ca. 1945.* (Marine Corps)

**884.** *Activities aboard USS* MONTEREY. *Navy pilots in the forward elevator well playing basketball. Jumper at left has been identified as Gerald Ford. June/July 1944. Attributed to Lt. Victor Jorgensen.* (Navy)

**885.** *U.S. Coast Guardsmen go for a swim under the hull of a famous Japanese landmark in the Solomons. It is the* KINUGAWA MARU, *beached by the Japanese after being riddled by American gunners. Ca. 1943–44.* (Coast Guard)

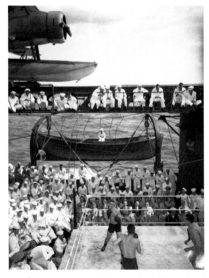

**886.** *The old (Pacific) swimmin' hole. Come on in mates; the water's fine. And there's plenty of it between the coast of California and the shores of the Philippines. Coast Guardsmen and Marines "beat the heat" by taking a dip from the side of the ship. 1944.* (Coast Guard)

**887.** *President Truman and party aboard USS* AUGUSTA *for return trip from the Potsdam Conference. Watching boxing bouts during smoker on well deck. August 1945.* (Navy)

**888.** *Maj. Gen. Gilbert Cheves (left) and Maj. Gen. Claire Chennault observe a typically American custom to open a softball game in China. Gen. Chennault pitched for the "Flying Tigers," while Gen. Cheves held down first base for the opposing team. 1945.* (Army)

**889.** *Neptune party on USS* ENTERPRISE. September 1944. (Navy)

**890.** *Neptune party on USS* ENTERPRISE. *Pollywog V. E. Christensen, S2c., gives his shipmates a song or two on the flight deck.* September 1944. (Navy)

**891.** *Personnel of USS* LEXINGTON *celebrate Christmas with make-shift decorations and a firefighting, helmeted Santa Claus.* December 1944. Lt. Barrett Gallagher. (Navy)

**892.** Personnel of OSS camp, Ceylon, 1945. (OSS)

**893.** *Cpl. Bernard Butnik, Cleveland Heights, Ohio, and Sgt. Richard Goodbar, Russellville, Ark., offer "Agnes" their snow woman, cigarettes and a "coke."* European theater, January 14, 1945. Sgt. G. W. Herold. (Army)

**894.** *Sailor eating sandwich beneath propellers of torpedo being loaded aboard U.S. submarine at New London, Conn.* August 1943. Lt. Comdr. Charles Fenno Jacobs. (Navy)

**895.** *Much tattooed sailor aboard the USS* NEW JERSEY.
December 1944. Lt. Comdr. Charles Fenno Jacobs.
(Navy)

**896.** *Sgt. Franklin Williams, home on leave from army duty, with his best girl Ellen Hardin, splitting a soda. They met at Douglas High School.* Baltimore, MD, May 1942. Arthur Rothstein. (OWI)

**897.** *Navy pilots relax and enjoy feminine companionship, sports and entertainment at Chris Holmes Rest Home, maintained for pilots on leave from combat. Fingers replace forks at chow-time.* Hawaii, March 1944. Lt. Comdr. Charles Fenno Jacobs. (Navy)

**898.** *U.S. Navy pilot and date stand under tropical vegetation at Glen Innis Rest Home in New Zealand.* March 1944. Lt. Comdr. Horace Bristol. (Navy)

**899.** *Liberty party. Liberty section personnel aboard LCM returning to USS CASABLANCA from Rara Island, off Pitylieu Island, Manus.* Admiralty Islands, April 19, 1945. PhoM1c. R. W. Mowday. (Navy)

**900.** *A youngster, clutching his soldier father, gazes upward while the latter lifts his wife from the ground to wish her a "Merry Christmas." The serviceman is one of those fortunate enough to be able to get home for the holidays.* December 1944. Acme. (OWI)

# ENTERTAINMENT

Photographs 901–905

**901.** *"This Is The Army," Irving Berlin's Broadway hit, with an all-soldier cast, is making $40,000 a week for Army Relief. Don't let them fool you, boys. They're chorus "gals," but tough as mule meat. 1942. (OWI)*

**902.** *Pfc. Mickey Rooney imitates some Hollywood actors for an audience of Infantrymen of the 44th Division. Rooney is a member of a three-man unit making a jeep tour to entertain the troops. Kist, Germany, April 13, 1945. T5c. Louis Weintraub. (Army)*

**903.** *Danny Kaye, well known stage and screen star, entertains 4,000 5th Marine Div. occupation troops at Sasebo, Japan. The crude sign across the front of the stage says: "Officers keep out! Enlisted men's country." October 25, 1945. Pfc. H. J. Grimm. (Marine Corps)*

**904.** *Bing Crosby, stage, screen and radio star, sings to Allied troops at the opening of the London stage door canteen in Piccadilly, London, England. August 31, 1944. Pearson. (Army)*

**905.** *A portion of the 10,000 GI's who were on hand to witness the showing of the Copacabana All Girl Review, listen attentively while the girls' trio sing from the stage of the Glenn Miller Theater, near Marseilles, France. August 29, 1945. Bransford. (Army)*

# AID & COMFORT

*Photographs 906–934*

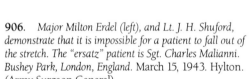

**906.** *Major Milton Erdel (left), and Lt. J. H. Shuford, demonstrate that it is impossible for a patient to fall out of the stretch. The "ersatz" patient is Sgt. Charles Malianni.* Bushey Park, London, England. March 15, 1943. Hylton. (Army Surgeon General)

**907.** *Crewmen lifting Kenneth Bratton (AOM) out of turret of TBF on the USS SARATOGA after raid on Rabaul.* November 1943. Lt. Wayne Miller. (Navy)

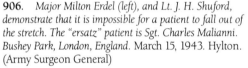

**908.** *They did their part. Wounded Marines are helped to an aid station by Navy corpsmen and Marine walking wounded.* Iwo Jima, ca. February/March 1945. Cpl. Eugene Jones. (Marine Corps)

**909.** Medics helping injured soldier, France, 1944. (OWI)

**910.** *An American medium tank hit a Jap land mine in surging forward to the Tacloban Air Strip during the early stages of the Philippines invasion on Oct. 20. Here, one of the wounded from the wrecked tank is being bandaged by a medical corpsman.* 1944. (Coast Guard)

**911.** *Pvt. W. D. Fuhlrodt is removed from the tank which carried him from the front lines. Japanese artillery and small arms fire made it impossible for ambulances to carry the wounded to the rear. Okinawa, 1945. Sgt. Thomas D. Barnett, Jr. (Marine Corps)*

**912.** *Medics remove a casualty from the battle field to an aid station in an air raid shelter, near Brest, France, formerly used by the Germans. August 28, 1944. Gilbert. (Army)*

**913.** *Marines wounded during the landing on Tarawa are towed out on rubber boats by their buddies to larger vessels that will take them to base hospitals for better medical care. November 1943. (Marine Corps)*

**914.** *Casualties shown lying on stretchers aboard lighter, Munda Point, New Georgia. Ca. July/August 1943. Wendlinger. (Army)*

**915.** *One of the first to fall. Wounded in the initial invasion at Empress Augusta Bay, Bougainville, this American is hoisted aboard a Coast Guard-manned transport off shore. November 1943. (Coast Guard)*

**916.** *Transfer of wounded from USS BUNKER HILL to USS WILKES BARRE, who were injured during fire aboard carrier following Jap suicide dive bombing attack off Okinawa in Ryukyus. May 11, 1945. PhoM3c. Kenneth E. Roberts. (Navy)*

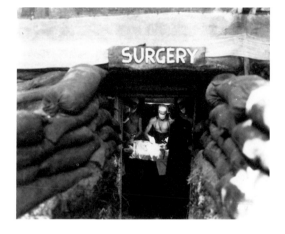

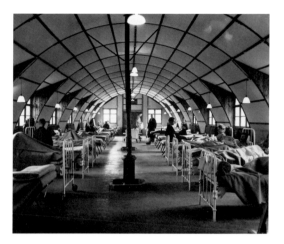

**917.**  *American medics treat casualties at an American portable surgical unit during the 36th Division drive on Pinwe, Burma.* November 12, 1944. Sgt. W. Lentz. (Army)

**918.**  *In an underground surgery room, behind the front lines on Bougainville, an American Army doctor operates on a U.S. soldier wounded by a Japanese sniper.* December 13, 1943. Attributed to Miller. (Army)

**919.**  *General view of a typical medical ward of the 2nd Evac. Hosp., Diddington, England.* June 3, 1943. Hedrich. (Army Surgeon General)

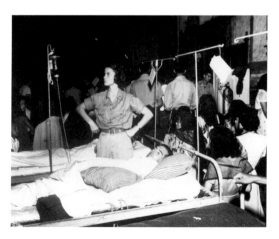

**920.**  *Pfc. Warren Capers recommended for Silver Star. With other members of his medical detachment Private Capers set up a dressing station and aided over 330 soldiers on a beachhead on D-Day.* August 18, 1944. Cunningham. (Army Surgeon General)

**921.**  *Nurses of a field hospital who arrived in France via England and Egypt after three years service.* August 12, 1944. Parker. (Army Surgeon General)

**922.**  *1st Lt. Phyllis Hocking adjusts glucose injection apparatus for a GI patient in the 36th Evac. Hospital, Palo, Leyte, P.I., quartered in the Church of the Transfiguration, as the congregation kneels during Christmas Eve services.* December 24, 1944. (Army Staff)

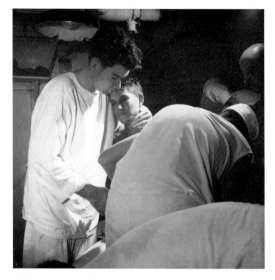

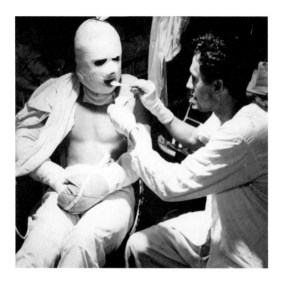

**923.**  *Pvt. J. B. Slagle, USA, receives his daily dressing of wounds on board USS SOLACE enroute from Okinawa to Guam. May 1945. Lt. Victor Jorgensen. (Navy)*

**924.**  *Pressure bandaged after they suffered burns when their ship was hit by a Kamikaze attack, men are fed aboard the USS SOLACE. 1945. Attributed to Lt. Victor Jorgensen. (Navy)*

**925.**  *Medicine in the form of ice-cream sundaes and banana splits are enjoyed by the convalescing battle casualties at the 1st U.S. General Hospital, Paris, France. February 22, 1945. T4c. Baum. (Army Surgeon General)*

**926.**  *These Marines, begrimed and weary from two days and two nights of fighting, are typical of the conquerors of Eniwetok Atoll. Pfc. Faris M. (Bob) Tuohy, 19, is the Marine holding the coffee cup. Ca. 1944. CPhoM. Ray R. Platnick. (Coast Guard)*

**927.**  *When land was sighted, even the wounded left their beds to have the first glimpse of home. Bed patients, they had to make sure it was true. Ca. July 1944. (OWI)*

**928.**  *Pfc. Troy Dixon, Leadhill, Ark., uses a Japanese barber chair to cut the hair of Sgt. John Anderson, Anita, Pa. Both men are members of the 363rd F.A. Bn., located near Shuri. Okinawa, June 10, 1945. Hendrickson. (Army)*

**929.** *Precious words from home. Eagerness and expectancy mark the faces of Coast Guardsmen jam-packed about No. 3 hatch as mail call takes place aboard a Coast Guard-manned troop transport in an advanced Pacific area. Ca. 1945. (Coast Guard)*

**930.** *Protestant Chaplain Rufus W. Oakley holding services within a few hundred yards of Japanese positions, well within range of their mortars if they had chosen to throw them. Peleliu, September 1944. McElroy. (Marine Corps)*

**931.** *With a canvas tarpaulin for a church and packing cases for an altar, a Navy chaplain holds mass for Marines at Saipan. The service was held in memory of brave buddies who lost their lives in the initial landings. June 1944. Sgt. Steele. (Marine Corps)*

**932.** *The crew of the USS SOUTH DAKOTA stands with bowed heads, while Chaplain N. D. Lindner reads the benediction held in honor of fellow shipmates killed in the air action off Guam on June 19, 1944. July 1, 1944. (Navy)*

**933.** *CB's of 50th Battalion sitting on sandbags in a Canvas, NCB, Chapel, bow their heads in prayer during candle light Holy Communion service, at Tinian, Marianas Islands. December 24, 1944. Chief Carpenter's Mate H. F. Merterns. (Navy)*

**934.** *U.S. wounded soldiers attend Mother's Day services in blitzed Coventry Cathedral, England. Men are patients in nearby convalescent hospitals. Mayor of Coventry attended ceremony. May 13, 1945. T3c. A. Cissna. (Army)*

# NAVY

Photographs 935–980

**935.** *Negro sailors of the USS* MASON *commissioned at Boston Navy Yard 20 March 1944 proudly look over their ship which is first to have predominantly Negro crew.* (Navy)

**936.** *On board the USS* SANDLANCE *on war patrol. R. H. Swickard (QM2/c) operating searchlight.* May 1945. (Navy)

**937.** *USS* SEA DOG *prowls the Pacific in search of enemy shipping.* May 1945. Lt. Comdr. Horace Bristol. (Navy)

**938.** *Lawrence Britton (SN2) on duty at prow lookout aboard USS* NASSAU. October 1943. Lt. Wayne Miller. (Navy)

**939.** *On bridge of U.S. submarine at submarine base New London, Conn. Relaying commands to quick firing 20mm gun crew.* August 1943. Lt. Comdr. Charles Fenno Jacobs. (Navy)

**940.** *Barbette of 16″ gun on board the USS* NEW JER-SEY. *Gunners packing in bags of powder which will fire the huge shell already in gun.* November 1944. Lt. Comdr. Charles Fenno Jacobs. (Navy)

**941.** *A PT marksman provides a striking camera study as he draws a bead with his 50 cal. machine gun on his boat off New Guinea.* July 1943. (Navy)

**942.** *Looking forward along deck from stern of U.S. submarine off coast of New London, Conn.* August 1943. Lt. Comdr. Charles Fenno Jacobs. (Navy)

**943.** *On board the USS* MARLIN *at New London, Conn. Sailor looks down the hatch.* August 1943. (Navy)

**944.** *Officer at periscope in control room of submarine.* Ca. 1942. (Navy)

**945.** *Sailor at work in the electric engine control room of USS* BATFISH *on war patrol.* May 1945. Lt. Comdr. Horace Bristol. (Navy)

**946.** *Conning tower of U.S. submarine.* August 1943. Comdr. Edward J. Steichen. (Navy)

**947.** *Inspection of personnel aboard a U.S. submarine at New London submarine base, Conn.* August 1943. Attributed to Comdr. Edward J. Steichen. (Navy)

**948.** *Survivors of USS* PRINCETON *adrift in life boat at sea as seen from USS* CASSIN YOUNG. October 1944. (Navy)

**949.** The U.S.S. *Queenfish* rescuing British and Australian prisoners of war, survivors of the Japanese ship *Rakuyo Maru,* sunk in the China Sea by the U.S.S. *Sealion,* September 1944. (Navy)

**950.** *British and Australian survivors rescued by the USS* SEALION *on Second War Patrol.* September 1944. (Navy)

**951.** *U.S. Navy seaman relaxes as two Coast Guardsmen scrape a thick coating of oil from his body. The survivor's ship, the USS* LANSDALE, *was sunk by Nazi planes off the coast of North Africa.* April 1944. (Coast Guard)

**952.** *PT's patrolling off coast of New Guinea. 1943.* (Navy)

**953.** Starboard bow view of U.S. ship LCI 772, Astoria, OR, July 30, 1944. PhoM2c. R. W. Mowday. (Navy)

**954.** *Adm. Lord Louis Mountbatten, RN, addresses personnel aboard the USS SARATOGA at Trincomalee, Ceylon. Adm. Mountbatten (center) on flight deck. April 1944.* Lt. Wayne Miller. (Navy)

**955.** *USS PENNSYLVANIA and battleship of COLORADO class followed by three cruisers move in line into Lingayen Gulf preceding the landing on Luzon. Philippines, January 1945.* (Navy)

**956.** *Task Group 38.3 in line as they enter Ulithi anchorage after strikes against the Japs in the Philippines. USS* LANGLEY, TICONDEROGA, WASHINGTON, NORTH CAROLINA, SOUTH DAKOTA, SANTA FE, BILOXI, MOBILE, *and* OAKLAND. December 1944. (Navy)

**957.** *Dirigible escort, U.S.S.* Casablanca. August 8, 1943. CPhoM. C. W. Overhulser. (Navy)

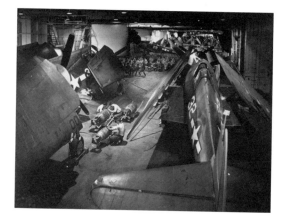

**958.** *Surrounded by F6F's, ordnancemen work on bombs on hangar deck of USS YORKTOWN. Officers and men in background watch movie. Ca. 1943. Lt. Comdr. Charles Kerlee. (Navy)*

**959.** *Pilots pleased over their victory during the Marshall Islands attack, grin across the tail of an F6F Hellcat on board the USS LEXINGTON, after shooting down 17 out of 20 Japanese planes heading for Tarawa. November 1943. Comdr. Edward J. Steichen. (Navy)*

**960.** *Flight Deck, USS CASABLANCA. Flight deck load, aircraft, P-47NE5, aft. Planes loaded at N.A.S. Alameda, California, enroute to Guam, from San Francisco. July 16, 1945. PhoM3c. D. C. Diers. (Navy)*

**961.** *Dynamic static. The motion of its props causes an "aura" to form around this F6F on USS YORKTOWN. Rapid change of pressure and drop in temperature create condensation. Rotating with blades, halo moves aft, giving depth and perspective. November 1943. (Navy)*

**962.** *TBF (Avengers) flying in formation over Norfolk, Va. September 1942. Attributed to Lt. Comdr. Horace Bristol. (Navy)*

**963.** *Aerial view of SB2C in upper landing circle showing USS YORKTOWN, below. July 1944. (Navy)*

**964.** *Crash landing of F6F on flight deck of USS ENTER-PRISE while enroute to attack Makin Island. Lt. Walter Chewning, catapult officer, clambering up the side of the plane to assist pilot, Ens. Byron Johnson, from the flaming cockpit.* November 1943. (Navy)

**965.** *Crash of TBM #11, VC-69, in port catwalk of USS BOGUE. #11 being raised from catwalk.* June 1944. L. F. Cirzan. (Navy)

**966.** *VMF-214 on Turtle Bay fighter strip, Espiritu Santo, New Hebrides. VMF-214 poses for a group picture before leaving for Munda, an F4U in background. Col. Gregory Boyington's Black Sheep Squadron, ca. September 1943.* (Navy)

**967.** *VF-17 ground crewmen await word to ready F4U for takeoff on Rabaul raid from Piva strip on Bougainville.* February 1944. Lt. Comdr. Charles Fenno Jacobs. (Navy)

**968.** *Pilots being briefed on board USS ESSEX the night before they were to raid Formosa.* December 1944. Ens. Thomas Binford. (Navy)

**969.** *Chart room on board USS LEXINGTON as ship maneuvers into enemy waters during strike in the Gilbert and Marshall Islands.* December 1943. Comdr. Edward J. Steichen. (Navy)

**970.** *Coast Guardsmen on the deck of the U.S. Coast Guard Cutter* Spencer *watch the explosion of a depth charge which blasted a Nazi U-boat's hope of breaking into the center of a large convoy. Sinking of U-175, April 17, 1943.* WO Jack January. (Coast Guard)

**971.** *Crewmen aboard USS* YORKTOWN *dash to stations as general quarters sound. May 1943.* Lt. Comdr. Charles Kerlee. (Navy)

**972.** *Navy fighters during the attack on the Japanese fleet off Midway, June 4th to 6th 1942. In the center is visible a burning Japanese ship.* (Navy)

**973.** *16″ guns of the USS* IOWA *firing during battle drill in the Pacific. Ca. 1944.* (Navy)

**974.** *Jap torpedo bomber explodes in air after direct hit by 5 inch shell from U.S. aircraft carrier as it attempted an unsuccessful attack on carrier, off Kwajalein. U.S.S. Yorktown, December 4, 1943.* CPhoM. Alfred N. Cooperman. (Navy)

**975.** *Japanese plane shot down as it attempted to attack USS* KITKUN BAY. *Near Mariana Islands, June 1944.* (Navy)

**976.** *Japanese attack on the USS* ENTERPRISE, *afternoon of 24 Aug 1942. Third Japanese bomb hit on the flight deck of the* ENTERPRISE. *The photographer lost his life while taking picture.* PhoM3c. Robert Frederick Read. (Navy)

**977.** *A Japanese bomb splashes astern of a U.S. carrier as the enemy plane pulls out of its dive above the carrier. In the center is another enemy plane that has made an unsuccessful dive. Battle of Santa Cruz.* October 26, 1942. (Navy)

**978.** *USS* BUNKER HILL *burning after Jap suicide attack.* Near Okinawa, May 11, 1945. (Navy)

**979.** *USS* SANTA FE *lays alongside of USS* FRANKLIN *rendering assistance after carrier had been hit and set afire by a Japanese dive bomber.* March 1945. (Navy)

**980.** *USS* BUNKER HILL *hit by two Kamikazes in 30 seconds on 11 May 1945 off Kyushu. Dead — 372. Wounded — 264.* (Navy)

# WAR IN THE WEST

## BACKGROUND
*Photographs 981–992*

**981.** Hitler at Nazi Party rally, Nuremberg, Germany, ca. 1928. Heinrich Hoffman Collection. (Foreign Records Seized)

**982.** *Reichsparteitag. Der Vorbeimarsch der SA am Führer.* Parade of SA troops past Hitler. Nuremberg, November 9, 1935. (National Archives Gift Collection)

**983.** *Reichsparteitag. Übersicht über den grossen Appell der SA, SS und des NSKK.* Overview of the mass roll call of SA, SS, and NSKK troops. Nuremberg, November 9, 1935. (National Archives Gift Collection)

**984.** *Reichsparteitag. Der grosse Appell der Politischen Leiter auf der von Scheinwerfern überstrahlten Zeppelinwiese in Nürnburg.* Grand review by political leaders on the searchlight-illuminated Zeppelin field in Nuremberg. September 1937. (Office of Alien Property)

**985.** *On April 1st, 1933, the boycott which was announced by the Nationalsocialistic party began.* Placard reads, "Germans, defend yourselves, do not buy from Jews," at the Jewish Tietz store. Berlin. New York Times Paris Bureau Collection. (USIA)

**986.** *Thousands of books smoulder in a huge bonfire as Germans give the Nazi salute during the wave of book-burnings that spread throughout Germany. 1933. INP. (OWI)*

**987.** *Firemen work on the burning Reichstag Building in February 1933, after fire broke out simultaneously at 20 places. This enabled Hitler to seize power under the pretext of "protecting" the country from the menace to its security. Berlin. Acme. (OWI)*

**988.** *Hitler accepts the ovation of the Reichstag after announcing the "peaceful" acquisition of Austria. It set the stage to annex the Czechoslovakian Sudetenland, largely inhabited by a German-speaking population. Berlin, March 1938. (OWI)*

**989.** *Österreich wird Deutsche. Einmarsch der Deutschen polizei in Imst (Tirol).* Austria becomes German. Entry of German police into Imst. March 1938. Heinrich Hoffman Collection. (Foreign Records Seized)

**990.** Soviet Foreign Minister Molotov signs the German-Soviet nonaggression pact; Joachim von Ribbentrop and Josef Stalin stand behind him, Moscow, August 23, 1939. Von Ribbentrop Collection. (Foreign Records Seized)

**991.** *Weihestunde der HJ vor dem Rathaus in Tomaschow am 11.5.1941.* Hitler Youth Hour of Commemoration in front of the Town Hall in Tomaszow, Poland, May 11, 1941. Otto Rösner. (WWII War Crimes Records)

# WAR IN THE WEST

## GERMANY ATTACKS

*Photographs 993–999*

**992.** *To another — Asia and the Pacific Ocean!* Watercolor illustration for filmstrip, "The Fruits of Aggression." (USIA)

**993.** *The tragedy of this Sudeten woman, unable to conceal her misery as she dutifully salutes the triumphant Hitler, is the tragedy of the silent millions who have been "won over" to Hitlerism by the "everlasting use" of ruthless force. Ca. 1938.* (OWI)

**994.** *Die Soldaten des Führers im Felde. Vor Warschau.* The soldiers of the Führer in the field, before Warsaw. Poland, 1939. PK Hugo Jäger. Stereo. (National Archives Gift Collection)

**995.** *Belgian refugees. Ca. 1940.* United Nations Information Office. (OWI)

**996.** German troops in Russia, 1941. (Foreign Records Seized)

**997.** *A Frenchman weeps as German soldiers march into the French capital, Paris, on June 14, 1940, after the Allied armies had been driven back across France.* (OWI)

**998.** *Der Führer in Paris.* Hitler in Paris. June 23, 1940. Heinrich Hoffman Collection. (Foreign Records Seized)

**999.** British prisoners at Dunkerque, France, June 1940. Eva Braun Collection. (Foreign Records Seized)

# War in the West

## Battle of Britain

*Photographs 1000–1014*

**1000.** Aircraft spotter on the roof of a building in London with St. Paul's Cathedral in the background. New York Times Paris Bureau Collection. (USIA)

**1001.** *Anti-aircraft guns in Hyde Park go into action as "enemy bombers" make a daylight raid on London, during giant air defence exercises in which over 20,000 men and 1,300 RAF planes are taking part.* August 1939. New York Times Paris Bureau Collection. (USIA)

**1002.** Big Ben and the Houses of Parliament, London. New York Times Paris Bureau Collection. (USIA)

**1003.** *Standing up gloriously out of the flames and smoke of surrounding buildings, St. Paul's Cathedral is pictured during the great fire raid of Sunday December 29th.* London, 1940. New York Times Paris Bureau Collection. (USIA)

**1004.** *This picture, taken during the first mass air raid on London, 7th Sep. 1940, describes more than words ever could, the scene in London's dock area. Tower Bridge stands out against a background of smoke and fires.* New York Times Paris Bureau Collection. (USIA)

**1005.** *A burning building in Sheffield which was raided recently.* December 1941. New York Times Paris Bureau Collection. (USIA)

**1006.** *Over 500 firemen and members of the London Auxiliary Fire Fighting Services, including many women, combined in a war exercise over the ground covered by Greenwich (London) Fire Station.* 1939. New York Times Paris Bureau Collection. (USIA)

**1007.** Firemen at work in bomb-damaged street in London, after Saturday night raid, ca. 1941. New York Times Paris Bureau Collection. (USIA)

**1008.** *La Vie a Londres pendant la guerre. Voici un homme blessé par la chute d'un V-1.* Life in London during the war. Here is a man who was injured by the fall of a V-1. Ca. 1940. New York Times Paris Bureau Collection. (USIA)

**1009.** *Children of an eastern suburb of London, who have been made homeless by the random bombs of the Nazi night raiders, waiting outside the wreckage of what was their home.* September 1940. New York Times Paris Bureau Collection. (USIA)

**1010.** *Demolishing a tower in London's Smithfield Market which was unsafe after it had been damaged by enemy action.* Ca. 1941. New York Times Paris Bureau Collection. (USIA)

1011. *London has its biggest raid of the war. Fire bombs and high explosives rained on the capital for many hours. A building completely wrecked after last night's all night raid. April 1941. New York Times Paris Bureau Collection. (USIA)*

1012. *The London Necropolis Railway Station, privately owned station in Westminster Bridge Road, after London's biggest night raid of the war. Ca. 1941. New York Times Paris Bureau Collection. (USIA)*

1013. *A scene at a London railway station showing troops arriving while kiddies who are being evacuated from London leave for the reception area. Ca. 1940. New York Times Paris Bureau Collection. (USIA)*

# WAR IN THE WEST

## NORTH AFRICA, SICILY, ITALY
*Photographs 1015–1036*

1014. *A 2,500 pound German bomb, buried opposite University College Hospital, London, was removed by Army sappers. Before the bomb, which fell in 1941, was de-fused, people in the area were evacuated to a safe distance. Ca. 1948. New York Times Paris Bureau Collection. (USIA)*

1015. *An Air Transport Command plane flies over the pyramids in Egypt. Loaded with urgent war supplies and materials, this plane is one of a fleet flying shipments from the U.S. across the Atlantic and the continent of Africa to strategic battle zones. 1943. (Army)*

**1016.** *General Rommel bei der 15. Panzer-Division zwischen Tobruk und Sidi Omar.* General Rommel with the 15th Panzer Division between Tobruk and Sidi Omar. Libya, January or November 24, 1941. Sdf. Zwilling. (Foreign Records Seized)

**1017.** *General Bernard L. Montgomery watches his tanks move up.* North Africa, November 1942. British Official. (OWI)

**1018.** *Ack-Ack fire during an air raid on Algiers, by the Nazis.* 1943. Lt. W. R. Wilson. (Army)

**1019.** *Thousands of used enemy shells in Bizerte. Note damaged building in background.* Tunisia, ca. May 1943. (OSS)

**1020.** *Bizerte Harbour. These ships were the first to enter Bizerte in May of 1943.* Tunisia. (OSS)

**1021.** *Row boat and rifle left on the beach of Cap Bon by the Germans.* Tunisia, ca. May 1943. (OSS)

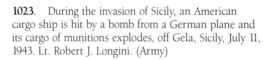

**1022.** *L.S.T.'s lined up and waiting for tanks to come aboard. Two days before invasion of Sicily. La Pecherie, French Naval Base.* Tunisia, July 1943. (OSS)

**1023.** During the invasion of Sicily, an American cargo ship is hit by a bomb from a German plane and its cargo of munitions explodes, off Gela, Sicily, July 11, 1943. Lt. Robert J. Longini. (Army)

**1024.** *Lt. Col. Lyle Bernard, CO, 30th Inf. Regt., a prominent figure in the second daring amphibious landing behind enemy lines on Sicily's north coast, discusses military strategy with Lt. Gen. George S. Patton. Near Brolo.* 1943. (Army)

**1025.** *Private Roy Humphrey of Toledo, Ohio, is being given blood plasma by Pfc. Harvey White of Minneapolis, Minn., after he was wounded by shrapnel, on 9 August 1943 in Sicily.* Wever. (Army)

**1026.** *Sgt. Norwood Dorman, Benson, N.C., stops to rest at the memorial to the Italian soldier of World War I. Brolo, Sicily.* August 14, 1943. Lt. Robert J. Longini. (Army)

**1027.** *Fliers of a P-51 Mustang Group of the 15th Air Force in Italy "shoot the breeze" in the shadow of one of the Mustangs they fly.* August 1944. (OWI)

**1028.** *Front view of 240mm howitzer of Btry. "B," 697th F.A. Bn., just before firing into German held territory. Mignano area, Italy.* January 30, 1944. Boyle. (Army)

**1029.** *Long Tom speaks. A 155mm gun ("Long Tom") is fired by American troops. Nettuno area, Italy.* February 13, 1944. Bonnard. (Army)

**1030.** *Moving up through Prato, Italy, men of the 370th Infantry Regiment have yet to climb the mountain which lies ahead.* April 9, 1945. Bull. (Army)

**1031.** *Americans of Japanese descent, Infantrymen of the 442nd Regiment, run for cover as a German artillery shell is about to land outside the building. Italy.* April 4, 1945. Levine. (Army)

**1032.** *Catholic Mass is held for two soldiers who were killed nearby. San Benedetto, Italy.* October 11, 1944. Schmidt. (Army)

**1033.** *Pvt. Paul Oglesby, 30th Inf., standing in reverence before an altar in a damaged Catholic Church. Note: pews at left appear undamaged, while bomb-shattered roof is strewn about the sanctuary. Acerno, Italy.* September 23, 1943. Benson. (Army)

**1034.** *Lt. Col. Woran, Chaplain of the 10th Mountain Div., leads a group of men in prayer at Torboli the day following the unconditional surrender of all German troops in Italy. May 3, 1945. Bull. (Army)*

**1035.** *There is no place safe from their attack.* Watercolor illustration for filmstrip, "The Fruits of Aggression." (USIA)

**1036.** *From Coast Guard-manned "sea-horse" landing craft, American troops leap forward to storm a North African beach during final amphibious maneuvers. Ca. 1944. James D. Rose, Jr. (Coast Guard)*

# War in the West

## France
*Photographs 1037–1060*

**1037.** *Jedburghs get instructions from Briefing Officer in London flat.* England, ca. 1944. (OSS)

**1038.** *Jedburghs in front of B-24 just before night takeoff.* Area T, Harrington Airdrome, England, ca. 1944. (OSS)

**1039.** *Father (Major) Edward J. Waters, Catholic Chaplain from Oswego, New York, conducts Divine Services on a pier for members of the first assault troops thrown against Hitler's forces on the continent. Weymouth, England. June 6, 1944. (Army)*

**1040.** *Gen. Dwight D. Eisenhower gives the order of the Day. "Full victory — nothing else" to paratroopers in England, just before they board their airplanes to participate in the first assault in the invasion of the continent of Europe. June 6, 1944. Moore. (Army)*

**1041.** *Landing on the coast of France under heavy Nazi machine gun fire are these American soldiers, shown just as they left the ramp of a Coast Guard landing boat. June 6, 1944. CPhoM. Robert F. Sargent. (Coast Guard)*

**1042.** *Members of an American landing party lend helping hands to others whose landing craft was sunk by enemy action off the coast of France. These survivors reached Utah Beach, near Cherbourg, by using a life raft. June 6, 1944. Weintraub. (Army)*

**1043.** *American assault troops of the 16th Infantry Regiment, injured while storming Omaha Beach, wait by the Chalk Cliffs for evacuation to a field hospital for further medical treatment. Collville-sur-Mer, Normandy, France. June 6, 1944. Taylor. (Army)*

**1044.** *Crossed rifles in the sand are a comrade's tribute to this American soldier who sprang ashore from a landing barge and died at the barricades of Western Europe. 1944. (Coast Guard)*

1045. *The beachhead is secure, but the price was high. A Coast Guard Combat Photographer came upon this monument to a dead American soldier somewhere on the shell-blasted shore of Normandy. Ca. June 1944. S. Scott Wigle. (Coast Guard)*

1046. *Monster Nazi gun battery silenced in France. This German gun emplacement has walls of concrete 13 feet thick and four guns each with a 10¼″ bore. This particular position was bombed out of action by Allied flyers. Ca. 1944. Albert Thompson. (Coast Guard)*

1047. *American howitzers shell German forces retreating near Carentan, France. July 11, 1944. Franklin. (Army)*

1048. *Infantrymen take a short rest before pushing on, in a deserted house in the French town of Tessy sur Vire. "Our 'foxhole' for the night was a beer cellar. There were beaucoup kegs down there but they were empty. Boy, were we sad sacks." August 3, 1944. Norbie. (Army)*

1049. *Lined up in front of a wrecked German tank and displaying a captured swastika, is a group of Yank infantrymen who were left behind to "mop-up" in Chambois, France, last stronghold of the Nazis in the Falaise Gap area. August 20, 1944. Tomko. (Army Surgeon General)*

1050. *This dead German soldier was one of the "last stand" defenders of German-held Cherbourg. Capt. Earl Topley, who led one of the first outfits into the fallen city, blamed him for killing three of his boys. France, June 27, 1944. Zwick. (Army)*

**1051.** *"We couldn't stick around long though. The Jerries were on the run and we wanted to keep them that way. The Tricolor flying from the Arc de Triomphe looked pretty good as we went through."* American tank in Paris, August 1944. (OWI)

**1052.** *Frenchwoman exclaims to neighbor and to American soldier: "Tout Belfort Est Libre" (All Belfort is liberated).* November 25, 1944. Leibowitz. (Army)

**1053.** *"Finally, I got me a 'souvenir.' Somehow the Jerries I got in my sights always seemed to have bad luck. Then one day in Illy, France, I spotted an officer inside a battered building and I yelled for him to come on out. He did."* Ca. September 1944. Army. (OWI)

**1054.** *Americans take shelter during mop-up of Brest. Crouching behind a pile of rubble, a U.S. soldier watches for German snipers in the streets of Brest, while a companion covers him from behind a doorway. September 1944. INP. (OWI)*

**1055.** American officer and French partisan crouch behind an auto during a street fight in a French city, ca. 1944. (Army)

**1056.** *General Charles de Gaulle, President of the French Committee of National Liberation, speaks to the people of Cherbourg from the balcony of the City Hall during his visit to the French port city on August 20. 1944. (OWI)*

**1057.** *Crowds of Parisians celebrating the entry of Allied troops into Paris scatter for cover as a sniper fires from a building on the place De La Concorde. Although the Germans surrendered the city, small bands of snipers still remained. August 26, 1944. Verna. (Army)*

**1058.** *Soldiers of the 4th U.S. Infantry Division look at the Eiffel Tower in Paris, after the French capital had been liberated on August 25, 1944. August 1944. John Downey. (OWI)*

**1059.** *American troops of the 28th Infantry Division march down the Champs Elysees, Paris, in the "Victory" Parade.* August 29, 1944. Poinsett. (Army)

**1060.** *Parisians line the Champs Elysees to cheer the massed infantry units of the American army as they march in review towards the Arc de Triomphe, celebrating the liberation of the capital of France from Nazi occupation.* August 29, 1944. Parker. (Army)

# WAR IN THE WEST

## THE LOW COUNTRIES

*Photographs 1061–1081*

**1061.** *Men of the 8th Infantry Regiment attempt to move forward and are pinned down by German small arms from within the Belgian town of Libin. Men seek cover behind hedges and signs to return the fire.* September 7, 1944. Gedicks. (Army)

**1062.** *Yanks of 60th Inf. Regt. advance into a Belgian town under the protection of a heavy tank.* September 9, 1944. Spangle. (Army)

**1063.** *Long, twin lines of C-47 transport planes are loaded with men and equipment at an airfield from which they took off for Holland September 17, 1944. The C-47's carried paratroopers of the First Allied Airborne Army. England. Army. (OWI)*

**1064.** *Brig. Gen. Anthony C. Mcauliffe, artillery commander of the 101st Airborne Division, gives his various glider pilots last minute instructions before the take-off on D plus 1. England, September 18, 1944. Klosterman. (Army)*

**1065.** *A fleet of Allied aircraft flies overhead as paratroopers of the Allied Airborne Command float groundward in the invasion of the Netherlands, still another step towards the liberation of Europe. September 17, 1944. Tischler, Air Transport Command. (Army)*

**1066.** *Parachutes open overhead as waves of paratroops land in Holland during operations by the 1st Allied Airborne Army. September 1944. (Army)*

**1067.** *A panoramic view of the city of Nijmegen, Holland, and the Nijmegen Bridge over the Waal (Rhine) River in the background. The city was hit by German and Allied bombardment and shelling. September 28, 1944. Poznak. (Army)*

**1068.** *A U.S. Infantry anti-tank crew fires on Nazis who machine-gunned their vehicle, somewhere in Holland. November 4, 1944. W. F. Stickle. (Army)*

**1069.** *Sergt. [or T4c.] Marvin E. Eans, Jr., demonstrates the new snow cape being used by First U.S. Army Infantrymen in snow-covered areas in Belgium. White rags are wrapped around his rifle for additional camouflage. St. Vith. December 15, 1944. T5c. Richard A. Massenge. (Army)*

**1070.** *A Nazi soldier, heavily armed, carries ammunition boxes forward with companion in territory taken by their counter-offensive in this scene from captured German film. Belgium, December 1944. (Army)*

**1071.** *A lanky GI, with hands clasped behind his head, leads a file of American prisoners marching along a road somewhere on the western front. Germans captured these American soldiers during the surprise enemy drive into Allied positions. December 1944. (Army)*

**1072.** *The pathfinder unit of the 101st Airborne Div., dropped by parachute, sets up radar equipment near Bastogne, Belgium. It is their job to guide planes with medical supplies and ammunition to the division, besieged by the Germans. December 23, 1944. T5c. Krochka. (Army)*

**1073.** *Infantryman goes out on a one-man sortie, covered by a buddy in the background. 82nd Airborne Division, Bra, Belgium. December 24, 1944. Edgren. (Army)*

**1074.** *Infantrymen, attached to the 4th Armored Division, fire at German troops, in the American advance to relieve the pressure on surrounded airborne troops in Bastogne, Belgium. December 27, 1944. Pfc. Donald R. Ornitz. (Army)*

**1075.** *Chow is served to American Infantrymen on their way to La Roche, Belgium. 347th Inf. Regt.* January 13, 1945. Newhouse. (Army)

**1076.** *Pfc. Margerum, Philadelphia, Pa., walks the road through a peaceful forest in the Bastogne area, as he returns from the front lines. Belgium or Luxembourg.* December 27, 1944. Pfc. Donald R. Ornitz. (Army)

**1077.** *American infantrymen of the 290th Regiment fight in fresh snowfall near Amonines, Belgium. January 4, 1945.* Braun. (Army)

**1078.** *After holding a woodland position all night near Wiltz, Luxembourg, against German counter attack, three men of B Co., 101st Engineers, emerge for a rest. January 14, 1945.* Gilbert. (Army)

**1079.** *American soldiers of the 289th Infantry Regiment march along the snow-covered road on their way to cut off the St. Vith-Houffalize road in Belgium. January 24, 1945.* Richard A. Massenge. (Army)

**1080.** *Deep snow banks on a narrow road halt military traffic in the woods of Wallerode, Belgium. 87th Inf. Div. January 30, 1945.* Norbuth. (Army)

**1081.** *Infantry of the Regiment de Maisonneuve moving through Holten to Rijssen, both towns in the Netherlands. 9 April 1945.* Lt. D. Guravitch. Canadian Military photograph. New York Times Paris Bureau Collection. (USIA)

# War in the West

## Germany

*Photographs 1082–1101*

**1082.** *First U.S. Army men and equipment pour across the Remagen Bridge; two knocked out jeeps in foreground.* Germany, March 11, 1945. Sgt. William Spangle. (Army)

**1083.** *"Then came the big day when we marched into Germany — right through the Siegfried Line."* 1945. Army. (OWI)

**1084.** *Alerted GIs of M-51 Anti-aircraft Battery are silhouetted against German sky streaked with vapor trails from allied and enemy planes engaged in Christmas Day dogfight. Near Puffendorf, Germany.* December 25, 1944. Pvt. M. S. Kelly. (Army)

**1085.** *"Getting across the Rhine wasn't all there was to it. There was the little matter of establishing a beachhead. We threw our mortars at them and everything else we had until they finally gave way."* 1945. Army. (OWI)

**1086.** *"I drew an assault boat to cross in — just my luck. We all tried to crawl under each other because the lead was flying around like hail."* Crossing the Rhine under enemy fire at St. Goar, March 1945. Army. (OWI)

**1087.** *"The first big raid by the 8th Air Force was on a Focke Wulf plant at Marienburg. Coming back, the Germans were up in full force and we lost at least 80 ships — 800 men, many of them pals."* 1943. Army Air Forces. (OWI)

**1088.** *Adolf Hitler, accompanied by other German officials, grimly inspects bomb damage in a German city in 1944, in this German film captured by the U.S. Army Signal Corps on the western front. Ca. 1944. (Army)*

**1089.** *British Trooper W. Williamson does his good deed for the day by rescuing a puppy dog from the ruins of a shelled German house on the outskirts of Geilenkirchen. Ca. November 1944. British Official. New York Times Paris Bureau Collection. (USIA)*

**1090.** *With German shells screaming overhead, American Infantrymen seek shelter behind a tank. In the background can be seen the ruins of the town of Geich, Germany, which is still under heavy shelling. December 11, 1944. Roberts. (Army)*

**1091.** *Two anti-tank Infantrymen of the 101st Infantry Regiment, dash past a blazing German gasoline trailer in square of Kronach, Germany. April 14, 1945. T4c. W. J. Rothenberger. (Army)*

**1092.** *German woman carrying a few possessions runs from burning building in Seigburg, Germany. Fire started by Nazi saboteur. April 13, 1945. T4c. Troy A. Peters, USA. (Roberts Commission)*

**1093.** *Alert for enemy movement, Pfc. Armand Rindone, Philadelphia, Pa., crouches with a carbine at the railroad station in the newly captured town of Hamm, Germany. April 6, 1945. T4c. Vernon M. Sharette. (Army)*

**1094.** *Soldiers of the 55th Armored Infantry Battalion and tank of the 22nd Tank Battalion, move through smoke filled street. Wernberg, Germany. April 22, 1945. Pvt. Joseph Scrippens. (Army)*

**1095.** *Infantrymen of the 255th Inf. Regt. move down a street in Waldenburg to hunt out the Hun after a recent raid by 63rd Division. April 16, 1945. 2d Lt. Jacob Harris. (Army)*

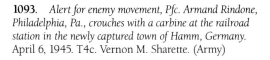

**1096.** *Happy 2nd Lt. William Robertson and Lt. Alexander Sylvashko, Russian Army, shown in front of sign [East Meets West] symbolizing the historic meeting of the Russian and American Armies, near Torgau, Germany. April 25, 1945. Pfc. William E. Poulson. (Army)*

**1097.** *Marshal Zhukov decorates Field Marshal Montgomery with the Russian Order of Victory. Allied chiefs who attended the ceremony at Gen. Eisenhower's Headquarters at Frankfurt are about to drink a toast. June 10, 1945. British Official. (OWI)*

**1098.** *Mammoth 274-mm railroad gun captured in the U.S. Seventh Army advance near Rentwertshausen easily holds these 22 men lined up on the barrel. Although of an 1887 French design, the gun packs a powerful wallop. April 10, 1945. T5c. Pat W. Kohl. (Army)*

**1099.** *General Dwight D. Eisenhower, Supreme Allied Commander, accompanied by Gen. Omar N. Bradley, and Lt. Gen. George S. Patton, Jr., inspects art treasures stolen by Germans and hidden in salt mine in Germany. April 12, 1945. Lt. Moore. (Army)*

**1100.** *In the cellar of the Race Institute in Frankfurt, Germany, Chaplain Samuel Blinder examines one of hundreds of "Saphor Torahs" (Sacred Scrolls), among the books stolen from every occupied country in Europe. July 6, 1945. T3c. Irving Katz. (Army)*

**1101.** *The 90th Division discovered this Reichsbank wealth, SS loot, and Berlin museum paintings that were removed from Berlin to a salt mine in Merkers, Germany. April 15, 1945. Cpl. Donald R. Ornitz, USA. (Roberts Commission)*

# War in the West

## The Holocaust
*Photographs 1102–1130*

**1102.** *Starving inmate of Camp Gusen, Austria. May 12, 1945. T4c. Sam Gilbert. (Army)*

**1103.** *Starved prisoners, nearly dead from hunger, pose in concentration camp in Ebensee, Austria. The camp was reputedly used for "scientific" experiments. It was liberated by the 80th Division. May 7, 1945. Lt. A. E. Samuelson. (Army)*

**1104.** *These two staring, emaciated men are liberated inmates of Lager Nordhausen, a Gestapo concentration camp. The camp had from 3,000 to 4,000 inmates. All were maltreated, beaten and starved. Germany, April 12, 1945. T4c. James E. Myers. (Army)*

**1105.** *These are slave laborers in the Buchenwald concentration camp near Jena; many had died from malnutrition when U.S. troops of the 80th Division entered the camp. Germany, April 16, 1945. Pvt. H. Miller. (Army)*

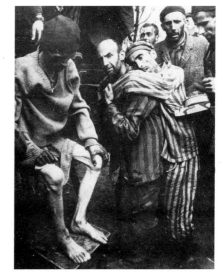

**1106.** *Wobbelin Concentration Camp, recently captured by troops of the 82nd Airborne Division. Many prisoners were found nearly starved to death. Here former prisoners are being taken to a hospital for medical attention. Germany, May 4, 1945. Pvt. Ralph Forney. (Army)*

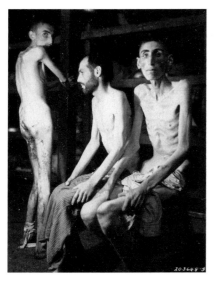

**1107.** *These Russian, Polish, and Dutch slave laborers interned at the Buchenwald concentration camp averaged 160 pounds each prior to entering camp 11 months ago. Their average weight is now 70 pounds. Germany, April 16, 1945. Pvt. H. Miller. (Army)*

**1108.** *At the German concentration camp at Wobbelin, many inmates were found by the U.S. Ninth Army in pitiful condition. Here one of them breaks out in tears when he finds he is not leaving with the first group to the hospital. Germany, May 4, 1945. Pvt. Ralph Forney. (Army)*

**1109.** *Six-year-old war orphan with Buchenwald badge on his sleeve waits for his name to be called at roll call at Buchenwald camp, Germany, for departure to Switzerland. June 19, 1945. Pfc. G. A. Haynia. (Army)*

**1110.** *These women and children were liberated when the concentration camp for Jewish prisoners at Lambach, Austria, was overrun by the 71st Inf. Div. Death rate at the camp, mostly from starvation, was reputed to be 200 to 300 a day.* May 7, 1945. Sgt. Robert Holliway. (Army)

**1111.** *Russian slave laborer among prisoners liberated by 3rd Armored Division points out former Nazi guard who brutally beat prisoners.* Germany, April 14, 1945. T4c. Harold M. Roberts. (Army)

**1112.** *Muhlhausen, Austria. Nador Livia, in pre-Nazi days, was a beautiful, talented, and famous actress on the Budapest stage. She was taken prisoner, eventually to Gusen where she is pictured. Reason for imprisonment: Jewish heritage.* May 12, 1945. T5c. Ignatius Gallo. (Army)

**1113.** *Gen. Dwight D. Eisenhower watches grimly while occupants of a German concentration camp at Gotha demonstrate how they were tortured by the Nazi sadists operating the camp. Generals Bradley and Patton are at his right. Germany, April 12, 1945. Lt. Moore. (Army)*

**1114.** *This Polish Jew was shot in cold blood by the retreating Germans as the 3rd U.S. Army advanced into the Ohrdruf area, Germany. April 12, 1945. Sgt. B. Hawkins. (Army)*

**1115.** *This victim of Nazi inhumanity still rests in the position in which he died, attempting to rise and escape his horrible death. He was one of 150 prisoners savagely burned to death by Nazi SS troops. Gardelegen, Germany. April 16, 1945. Sgt. E. R. Allen. (Army)*

**1116.** *At the doorway of this railroad car may be seen the bodies of 3 political prisoners, shot as they tried to flee massacre at Seeshaupt. All prisoners on train were killed by machine guns at the hands of SS troops. Germany, May 1, 1945. T4c. Albert Gretz. (Army)*

**1117.** *Some of the bodies being removed by German civilians for decent burial at Gusen Concentration Camp, Muhlhausen, near Linz, Austria. Men were worked in nearby stone quarries until too weak for more, then killed. May 12, 1945. T4c. Sam Gilbert. (Army)*

**1118.** *Starved bodies of prisoners who were transported to Dachau from another concentration camp, lie grotesquely as they died enroute. This is contents of one of 50 similar freight cars. Germany, April 30, 1945. T4c. Sidney Blau. (Army)*

**1119.** *Political prisoners of the Nazis who met their deaths at the hands of SS troops who set the barn afire. This group tried to escape and was shot. Of the 1100 prisoners, only 12 managed to escape. Gardelegen, Germany, April 16, 1945. T5c. P. R. Mark. (Army)*

**1120.** *A truck load of bodies of prisoners of the Nazis, in the Buchenwald concentration camp at Weimar, Germany. The bodies were about to be disposed of by burning when the camp was captured by troops of the 3rd U.S. Army. April 14, 1945. Pfc. W. Chichersky. (Army)*

**1121.** *Rows of bodies of dead inmates fill the yard of Lager Nordhausen, a Gestapo concentration camp. This photo shows less than half of the bodies of the several hundred inmates who died of starvation or were shot by Gestapo men. Germany, April 12, 1945. Myers. (Army)*

**1122.** *Bones of anti-Nazi German women still are in the crematoriums in the German concentration camp at Weimar, Germany, taken by the 3rd U.S. Army. Prisoners of all nationalities were tortured and killed. April 14, 1945. Pfc. W. Chichersky. (Army)*

**1123.** *Citizens of Ludwigslust, Germany, inspect a nearby concentration camp under orders of the 82nd Airborne Division. Bodies of victims of Nazi torture were found dumped in pits in yard, one pit containing 300 bodies. May 6, 1945. T4c. Jack Clemmer. (Army)*

**1124.** *A German girl is overcome as she walks past the exhumed bodies of some of the 800 slave workers murdered by SS guards near Namering, Germany, and laid here so that townspeople may view the work of their Nazi leaders. May 17, 1945. Cpl. Edward Belfer. (Army)*

**1125.** *Civilians of Neunburg bear victims of SS killings to burial ground, after bodies were exhumed from mass grave where their murderers had dumped them. Chaplains of U.S. Third Army will conduct burial services. April 29, 1945. Pfc. Wendell N. Hustead. (Army)*

**1126.** *Chaplains of the U.S. Third Army conduct burial services for the 120 Russian and Polish Jews, victims of SS troopers' killing in a wood near Neunburg, Germany. April 29, 1945. Pfc. Wendell N. Hustead. (Army)*

**1127.** *Civilians of Namering, Germany give burial to 800 victims of an SS killing three weeks ago. The bodies had lain in the open for five days. Burial was ordered by the military government. May 19, 1945. Pfc. J. Nestereck. (Army)*

**1128.** *These markers are for the graves of 80 victims of the Nazis found in Ludwigslust. The entire population of Schwerin, Germany, was ordered by the Military Government to attend funeral rites conducted by U.S. Army chaplains. May 8, 1945. A. Drummond, Jr. (Army)*

**1129.** *This pile of clothes belonged to prisoners of the Dachau concentration camp, recently liberated by troops of the U.S. Seventh Army. Slave laborers were compelled to strip before they were killed. Germany, April 30, 1945. T4c. Sidney Blau. (Army)*

**1130.** *A few of the thousands of wedding rings the Germans removed from their victims to salvage the gold. U.S. troops found rings, watches, precious stones, eyeglasses, and gold fillings, near Buchenwald concentration camp. Germany, May 5, 1945. T4c. Roberts. (Army)*

# WAR IN THE EAST

## JAPAN ATTACKS
*Photographs 1131–1147*

**1131.** *This terrified baby was almost the only human being left alive in Shanghai's South Station after brutal Japanese bombing.* China, August 28, 1937. H. S. Wong. (OWI)

**1132.** Captured Japanese photograph taken aboard a Japanese carrier before the attack on Pearl Harbor, December 7, 1941. (Navy)

**1133.** Captured Japanese photograph taken during the attack on Pearl Harbor, December 7, 1941. In the distance, the smoke rises from Hickam Field. (Navy)

**1134.** *Pearl Harbor, taken by surprise, during the Japanese aerial attack. Wreckage at NAS, Pearl Harbor.* (Navy)

**1135.** *USS SHAW exploding during the Japanese raid on Pearl Harbor.* December 7, 1941. (Navy)

**1136.** *The USS ARIZONA burning after the Japanese attack on Pearl Harbor.* December 7, 1941. (Navy)

**1137.** *Pearl Harbor, taken by surprise, during the Japanese aerial attack. USS WEST VIRGINIA aflame.* December 7, 1941. (Navy)

**1138.** *Japanese attack on Pearl Harbor. Wrecked USS DOWNES at left and USS CASSIN at right. In the rear is the USS PENNSYLVANIA, 33,100-ton Flagship of the Pacific Fleet, which suffered only light damage.* December 1941. Attributed to CPhoM. H. S. Fawcett. (Navy)

**1139.** *A burned B-17C aircraft rests near Hangar Number Five, Hickam Field, following the attack by Japanese aircraft. Pearl Harbor, Hawaii.* December 7, 1941. (Navy)

**1140.** Japanese troops on Bataan, Philippine Islands, ca. 1942. Captured Japanese photograph. (Army)

**1141.** *During the siege of Corregidor, P.I., the Finance Office, U.S. Army, Manila, shared lateral No. 12 of Melinta Tunnel with the Signal Corps. Members of the Finance Office staff appear in the foreground.* Ca. March/April 1942. Maj. Paul Wing. (Army)

1142.  Surrender of American troops at Corregidor, Philippine Islands, May 1942. INP. (OWI)

1143.  *Captured Japanese photograph. U.S. soldiers and sailors surrendering to Jap forces at Corregidor, P.I. May 1942.* (Army)

1144.  *The March of Death. Along the March [on which] these prisoners were photographed, they have their hands tied behind their backs. The March of Death was about May 1942, from Bataan to Cabanatuan, the prison camp.* (Marine Corps)

1145.  *This picture, captured from the Japanese, shows American prisoners using improvised litters to carry those of their comrades who, from the lack of food or water on the march from Bataan, fell along the road. Philippines, May 1942.* (OWI)

1146.  *On high ground overlooking an icy inlet in Alaska, U.S. Marines man a machine gun at a lookout post. Ca. 1942–43. Marine Corps.* (OWI)

1147.  *Japanese attack on Dutch Harbor, June 3, 1942. Group of Marines on the "alert" between attacks. Smoke from burning fuel tanks in background had been set afire by a dive bomber the previous day. Alaska.* (Navy)

# War in the East

## America Fights Back

*Photograph 1148*

**1148.** *Take off from the deck of the USS* HORNET *of an Army B-25 on its way to take part in first U.S. air raid on Japan.* Doolittle Raid, April 1942. (Navy)

# War in the East

## China, Burma, India

*Photographs 1149–1161*

**1149.** *A Chinese soldier guards a line of American P-40 fighter planes, painted with the shark-face emblem of the "Flying Tigers," at a flying field somewhere in China. The American pursuit planes have a 12-to-1 victory ratio over the Japanese.* Ca. 1942. (OWI)

**1150.** *Landing wheels recede as this U.S. Army Air Forces Liberator bomber crosses the shark-nosed bows of U.S. P-40 fighter planes at an advanced U.S. base in China. An American soldier waves good luck to the crew, off to bomb Japan.* Ca. 1943. Acme. (OWI)

**1151.** *This Chinese soldier, age 10, with heavy pack, is a member of a Chinese division which is boarding planes at the North Airstrip, Myitkyina, Burma, bound for China.* December 5, 1944. Henry Allen. (Army)

**1152.** *Conference at Yenan Communist Headquarters before Mao Tze Tung, chairman, left for Chungking meeting. Central figures are U.S. Ambassador Patrick J. Hurley, Col. I. V. Yeaton, U.S. Army Observer, and Mao Tze Tung.* August 27, 1945. T5c. Frayne. (Army)

**1153.** *Camp "Y." Captain Derby.* Trincomallee, Ceylon, July 24, 1945. (OSS)

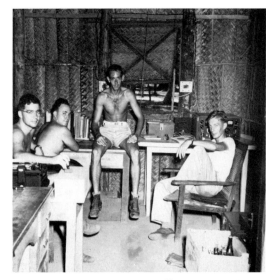

**1154.** *Camp "Y." Maj. S. Karr, Camp Commandant.* Trincomallee, Ceylon, July 24, 1945. (OSS)

**1155.** *Commo Camp "Y." Commo officers.* Trincomallee, Ceylon, July 24, 1945. (OSS)

**1156.** *Mule skinners attached to 2nd Bn., 475th Inf. Regt., Mars Task Force, stripped down to their bare skin to lead mules through the swift river that impeded their progress to Bhamo.* Burma, November 17, 1944. S.Sgt. Quaid. (Army)

**1157.** *A barge, powered by outboard motors, crosses the Irrawaddy River near Tigyiang, Burma. The men, their truck and ammunition all make the crossing at once in this way. December 30, 1944. Sgt. William Lentz. (Army)*

**1158.** *U.S. Convoy which operates between Chen-Yi and Kweiyang, China, is ascending the famous twenty-one curves at Annan, China. March 26, 1945. Pfc. John F. Albert. (Army)*

**1159.** *Silhouette of troops at Pandu Ghat. 124th Cavalry Regt., 5332nd Brigade (Prov) on move from Ramgarh Training Center to Myitkyina, Burma. October 25, 1944. T5c. Kirsten. (Army)*

**1160.** *Aerial of Stinson L-5's used for ferry service from Akyab to Kyaukpyu. Each plane carries one passenger. The flight takes 55 minutes. Burma, May 5, 1945. (OSS)*

**1161.** *Pfc. Edeleanu prints news bulletin on bulletin board outside Intelligence tent of Kyaukpyu Camp the day before OSS, AFU, departure via convoy for Rangoon. Detachment 101, Ramree Island, Burma, May 6, 1945. (OSS)*

# WAR IN THE EAST

## ISLAND CAMPAIGNS
*Photographs 1162–1200*

**1162.** *Three Coast Guardsmen, silhouetted at the stern of a Coast Guard-manned LST. Their destination is Morotai in the Halmaheras, as the powerful attacking force penetrates deep into the crumbling Japanese sea empire. September 1944. (Coast Guard)*

**1163.** *Columns of troop-packed LCIs trail in the wake of a Coast Guard-manned LST en route for the invasion of Cape Sansapor, New Guinea. The deck of the LST is closely packed with motorized fighting equipment. 1944. PhoM1c. Harry R. Watson.* (Coast Guard)

**1164.** *U.S. troops go over the side of a Coast Guard manned combat transport to enter the landing barges at Empress Augusta Bay, Bougainville, as the invasion gets under way. November 1943.* (Coast Guard)

**1165.** *A Water Buffalo, loaded with Marines, churns through the sea bound for beaches of Tinian Island near Guam. July 1944.* (Coast Guard)

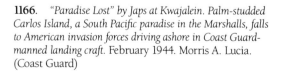

**1166.** *"Paradise Lost" by Japs at Kwajalein. Palm-studded Carlos Island, a South Pacific paradise in the Marshalls, falls to American invasion forces driving ashore in Coast Guard-manned landing craft. February 1944. Morris A. Lucia.* (Coast Guard)

**1167.** *165th Inf. assault wave attacking Butaritari, Yellow Beach Two, find it slow going in the coral bottom waters. Jap machine gun fire from the right flank makes it more difficult for them. Makin Atoll, Gilbert Islands, November 20, 1943. Dargis.* (Army)

**1168.** *Army reinforcements disembarking from LST's form a graceful curve as they proceed across coral reef toward the beach. Saipan, ca. June/July 1944. Laudansky.* (Army)

**1169.** *Marines hit three feet of rough water as they leave their LST to take the beach at Cape Gloucester, New Britain. December 26, 1943. Sgt. Robert M. Howard. (Marine Corps)*

**1170.** *From Coast Guard-manned landing craft, American invaders wade through a golden, shallow surf to hit the beach of Tinian Island. Units of a mighty task force stand on the horizon — Navy warships, transports and LSTs. July 1944. (Coast Guard)*

**1171.** *Australian troops storm ashore in the first assault wave to hit Balikpapan on the southeast coast of oil-rich Borneo. Coast Guard Combat Photographer James L. Lonergan stands in the landing craft. July 1945. Gerald C. Anker. (Coast Guard)*

**1172.** *American troops of the 160th Infantry Regiment rush ashore from a landing boat during amphibious training here. Guadalcanal, March 1, 1944. Preston. (Army)*

**1173.** *American troops of the 163rd Inf. Regt., hit the beach from Higgins boats during the invasion of Wadke Island, Dutch New Guinea. May 18, 1944. Lt. Kent Rooks. (Army)*

**1174.** *It appears that one Marine is relieving another on the beach at Saipan but they are really crawling under enemy fire, to their assigned positions. June 1944. Sgt. James Burns. (Marine Corps)*

**1175.** *The first wave of Marines to hit the Saipan beach in the Marianas invasion take cover behind a sand dune, while waiting for the following three waves to come in. June 1944. Sgt. James Burns. (Marine Corps)*

**1176.** *Landing operations on Rendova Island, Solomon Islands, 30 June 1943. Attacking at the break of day in a heavy rainstorm, the first Americans ashore huddle behind tree trunks and any other cover they can find. (Navy)*

**1177.** *First flag on Guam on boat hook mast. Two U.S. officers plant the American flag on Guam eight minutes after U.S. Marines and Army assault troops landed on the Central Pacific island on July 20, 1944. Batts. (Marine Corps)*

**1178.** *An amphibious tractor burns on the beach as Marines take shelter under a duck. Peleliu, September 1944. Pfc. John J. Smith. (Marine Corps)*

**1179.** *Marines storm Tarawa. Gilbert Islands. November 1943. WO Obie Newcomb, Jr. (Marine Corps)*

**1180.** *Marines take cover behind a sea wall on Red Beach #3, Tarawa. November 1943. (Marine Corps)*

**1181.** *A US Marine charges across the beach on Peleliu Island, Palau Islands, the "walkie talkie" firmly strapped to his back and clutching a radio phone in his right hand. Ca. September 1944.* (Navy)

**1182.** *US Marine in action at Peleliu Island, Palau Islands. Ca. September 1944.* (Navy)

**1183.** *Taking the slim protection that a blasted tree affords, this Marine picks-off the Japs in a pill box. A Jap in a pill box must be shot through the small opening he uses to sight through, but that didn't bother this Marine on Tarawa. November 1943.* (Marine Corps)

**1184.** *An American plane sweeps overhead to strafe the enemy hidden in their coral trenches, while a group of Marines lie prone in the sand peppering the Japs across smoking No-Man's Land with rifle fire. Eniwetok Atoll, Marshall Islands, February 1944.* (Coast Guard)

**1185.** *The Yanks mop up on Bougainville. At night the Japs would infiltrate American lines. At Dawn, the doughboys went out and killed them. This photo shows tank going forward, infantrymen following in its cover. March 1944.* (Army)

**1186.** *Retreating at first into the jungle of Cape Gloucester, Japanese soldiers finally gathered strength and counterattacked their Marine pursuers. These machine gunners pushed them back. January 1944. Brenner.* (Marine Corps)

**1187.** *Men of the 7th Div. using flame throwers to smoke out Japs from a block house on Kwajalein Island, while others wait with rifles ready in case Japs come out.* February 4, 1944. Cordray. (Army)

**1188.** *After the Marines captured this mountain gun from the Japs at Saipan, they put it into use during the attack on Garapan, administrative center of the island. Ca. July 1944. Cpl. Angus Robertson. (Marine Corps)*

**1189.** *Night firing of 155mm rifle. Guam, July 29, 1944. Cpl. A. F. Hager, Jr. (Marine Corps)*

**1190.** *A Marine from the Third Marine Division goes after a sniper in a shelled building. Guam, August 1944. Cpl. J. F. Andrejka. (Marine Corps)*

**1191.** *Using every available means of transporting supplies to the front lines on Saipan, these Marines loaded this ox cart but had to use a lot of persuasion and a little teamwork to get the ox under way. Ca. June 1944. Cpl. Angus Robertson, USMC. (OWI)*

**1192.** *Lt. Col. John Weber, commanding officer of a Marine battalion on Cape Gloucester, sitting on his helmet, receives a report from one of his company commanders. Pfc. Vincent Miley, looking on, blows cigarette smoke out of his nose. January 1944. Brenner. (Marine Corps)*

**1193.** *Navajo Indian communication men with the Marines on Saipan landed with the first assault waves to hit the beach. Ca. June 1944. J. L. Burns. (Marine Corps)*

**1194.** *Marine awaits signal to go ahead in battle to recapture Guam from Japs. July 1944. Lt. Paul Dorsey. (Navy)*

**1195.** *Tired member of VF-17 pauses under squadron scoreboard at Bougainville. February 1944. Lt. Comdr. Charles Fenno Jacobs. (Navy)*

**1196.** *The U.S. Marines salute the U.S. Coast Guard after the fury of battle had subsided and the Japs on Guam had been defeated. "They (the Coast Guard) Put Us Here and We Intend to Stay" is the way the Marines felt about it. Ca. August 1944. (Coast Guard)*

**1197.** *Sign on Tarawa illustrates Marine humor and possible lack of optimism as to duration of war. June 1944. Lt. Comdr. Charles Fenno Jacobs. (Navy)*

**1198.** *Back to a Coast Guard assault transport comes this Marine after two days and nights of Hell on the beach of Eniwetok in the Marshall Islands. His face is grimey with coral dust but the light of battle stays in his eyes. February 1944. (Coast Guard)*

**1199.** *Through the porthole of a Coast Guard combat transport in the Pacific, landing craft can be seen circling in the water just after dawn. The Coast Guard coxswains are awaiting orders to pick up troops and equipment to be ferried ashore during maneuvers. (Coast Guard)*

**1200.**    *These men have earned the bloody reputation of being skillful jungle fighters. They are U.S. Marine Raiders gathered in front of a Jap dugout on Cape Totkina on Bougainville, Solomon Islands, which they helped to take. January 1944. (Navy)*

# War in the East

## The Philippines

*Photographs 1201–1214*

**1201.** *Ships of the fighting fleet in Ulithi Atoll. Foreground to background: USS* WASP, *USS* YORKTOWN, *USS* HORNET, *USS* HANCOCK, *USS* TICONDEROGA, *USS* LEXINGTON. December 1944. (Navy)

**1202.** *The liberators move against the Philippines. An armada of American power steams in impressive array along the coast of Leyte Island in the Philippines as dawn of A-Day bathes the Pacific in golden glory. October 1944. (Coast Guard)*

**1203.** *The gun crews of a Navy cruiser covering American landing on the island of Mindoro, Dec. 15, 1944, scan the skies in an effort to identify a plane overhead. Two 5″ (127mm) guns are ready while inboard 20mm anti-aircraft crews are ready to act. Navy. (OWI)*

**1204.** *Eyes of 20mm anti-aircraft gun crews of a Navy cruiser covering the Mindoro landing, strain to spot the status of an unidentified plane overhead. December 15, 1944. Navy. (OWI)*

**1205.** *Landing barges loaded with troops sweep toward the beaches of Leyte Island as American and Jap planes duel to the death overhead. Troops watch the drama being written in the skies as they approach the hellfire on the shore. October 1944. (Coast Guard)*

**1206.** *A line of Coast Guard landing barges, sweeping through the waters of Lingayen Gulf, carries the first wave of invaders to the beaches of Luzon, after a terrific naval bombardment of Jap shore positions on Jan. 9. 1945.* PhoM1c. Ted Needham. (Coast Guard)

**1207.** *Gen. Douglas MacArthur wades ashore during initial landings at Leyte, P.I. October 1944.* (Army)

**1208.** *"Hug the dirt, mates, or you'll get your back scratched." Yankee invaders bellyflop into the sands of Leyte Island's beaches, after rushing ashore from the landing barges of a Coast Guard-manned invasion transport. October 1944.* (Coast Guard)

**1209.** *LST's pouring army equipment ashore on Leyte Is. in the Philippines. 1944.* (Navy)

**1210.** *Two Coast Guard-manned LST's open their great jaws in the surf that washes on Leyte Island beach, as soldiers strip down and build sandbag piers out to the ramps to speed up unloading operations. 1944.* (Coast Guard)

**1211.** *Veteran Artillery men of the "C" Btry., 90th F.A., lay down a murderous barrage on troublesome Jap artillery positions in Balete Pass, Luzon, P.I. April 19, 1945.* Morton. (Army)

**1212.** *Three Jap snipers elected to shoot it out during the battle for Leyte Island. Yankee bullets drilled the Nips and dropped them in the muddy water of a bomb crater, where they sought shelter in a running rifle fight. 1944. PhoM1c. Harry R. Watson. (Coast Guard)*

**1213.** *It doesn't seem to matter where the war has carried the GI. He retains a keen sense of humor and an equally sharp yearning for home. Signpost at a crossroads in Tacloban on Leyte reflects Joe's love of a gag and names and places he misses. Ca. 1944–45. (Coast Guard)*

**1214.** *The look of the vanquished Jap was caught as the surrender party walked down the ramp of a plane at Manila. The trilogy of expressions range from sorrow (top), through stoic pride (middle), to surliness (right). 1945. PhoM2c. James T. Seright. (Coast Guard)*

# WAR IN THE EAST

## IWO JIMA & OKINAWA

*Photographs 1215–1237*

**1215.** *Lieutenant Wade discusses overall importance of target at pre-invasion briefing. Invasion of Iwo Jima, ca. February 1945. Morejohn. (Marine Corps)*

**1216.** *Landing craft brings first wave of invading Yanks to Iwo Jima. February 1945. (Navy)*

**1217.** *Marines of the 5th Division inch their way up a slope on Red Beach No. 1 toward Surbachi Yama as the smoke of the battle drifts about them. Iwo Jima, February 19, 1945. Dreyfuss. (Marine Corps)*

**1218.** *Observer who spotted a machine gun nest finds its location on a map so they can send the information to artillery or mortars to wipe out the position. Iwo Jima, February 1945. Dreyfuss. (Marine Corps)*

**1219.** *Across the litter on Iwo Jima's black sands, Marines of the 4th Division shell Jap positions cleverly concealed back from the beaches. Here, a gun pumps a stream of shells into Jap positions inland on the tiny volcanic island. Ca. February 1945. (Coast Guard)*

**1220.** *Smashed by Jap mortar and shellfire, trapped by Iwo's treacherous black-ash sands, amtracs and other vehicles of war lay knocked out on the black sands of the volcanic fortress. Ca. February/March 1945. PhoM3c. Robert M. Warren. (Coast Guard)*

**1221.** *Flag raising on Iwo Jima. February 23, 1945.* Joe Rosenthal, Associated Press. (Navy)

**1222.** *From the crest of Mount Suribachi, the Stars and Stripes wave in triumph over Iwo Jima after U.S. Marines had fought their way inch by inch up its steep lava-encrusted slopes. Ca. February 1945. PhoM3c. John Papsun. (Coast Guard)*

**1223.** *This Marine, member of the "Fighting Fourth Marine Division," threatens the enemy even in death. His bayonet fixed at the Charge, he was killed by intense Japanese sniper fire as he advanced. February 19, 1945. Sgt. Bob Cooke. (Marine Corps)*

**1224.** *Corsair fighter looses its load of rocket projectiles on a run against a Jap stronghold on Okinawa. In the lower background is the smoke of battle as Marine units move in to follow up with a Sunday punch. Ca. June 1945. Lt. David D. Duncan. (Marine Corps)*

**1225.** *View of #4 90mm AAA gun emplacement with crew in pit. "D" Battery, 98th AAA Gun Bn., 137th AAA Gp. Okinawa, July 18, 1945. Hendrickson. (Army)*

**1226.** *A formidable task force carves out a beachhead, about 350 miles from the Japanese mainland. Landing craft of all kinds blacken the sea out to the horizon, where stand the battlewagons, cruisers and destroyers. Okinawa, April 13, 1945. (Coast Guard)*

**1227.** *A demolition crew from the 6th Marine Division watch dynamite charges explode and destroy a Japanese cave. Okinawa, May 1945. Robert M. Cusack. (Marine Corps)*

**1228.** *A Marine of the 1st Marine Division draws a bead on a Japanese sniper with his tommy-gun as his companion ducks for cover. The division is working to take Wana Ridge before the town of Shuri. Okinawa, 1945. S.Sgt. Walter F. Kleine. (Marine Corps)*

**1229.** *A Marine dashes through Japanese machine gun fire while crossing a draw, called Death Valley by the men fighting there. Marines sustained more than 125 casualties in eight hours crossing this valley. Okinawa, May 10, 1945. Pvt. Bob Bailey. (Marine Corps)*

**1230.** *With the captured capital of Naha as a background, Marine Maj. Gen. Lemuel Shepherd, commanding general of the 6th Marine Division, relaxes on an Okinawan ridge long enough to consult a map of the terrain. Ca. June 1945. Pfc. Sam Weiner. (Marine Corps)*

**1231.** *Marines pass through a small village where Japanese soldiers lay dead. Okinawa, April 1945. Norris G. McElroy. (Marine Corps)*

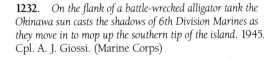

**1232.** *On the flank of a battle-wrecked alligator tank the Okinawa sun casts the shadows of 6th Division Marines as they move in to mop up the southern tip of the island. 1945. Cpl. A. J. Giossi. (Marine Corps)*

**1233.** *Tank-borne infantry moving up to take the town of Ghuta before the Japanese can occupy it. The men are members of the 29th Marines. Okinawa, April 1, 1945. Pfc. Robert L. Keller. (Marine Corps)*

**1234.** *A tank sunk in 5 feet of water waits for towing equipment. The Tank Commander gives vent to his feelings with a string of unprintable phraseology, while his driver uses a helmet to bale out the interior. Okinawa, May 1945. Alexander Roberts. (Army)*

**1235.** *Japanese night raiders are greeted with a lacework of anti-aircraft fire by the Marine defenders of Yontan airfield, on Okinawa. In the foreground are Marine Corsair fighter planes of the "Hell's Belles" squadron. 1945.* T.Sgt. Chorlest. (Marine Corps)

**1236.** *Harassing fire directed towards Japanese positions in Southern Okinawa begins during the early morning hours of May 11, 1945 as an all out offensive gets underway.* Cpl. Eastman. (Marine Corps)

**1237.** *Silhouetted against the entrance to one of the caves that honeycomb the Okinawa hills, a Marine rifleman resorts to cat-and-mouse tactics to pick off enemy snipers in the surrounding ridges. Ca. June 1945.* Cpl. F. E. Kershaw. (Marine Corps)

# War in the East

## Japan
*Photographs 1238–1248*

**1238.** *USS ESSEX based TBMs and SB2Cs dropping bombs on Hokadate, Japan. July 1945.* (Navy)

**1239.** *Task Force 58 raid on Japan. 40mm guns firing aboard USS HORNET on 16 February 1945, as the carrier's planes were raiding Tokyo. Note expended shells and ready-service ammunition at right. February 1945.* Lt. Comdr. Charles Kerlee. (Navy)

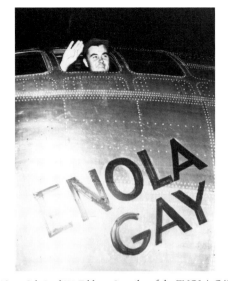

**1240.** *Col. Paul W. Tibbets, Jr., pilot of the ENOLA GAY, the plane that dropped the atomic bomb on Hiroshima, waves from his cockpit before the takeoff, 6 August 1945.* Army Air Forces. (OWI)

**1241.** *Battered religious figures stand watch on a hill above a tattered valley. Nagasaki, Japan. September 24, 1945.* Cpl. Lynn P. Walker, Jr. (Marine Corps)

**1242.** *A dense column of smoke rises more than 60,000 feet into the air over the Japanese port of Nagasaki, the result of an atomic bomb, the second ever used in warfare, dropped on the industrial center August 8, 1945, from a U.S. B-29 Superfortress.* (OWI)

**1243.** Roman Catholic cathedral, Nagasaki, ca. 1945. (Corps of Engineers)

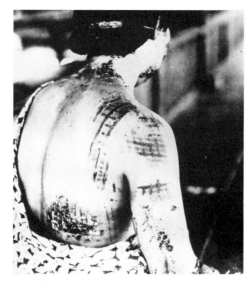

**1244.** *The patient's skin is burned in a pattern corresponding to the dark portions of a kimono worn at the time of the explosion.* Japan, ca. 1945. (Corps of Engineers)

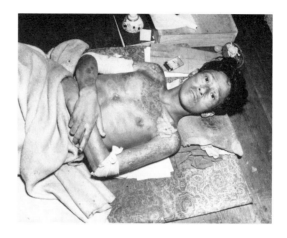

**1245.** *Victim of the Atom Bomb Explosion over Nagasaki.* Ca. 1945. (Corps of Engineers)

**1246.** Roman Catholic cathedral in background on hill, Nagasaki, ca. 1945. (Corps of Engineers)

**1247.** *Demobilized Japanese soldiers crowd trains at Hiroshima on way to homes.* September 1945. Lt. Wayne Miller. (Navy)

**1248.** *Discharged Japanese soldiers crowd trains as they take advantage of free transportation to their homes after end of World War II in Hiroshima, Japan.* September 1945. Lt. Wayne Miller. (Navy)

# WAR IN THE EAST

## ATROCITIES
### Photographs 1249–1253

**1249.** *Casualties of a mass panic; during Japanese air raid, 4,000 people were trampled or suffocated to death trying to return to shelters. Chungking, China, June 5, 1941. (OWI)*

**1250.** *The Tapel Massacre on 1 July 1945. Picture shows Pedro Cerono, the man who discovered the group of 8 skulls. Tapel, Cagayan Province, Luzon, Philippine Islands. November 23, 1945. T5c. Lewis D. Klein. (Army)*

**1251.** *Atrocity committed by the Japs on 9 April 1945 at Bingas, Luzon, Philippine Islands. Child laying in mud of creek. April 11, 1945. T5c. J. Jepson. (Army)*

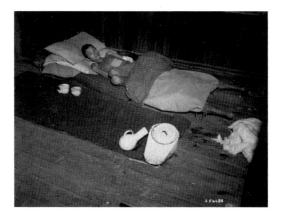

**1252.** *A 12-year old Burmese boy beaten by Japs with shovels and rifle butts, suffers from bayonet wounds. He was buried alive in a shallow grave, but crawled out. He was found by a patrol of the 1st Royal Scots Fusiliers. Burma, January 14, 1945. Lentz. (Army)*

**1253.** *U.S. medical men are attempting to identify more than 100 American POWs captured at Bataan and Corregidor and burned alive by the Japs at a POW camp, Puerto Princesa, Palawan, P.I. Picture shows charred remains being interred in grave. March 20, 1945. Lt. Rothberg. (Army)*

# CIVILIANS & REFUGEES

*Photographs 1254–1271*

**1254.** *Wearing a civilian hat salvaged along the way, a bearded GI amuses both GI's and French civilians as he tries to make himself understood with the aid of a French dictionary in the town of Orleans, France. August 19, 1944. Salvas. (Army Surgeon General)*

**1255.** *Army Ordnance men await the "go" signal for cross channel trip to France. British civilians serve hot coffee as the men await the word to move out in an English town. July 24, 1944. Messerlin. (Army)*

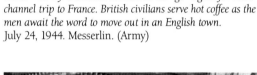

**1256.** *Polish youngster with his arms loaded down with bread made from flour supplied by the American Red Cross. Smile is in anticipation of enough bread to eat, something he would not get if he had stayed in his native Poland. Russia, ca. 1943. OWI. (Army)*

**1257.** *Cpl. Paul Opperer, New York City, amuses a group of French children who have taken refuge at a church near Plaennec, in the Brest area, France. His GI prestidigitations amused the children and took their minds off their troubles. August 20, 1944. Hall. (Army)*

**1258.** *Lad with mother pushing from behind rolls cartload of possessions out of Uerdingen, Germany, moved out by allied military government seeking to prevent loss of life from shelling by Germans on other side of Rhine. March 19, 1945. T4c. George J. Barry. (Army)*

**1259.** *This girl pays the penalty for having had personal relations with the Germans. Here, in the Montelimar area, France, French civilians shave her head as punishment.* August 29, 1944. Smith. (Army)

**1260.** *Children in Naples, Italy. Little boy helps one-legged companion across street.* August 1944. Lt. Wayne Miller. (Navy)

**1261.** *Two bewildered old ladies stand amid the leveled ruins of the almshouse which was Home; until Jerry dropped his bombs. Total war knows no bounds. Almshouse bombed Feb. 10, Newbury, Berks., England. February 11, 1943. Naccarata.* (Army)

**1262.** *These Jewish children are on their way to Palestine after having been released from the Buchenwald Concentration Camp. The girl on the left is from Poland, the boy in the center from Latvia, and the girl on right from Hungary. June 5, 1945. T4c. J. E. Myers.* (Army)

**1263.** *Verboten! Men of 101st Airborne Div. remember they can not fraternize as they watch a shapely fraulein swing up the walk to their rest center in Konigsee, Germany. June 18, 1945. Sgt. R. Sawyer.* (Army)

**1264.** *Native outrigger canoes approach a Coast Guard troop transport. The Moros have come for two purposes: to trade their souvenirs and to dive for coins thrown into the sea by Coast Guard crew members and GI's. Philippines, ca. 1945.* (Coast Guard)

**1265.** *These two Chinese youngsters are fascinated by the sight of an American soldier shaving in the open. Yunnan, China. June 1944.* (Army)

**1266.** *The salute was the little Filipino lad's own idea, when a Coast Guard Combat Photographer encountered him somewhere on liberated Leyte Island. Ca. 1945.* (Coast Guard)

**1267.** *A member of a Marine patrol on Saipan found this family of Japs hiding in a hillside cave. The mother, four children and a dog, took shelter from the fierce fighting in that area.* June 21, 1944. Cpl. Angus Robertson. (Marine Corps)

**1268.** *Marines try to soothe a crying child by offering a shiny rations tin. Children are sheltered with their families in a camp set up for refugees from battle areas by U.S. Marine Civil Affairs authorities on Saipan.* July 1944. PhoM1c. Ted Needham. (Coast Guard)

**1269.** *While big brother's attention is riveted on some object up the road on Okinawa, the little fellow protests against the delay, for all he wants is to get home.* 1945. T.Sgt. Glen A. Fitzgerald. (Marine Corps)

**1270.** *"The Fighting Irish," Good Shepherd Convent. Thirteen Irish nuns who had been interned in the Rangoon City Jail by the Japanese, but were later released as neutrals.* Burma, May 28, 1945. Attributed to Cpl. Rodney C. Ferguson. (OSS)

**1271.** *The Angel Guardian Home, a Catholic home for orphans, in Kumamoto, Japan. As Pvt. Louis Miller, Brooklyn, New York, was about to leave, Sister St. Paul had the orphans dress in their finest clothes to have their picture taken.* October 25, 1945. F. C. Rogers. (Marine Corps)

# PRISONERS

*Photographs 1272–1314*

**1272.** Prisoners in the concentration camp at Sachsenhausen, Germany, December 19, 1938. Heinrich Hoffman Collection. (Foreign Records Seized)

**1273.** Prisoners in the concentration camp at Sachsenhausen, Germany, December 19, 1938. Heinrich Hoffman Collection. (Foreign Records Seized)

**1274.** Prisoners in the concentration camp at Sachsenhausen, Germany, December 19, 1938. Heinrich Hoffman Collection. (Foreign Records Seized)

**1275.** *Himmler besichtigt die Gefangenenlager in Russland.* Heinrich Himmler inspects a prisoner-of-war camp in Russia. Ca. 1940–41. Heinrich Hoffman Collection. (Foreign Records Seized)

**1276.** *The captured French General Giraud, during his daily walk.* Germany, ca. 1940–41. (Office of Alien Property)

**1277.** Women prisoners. Copy of German photograph taken during the destruction of the Warsaw Ghetto, Poland, 1943. (WWII War Crimes Records)

**1278.** Jewish Rabbis. Copy of German photograph taken during the destruction of the Warsaw Ghetto, Poland, 1943. (WWII War Crimes Records)

**1279.** Prisoners. Copy of German photograph taken during the destruction of the Warsaw Ghetto, Poland, 1943. (WWII War Crimes Records)

**1280.** Jewish civilians. Copy of German photograph taken during the destruction of the Warsaw Ghetto, Poland, 1943. (WWII War Crimes Records)

**1281.** *With his feuhrer's trademark on his scivy shirt, a captured German U-boat seaman seems pretty glum about the fortunes of war after a Coast Guard fighting craft had depth-charged the submarine to its grave deep under the Allied shipping lanes.* (Coast Guard)

**1282.** *A Negro soldier of the 12th Armored Division stands guard over a group of Nazi prisoners captured in the surrounding German forest. April 1945. (OWI)*

**1283.** *"We were getting our second wind now and started flattening out that bulge. We took 50,000 prisoners in December alone."* Ca. 1944. Army. (OWI)

**1284.** *Two German prisoners of war are being taken to the 6th Div. POW Encampment for interrogation and searching. There were 218 captured by the Free French Infantry and 6th Armored Div. troops. Plouay, France. August 28, 1944. Pfc. H. M. Kuehne. (Army)*

**1285.** *German prisoners, Anzio Beachhead below Rome, on their way to prison camp. Italy, February 1944. (Navy)*

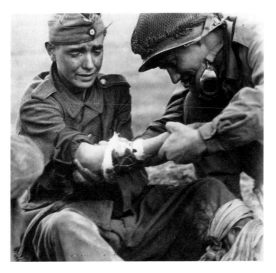

**1286.** *Dismay and loneliness is written on the face of this young Jap, wearing a Nazi uniform, in a roundup of German prisoners on the beaches of France. The Jap is giving his name and number to an American Army captain. 1944. (Coast Guard)*

**1287.** *This Nazi "Superman" appears to be in his "teens" and his expression is not exactly that of the conquering hero as an American soldier looks at the lad's injury while awaiting the arrival of a medic. September 6, 1944. Waks. (Army Surgeon General)*

**1288.** *A German prisoner of war captured near Ubach, Germany, wears a tag telling his captors that he has an injured back and should be handled carefully. December 1, 1944. Sgt. Miller. (Army Surgeon General)*

**1289.** *A German prisoner captured by the 16th Infantry Regiment, near Weywertz.* Belgium, January 15, 1945. Sgt. Bill Augustine. (Army)

**1290.** *The endless procession of German prisoners captured with the fall of Aachen marching through the ruined city streets to captivity.* Germany, October 1944. Associated Press Ltd. (U.S. Occupation Headquarters)

**1291.** *"This Nazi officer is eating his words, and a can of C-rations, in the ruins of Saarbrucken. The day we hung our washing on this Siegfried line stronghold, we of the Seventh linked up with Third Army armor west of Kaiserlautern. Was that a day."* Germany, 1945. (OWI)

**1292.** *Female members of the Wehrmacht are among the inmates of the Third U.S. Army prisoner of war enclosure at Regansburg, Germany.* May 8, 1945. T5c. R. Grant. (Army)

**1293.** *High ranking German officers seized by Free French troops which liberated their country's capital are lodged in the hotel Majestic, headquarters for the Wehrmacht in the days of the Nazi occupation.* Paris, France, August 26, 1944. Lovell. (Army)

**1294.** *Maj. Gen. Walther Dornberger, Commander of the V-2 laboratory at Peenemünde; Lt. Col. Herbert Axter; Prof. Wernher von Braun, inventor of the V-2 rocket; and Hans Lindenberg, after they surrendered to U.S. troops.* Austria, May 3, 1945. T5c. Louis Weintraub. (Army)

**1295.** *German Gestapo agents arrested after the fall of Liege, Belgium, are herded together in a cell in the citadel of Liege. Ca. October 1944.* La Frano. (Army)

**1296.** Nuremberg Trials. Looking down on defendants' dock, ca. 1945–46. (WWII War Crimes Records)

**1297.** Nuremberg Trials. Defendants in their dock: Goering, Hess, von Ribbentrop, and Keitel in front row, ca. 1945–46. (WWII War Crimes Records)

**1298.** *German Gen. Anton Dostler is tied to a stake before his execution by a firing squad in the Aversa stockade. The General was convicted and sentenced to death by an American military tribunal. Aversa, Italy.* December 1, 1945. Blomgren. (Army)

**1299.** *Liberated prisoners in the Mauthausen concentration camp near Linz, Austria, give rousing welcome to Cavalrymen of the 11th Armored Division. The banner across the wall was made by Spanish Loyalist prisoners.* May 6, 1945. Cpl. Donald R. Ornitz. (Army)

**1300.** *A returned German prisoner of war identified this woman's son. He will never return because he is dead. Prisoners released by the Soviet Union, Germany, 1955.* (USIA)

**1301.** *American prisoners of war celebrate the 4th of July in the Japanese prison camp of Casisange in Malaybalay, on Mindanao, P.I. It was against Japanese regulations and discovery would have meant death, but the men celebrated the occasion anyway. July 4, 1942.* (Army)

**1302.** *Service for deceased souls, 3rd Branch Camp.* American prisoners of war at Airyokei, Takao Province, Formosa, ca. 1943–44. (Army Staff)

**1303.** *Battle of Tarawa: Prisoners.* November 1943. (Marine Corps)

**1304.** *A further indication that not all Japanese fight to the death is this bag of 221 Nip prisoners of war. Sprawled on the deck of an LCT, they are being brought to a Coast Guard-manned troop transport at Guam for transfer to Pearl Harbor. Ca. 1945.* (Coast Guard)

**1305.** *Japanese prisoners of war are bathed, clipped, "deloused," and issued GI clothing as soon as they are taken aboard the USS NEW JERSEY. Prisoner bathing.* December 1944. Lt. Comdr. Charles Fenno Jacobs. (Navy)

**1306.** *Marines unloading Japanese POW from a submarine returned from war patrol.* Ca. May 1945. Lt. Comdr. Horace Bristol. (Navy)

**1307.** *This disconsolate Japanese prisoner of war sits dejectedly behind barbed wire after he and some 306 others were captured within the last 24 hours of the Okinawa battle by Sixth Marine Division. Okinawa, June 1945.* A. F. Hager, Jr. (Marine Corps)

**1308.** *Correspondents interview "Tokyo Rose." Iva Toguri, American-born Japanese.* September 1945. (Navy)

**1309.** *The Battle of the Marshall Islands. Namur. February 2, 1944. Cpl. John Fabian. (Marine Corps)*

**1310.** *Japanese POW at Guam, with bowed head after hearing Emperor Hirohito make announcement of Japan's unconditional surrender. August 15, 1945. (Navy)*

**1311.** *The Jap that surrendered at Kerama Retto, Ryukyu Islands. Ca. June 1945. (Navy)*

**1312.** *Japanese POW's at Guam, with bowed heads after hearing Emperor Hirohito make announcement of Japan's unconditional surrender. August 15, 1945. (Navy)*

**1313.** *On the porch of an emergency hospital these released American prisoners of war, liberated by U.S. Rangers from Cabanatuan prison camp on Luzon, P.I., wait for transfer to a base hospital. January 1945. (Army)*

**1314.** *Gaunt allied prisoners of war at Aomori camp near Yokohama cheer rescuers from U.S. Navy. Waving flags of the United States, Great Britain and Holland. Japan, August 29, 1945. (Navy)*

# Death &
# Destruction

*Photographs 1315–1352*

**1315.** Torpedoed Japanese destroyer photographed through periscope of U.S.S. *Wahoo* or U.S.S. *Nautilus*, June 1942. (Navy)

**1316.** *Allied tanker torpedoed in Atlantic Ocean by German submarine. Ship crumbling amidship under heat of fire, settles toward bottom of ocean.* 1942. (Navy)

**1317.** *Damaged USS RANDOLPH resulting from a Jap suicide attack. Damage to overhead hangar and flight deck aft.* March 11, 1945. PhoM1c. R. N. Cudabac and PhoM1c. W. E. Kruse. (Navy)

**1318.** *Sunken Japanese ships in Manila Bay are being refloated by Navy salvage crews, towed to deeper water, and re-sunk. Battered ships are afloat again.* August 1945. Lt. Comdr. Charles Fenno Jacobs. (Navy)

**1319.** *Infra red view of wrecked Jap plane near Angeles, Pampanga, on Luzon, P.I. In the background is Mt. Arayat, some 10 to 15 miles away.* May 29, 1945. S.Sgt. Harry Young. (Army)

**1320.** *U.S. Army troops pause for a look at a Japanese sea-plane during the battle of Makin. The plane was under repair in the lagoon when the invasion started. The Japanese used it as a machine gun nest until American fliers took care of it.* November 1943. (Coast Guard)

**1321.** Wrecked plane in Nuremberg, Germany, 1946. Goddard Collection. (Air Force)

**1322.** *Photograph made from B-17 Flying Fortress of the 8th AAF Bomber Command on 31 Dec. when they attacked the vital CAM ball-bearing plant and the nearby Hispano Suiza aircraft engine repair depot in Paris. France, 1943.* Army Air Forces. (OWI)

**1323.** *La Vie a Londres pendant la guerre. Vue d'un V-1 dans son vol.* Life in London during the war. View of a V-1 in flight. Ca. 1944. New York Times Paris Bureau Collection. (USIA)

**1324.** *A British Flag lies among the rubble of homes smashed by the Camberwell Rd. Rocket explosion.* V-bomb damage, London, ca. 1944. (OSS)

**1325.** Bomb damage in Cherbourg, France, after its liberation, ca. June/July 1944. (OSS)

**1326.** *"All this inanimate wreckage around us was little enough compensation for the human wreckage we hauled back and forth, back and forth."* Lunebach, Germany, ca. March 1945. Army. (OWI)

**1327.** *Choked with debris, a bombed water intake of the Pegnitz River no longer supplies war factories in Nuremberg, vital Reich industrial city and festival center of the Nazi party, which was captured April 20, 1945, by troops of the U.S. Army. April 1945.* (OWI)

**1328.** *General view of the Bavarian city of Nuremberg, following the cessation of organized resistance. In the distance, the twin-spired Lorenz Church; on the right and surrounded with rubble is a statue of Kaiser William I. 1945.* Keystone. (Roberts Commission)

**1329.** *Pfc. Lawrence Bartlett, Niagara Falls, N.Y., examines the 4 fallen lions which once adorned the top of the Siegestor, built by King Ludwig I, in 1844–1852 in tribute to the Bavarian Army. Munich, Germany, June 13, 1945.* Army. (Roberts Commission)

**1330.** *Heilbronn in a panorama. It was one of the three or four most devastated cities in all Europe. Germany, ca. April 1945.* Harold W. Clover. (National Archives Gift Collection)

**1331.** *Still standing in the rubble of a church in the war-blasted town of Dulag, a statue of the sacred heart appears to gaze in quiet sorrow on the destruction wrought by battle's fury seething over Leyte Island. Philippines, 1944.* (Coast Guard)

**1332.** *Rangoon Railway station, Rangoon, Burma. Repair Shed, 10′ in height at West end. May 25, 1945.* (OSS)

**1333.** *All that is left of one Shinto shrine in Nagasaki. The arch is made of elements. This plus the fact that the blast could go through and around the structure, enabled it to escape destruction.* Japan, October 1945. Lt. R. J. Battersby. (Marine Corps)

**1334.** *The German ultimatum ordering the Dutch commander of Rotterdam to cease fire was delivered to him at 10:30 a.m. on May 14, 1940. At 1:22 p.m., German bombers set the whole inner city of Rotterdam ablaze, killing 30,000 of its inhabitants.* (OWI)

**1335.** *A Marine observation plane flies low over Naha, capital of Okinawa. On this flight, the tiny ship drew small arms and antiaircraft fire from the city which was in Japanese control at the time.* Ca. May 1945. Lt. David D. Duncan. (Marine Corps)

**1336.** *Walls of houses of Wesel still stand, as do the churches, but a great part of the town was destroyed when the German commander forced the Allied troops to fight their way street by street through the ruins.* Germany, 1945. Army. (OWI)

**1337.** *Cologne Cathedral stands undamaged while entire area surrounding it is completely devastated. Railroad station and Hohenzollern Bridge lie damaged to the north and east of the cathedral.* Germany, April 24, 1945. T4c. Jack Clemmer. (Army)

**1338.** *Wounded once, this German wouldn't quit and was grenaded to death.* Germany, ca. April 1945. Harold W. Clover. (National Archives Gift Collection)

**1339.** *American soldiers, stripped of all equipment, lie dead, face down in the slush of a crossroads somewhere on the western front. Note the bare feet of the soldier in the foreground. Captured German photograph. Belgium, ca. December 1944. (Army)*

**1340.** *This boy's dead body, aflame, bears ghastly witness of the horror of the damage done by V-2 on main intersection in Antwerp on main supply line to Holland. Belgium, November 27, 1944. T3c. Ingeldew. (Army)*

**1341.** *American soldier lies dead in gutter of Schevenhutte, Germany, after being hit by flak from German guns. Medics had just given first aid, to no avail. December 22, 1944. Sgt. J. A. DeMarco. (Army Surgeon General)*

**1342.** *Sprawled bodies on beach of Tarawa, testifying to ferocity of the struggle for this stretch of sand. November 1943. (Navy)*

**1343.** *Trapped Japs, north of the town of Garapan, attempted to gain refuge by getting to their few ships in Tanapag harbor. On the beach is one Jap who didn't make the boat. Saipan, July 5, 1944. Cpl. Angus Robertson. (Marine Corps)*

**1344.** *Two enlisted men of the ill-fated U.S. Navy aircraft carrier LISCOME BAY, torpedoed by a Japanese submarine in the Gilbert Islands, are buried at sea from the deck of a Coast Guard-manned assault transport. November 1943. (Coast Guard)*

**1345.** *Burgomeister of Leipzig a suicide in his office together with wife and daughter as 69th Infantry Division and 9th Armored Division closed on city. Germany, April 20, 1945.* T5c. J. M. Heslop. (Army)

**1346.** *With torn picture of his feuhrer beside his clenched fist, a dead general of the Volkssturm lies on the floor of city hall, Leipzig, Germany. He committed suicide rather than face U.S. Army troops who captured the city on April 19.* 1945. T5c. J. M. Heslop. Army. (OWI)

**1347.** *Photo taken at the instant bullets from a French firing squad hit a Frenchman who collaborated with the Germans. This execution took place in Rennes, France.* November 21, 1944. Himes. (Army)

**1348.** *A bugler blows taps at the close of Memorial Day service at Margraten Cemetery, Holland, where lie thousands of American heroes of World War II. May 30, 1945.* Pfc. Richard G. Thompson. (Army)

**1349.** *French civilians erected this silent tribute to an American solider who has fallen in the crusade to liberate France from Nazi domination. Carentan, France. June 17, 1944.* Himes. (Army)

**1350.** *Silhouetted in the golden glory of a Pacific sunrise, crosses mark the graves of American boys who gave their lives to win a small atoll on the road to the Philippines. A Coast Guardsman stands in silent reverence beside the resting place of a comrade. 1944.* (Coast Guard)

**1351.** *A Coast Guard seaman died at his battle station aboard the USS* MENGES, *torpedoed by a Nazi sub in the Mediterranean. He represents the old Coast Guard expression, "You have to go out, but you don't have to come back."* PhoM1c. Arthur Green. (Coast Guard)

**1352.** *Standing in the grassy sod bordering row upon row of white crosses in an American cemetery, two dungaree-clad Coast Guardsmen pay silent homage to the memory of a fellow Coast Guardsman who lost his life in action in the Ryukyu Islands. Ca. 1945. Benrud. (Coast Guard)*

# VICTORY & PEACE

*Photographs 1353–1371*

**1353.** *Field Marshall Wilhelm Keitel, signing the ratified surrender terms for the German Army at Russian Headquarters in Berlin. Germany, May 7, 1945. Lt. Moore. (Army)*

**1354.** *Jubilant American soldier hugs motherly English woman and victory smiles light the faces of happy service men and civilians at Piccadilly Circus, London, celebrating Germany's unconditional surrender. England, May 7, 1945. Pfc. Melvin Weiss. (Army)*

**1355.** *At 1000 hours on 8 May 1945 aboard HM-LST 538, word was received via radio from Delhi announcing the end of hostilities in Europe. Immediately ship's signal flags were hoisted in gay display of victory. Kyaukpyu, Ramree Island, Burma. (OSS)*

**1356.** President Truman announces Japan's surrender, at the White House, Washington, DC, August 14, 1945. Abbie Rowe. (National Park Service)

**1357.** *GI's at the Rainbow Corner Red Cross Club in Paris, France, whoop it up after buying the special edition of the Paris Post, which carried the banner headline, "JAPS QUIT." August 10, 1945. T3c. G. Lempeotis. (Army)*

**1358.** *New York City celebrating the surrender of Japan. They threw anything and kissed anybody in Times Square.* August 14, 1945. Lt. Victor Jorgensen. (Navy)

**1359.** *V-J Day in New York City. Crowds gather in Times Square to celebrate the surrender of Japan.* August 15, 1945. Sgt. Reg Kenny. (Army)

**1360.** *Americans of Italian descent in New York City wave flags and toss paper into the air as they celebrate the news of Japan's unconditional surrender to the Allies on August 14, 1945.* Press Association. (OWI)

**1362.** *Japanese surrender signatories arrive aboard the USS* MISSOURI *in Tokyo Bay to participate in surrender ceremonies.* September 2, 1945. (Army)

**1363.** *Gen. Douglas MacArthur signs as Supreme Allied Commander during formal surrender ceremonies on the USS* MISSOURI *in Tokyo Bay. Behind Gen. MacArthur are Lt. Gen. Jonathan Wainwright and Lt. Gen. A. E. Percival.* September 2, 1945. Lt. C. F. Wheeler. (Navy)

**1361.** *Spectators and photographers pick vantage spots on the deck of the USS* MISSOURI *in Tokyo Bay, to witness the formal Japanese surrender proceedings.* September 2, 1945. (Army)

**1364.** *Second Division high pointers returning to the states. Nagasaki, Japan. October 1945. Cohn. (Marine Corps)*

**1365.** *Happy veterans head for harbor of Le Havre, France, the first to be sent home and discharged under the Army's new point system. May 25, 1945. Pfc. Stedman. (Army)*

**1366.** *These Yank airmen beam broadly as they look out from their bomber, following their arrival at Bradley Field, Windsor Locks, Conn., May 22, on a flight from Europe. In their bomber "Hell Hen," they helped to bomb Germany out of the war. 1945. Press Association. (OWI)*

**1367.** *The famous British liner, QUEEN MARY, arrives in New York Harbor, June 20, 1945, with thousands of U.S. troops from European battles. (Navy)*

**1368.** *Cheering U.S. veterans of the China-Burma-India campaigns arrive in New York Sept. 27, 1945, aboard the Army transport General A. W. Greely. The men and women were members of the Flying Tigers, Merrill's Marauders, and other heroic outfits. INP. (OWI)*

**1369.** *Pfc. Lee Harper, who was wounded in Normandy, is greeted by his 2½ year old sister, Janet, whom he had never seen before, on his arrival in New York City on Aug. 1, 1945. His mother and his wife look on. Press Association. (OWI)*

**1370.** *F4U's and F6F's fly in formation during surrender ceremonies; Tokyo, Japan. USS* MISSOURI [in] *left fore-ground.* September 2, 1945. (Navy)

**1371.** *Mount Fujiyama, Japan as seen from the USS* SOUTH DAKOTA *in Tokyo Bay.* August 1945. (Navy)

# KOREAN WAR

*Right after this we got so much fire of all kinds that I lost count. There were more mortar shells, more antitank stuff and more small-arms fire and then it started all over again. In a few minutes the little area back of the burning building which gave us cover was crowded with wounded men. They lay there in pain among burning debris and hot embers, hugging the ground to keep from getting hit again.*

*There was only one medic — A Navy corpsman — so I put my camera aside and gave him a hand. I missed a lot of good pictures but there is no need to say the pictures were not that important. . . .*

LT. ROBERT L. STRICKLAND
71st Signal Service Battalion
September 1950

John G. Westover, *Combat Support in Korea*. U.S. Army in Action Series. (reprint, Washington, DC: Center of Military History, 1987), p. 105.

In a world tired of war, the intransigence of political ideology led to the outbreak of war in Korea in 1950. The invasion of South Korea by the North Koreans led to the involvement on a large scale of American troops, part of the United Nations forces sent to fight the Communist aggression. A seesaw war had the North pushing through most of the South before U.N. troops drove them back almost to the Chinese border. Then Chinese and North Korean forces pushed back the advance almost all the way to the original boundary between North and South. Stalemate ensued and an uneasy armistice was reached in 1953.

*Opposite: Photo 1424*

# PERSONALITIES & POLITICS

*Photographs 1372–1379*

**1372.** *President Harry S. Truman is shown at his desk at the White House signing a proclamation declaring a national emergency.* December 16, 1950. Acme. (USIA)

**1373.** *Jacob A. Malik, Soviet representative on the U.N. Security Council, raises his hand to cast the only dissenting vote to the resolution calling on the Chinese Communists to withdraw troops from Korea.* Lake Success, NY, December 1950. INP. (USIA)

**1374.** Brig. Gen. Courtney Whitney; Gen. Douglas MacArthur, Commander in Chief of U.N. Forces; and Maj. Gen. Edward M. Almond observe the shelling of Inchon from the U.S.S. *Mt. McKinley,* September 15, 1950. Nutter. (Army)

**1375.** *General of the Army Douglas MacArthur is shown inspecting troops of the 24th Inf. on his arrival at Kimpo airfield for a tour of the battlefront.* February 21, 1951. INP. (USIA)

**1376.** Lt. Gen. Matthew Ridgway; Maj. Gen. Doyle Hickey; and Gen. Douglas MacArthur, Commander in Chief of U.N. Forces in Korea, in a jeep at a command post, Yang Yang, approximately 15 miles north of the 38th parallel, April 3, 1951. Grigg. (Army)

**1377.** Gen. Douglas MacArthur addressing an audience of 50,000 at Soldier's Field, Chicago, on his first visit to the United States in 14 years, April 1951. Acme. (USIA)

**1378.** At U.N. Security Council, Warren Austin, U.S. delegate, holds Russian-made submachine gun dated 1950, captured by American troops in July 1950. He charges that Russia is delivering arms to North Koreans. Lake Success, NY, September 18, 1951. INP. (USIA)

**1379.** *The Hon. S.Y. Lee, Vice President of South Korea, leads cheers at the close of the UN Day ceremony at Seoul.* October 24, 1950. Sgt. Ray Turnbull. (Army)

# TROOPS

*Photographs 1380–1401*

**1380.** Cpl. John W. Simms of Bradbury Heights, MD, is shown bidding his wife, Ann, and their 8-month-old son, John Jr., goodbye as he leaves for Korea, 1950. *Washington Post.* (USIA)

**1381.** *San Diego, Calif. A young officer and his wife sitting in their car at the dock and staring quietly at the waiting aircraft carrier before he leaves for Korea,* 1950. Black Star. (USIA)

**1382.** *U.S. troops are pictured on pier after debarking from ship, somewhere in Korea.* August 6, 1950. Sgt. Dunlap. (Army)

**1383.** *Troops of the 31st Inf. Regt. land at Inchon Harbor, Korea, aboard LST's.* September 18, 1950. Hunkins. (Army)

**1384.** *Officers and men of the 62nd Engineers stand in front of the first train to cross the new railroad bridge which they built across the Han River at Seoul, Korea.* October 19, 1950. Sfc. Albert Guyette. (Army)

**1385.** *Men of the 24th Inf. Regt. move up to the firing line in Korea.* July 18, 1950. Breeding. (Army)

**1386.** *Fresh and eager U.S. Marine troops, newly-arrived at the vital southern supply port of Pusan, are shown prior to moving up to the front lines.* August 1950. INP. (USIA)

**1387.** *During South Korean evacuation of Suwon Airfield, a 37-mm anti-tank gun is hauled out of the area for repairs, by a weapons carrier.* 1950. INP. (USIA)

**1388.** *An ROK soldier guards the Panmunjom road near the UN delegates' base camp, Munsan-ni.* March 15, 1952. G. Dimitri Boria. (Army)

**1389.** *Ethiopian troops training in Korea. A class in military intelligence instructed by Lt. Solomon Mokria of Addis Ababa.* May 1951. Gahn, State Dept. (USIA)

**1390.** *Men at Munsan-ni, preparing for inspection prior to acting as honor guard at signing of armistice at Panmunjom, Korea. Navy men shining their shoes.* July 23, 1953. (Navy)

**1391.** *Marines of the 1st Marine Division relax by a Korean hut after destroying an enemy sniper housed there.* September 24, 1951. T. Sgt. Frank W. Sewell. (Marine Corps)

**1392.** *Astonished Marines of the 5th and 7th Regiments, who hurled back a surprise onslaught by three Chinese communist divisions, hear that they are to withdraw!* Ca. December 1950. Sgt. Frank C. Kerr. (Marine Corps)

**1393.** *Pfc. Preston McKnight, 19th Inf. Regt., uses his poncho to get protection from the biting wind and cold, in the Yoju area, during break in action against the Chinese Communist aggressors.* January 10, 1951. Cpl. E. Watson. (Army)

**1394.** *Pfc. Edward Wilson, 24th Inf. Regt., wounded in leg while engaged in action against the enemy forces near the front lines in Korea, waits to be evacuated to aid station behind the lines.* February 16, 1951. Pfc. Charles Fabiszak. (Army)

**1395.** *Catching up on his letters to the folks at home during a break in action against the Chinese Communist forces along the fighting front in Korea, is Pfc. Dwight Exe, 5th Cav. Regt.* November 15, 1951. Cpl. James L. Chancellor. (Army)

**1396.** *Pfc. Clarence Whitmore, voice radio operator, 24th Infantry Regiment, reads the latest news while enjoying chow during lull in battle, near Sangju, Korea.* August 9, 1950. Pfc. Charles Fabiszak, Army. (USIA)

**1397.** Former American and Australian prisoners of war warming up before a stove in the 24th Division medical clearing station after being returned to U.S. lines by Chinese Communists, February 10, 1951. Sfc. Al Chang. (Army)

**1398.** With nearly 3,000 pin-ups (including over 200 shots of Marilyn Monroe) serving as wallpaper for their Quonset hut, these Marines of the "Devil-cats" squadron are still looking for more, October 28, 1952. Sgt. Curt Giese. (Marine Corps)

**1399.** *Missouri infantrymen with the 19th Inf. Regt. along the Kumsong front wish Happy New Year to the stateside folks.* December 14, 1951. Cpl. Mervyn Lew. (Army)

**1400.** *U.S. Marines stand along the rail and watch the ocean aboard the USS* Clymer. *To the aft a Marine is washing his dungarees by dragging them along behind the ship.* July 1950. Sgt. Frank C. Kerr. (Marine Corps)

**1401.** *Lt. Col. John Hopkins, commanding officer of the First Battalion, Fifth Marine Regiment, leads in singing the "Star Spangled Banner" during Memorial Services held in the field during the Korean campaign.* June 21, 1951. Cpl. Valle. (Marine Corps)

# SUPPLY & SUPPORT

*Photographs 1402–1415*

**1402.** *A view of the U.N. fuel dump at Inchon Harbor, Korea. Hundreds of fuel drums are lifted and moved with cranes from a tanker onto the ground.* March 7, 1952. G. Dimitri Boria. (Army)

**1403.** *Marine Corps tanks — ready for the front lines — are swung aboard a barge at the Naval Supply Center by crane, for transhipment to our forces in the Pacific Far Eastern Command.* Oakland, CA, 1950. Acme. (USIA)

**1404.** *Railroad cars loaded with barbed wire at Taegu RTO [Railway Transportation Office], Korea.* July 24, 1950. Sgt. Riley. (Army)

**1405.** *Supplies and equipment are also evacuated from the onslaught of the Communist Forces bearing down on Hungnam, Korea.* December 11, 1950. Pfc. Emerich M. Christ. (Army)

**1406.** *Invasion of Inchon, Korea. Four LST's unload men and equipment on beach. Three of the LST's shown are LST-611, LST-745, and LST-715.* September 15, 1950. C. K. Rose. (Navy)

**1407.** *"Freedom Gate Bridge" spanning the Imjin River, built by the 84th Engineer Construction Bn. This bridge temporarily replaces the original structure which was destroyed by bombs. March 10, 1952. G. Dimitri Boria. (Army)*

**1408.** *Three BD-110A switchboards on left and one BD-96 on extreme right being operated by Pfc. James Grahn of Co. B, 71st Sig. Svc. Bn., Pusan, Korea. August 1, 1950. Cpl. Crowe. (Army)*

**1409.** *Maj. Gen. Frank Lowe, USA, presidential representative in Korea, examines "flash range" instruments on the Marine front lines. Explaining the instrument is Marine S/Sgt. Charles Kitching of Redlands, Calif. March 1951. T.Sgt. Vance Jobe. (Marine Corps)*

**1410.** *An HRS-1 Sikorsky helicopter hovers close to the ground while Marines hook a cargo net loaded with 1,000 pounds of supplies for transportation to the front 12 miles away. Ca. 1951. M.Sgt. Ed Waite. (Marine Corps)*

**1411.** *An aircraft maintenance crew of the U.S. Air Forces 4th Fighter-Interceptor Wing in Korea, photographed through the tail-pipe of an F-86 Sabre, hoists an engine into place for installation on one of the jet fighter planes. September 1951. (USIA)*

**1412.** *Two Pantherjets are refueling after rockets have been "hung" under the wings. Ca. 1951. M.Sgt. C. D. Prindle. (Marine Corps)*

**1413.** *View of F-86 airplanes on the flight line getting ready for combat.* June 1951. Air Force. (USIA)

**1414.** *F4U's (Corsairs) returning from a combat mission over North Korea circle the USS* Boxer *as they wait for planes in the next strike to be launched from her flight deck — a helicopter hovers above the ship.* September 4, 1951. (Navy)

**1415.** *A U.N. LST slips into the harbor at Inchon prior to invasion by U.S. Marines.* December 13, 1950. (Navy)

# COMBAT

*Photographs 1416–1445*

**1416.** *Landing craft loaded with Marines head for the smoking beach in invasion of Inchon, September 15, 1950.* Sgt. Frank C. Kerr. (Marine Corps)

**1417.** *Troops are climbing down cargo net to waiting LCVP's as they land.* January 9, 1953. (Army)

**1418.** *Carrying scaling ladders, U.S. Marines in landing crafts head for the seawall at Inchon.* September 15, 1950. S.Sgt. W. W. Frank. (Marine Corps)

**1419.** *As against "The Shores of Tripoli" in the Marine Hymn, Leathernecks use scaling ladders to storm ashore at Inchon in amphibious invasion September 15, 1950. The attack was so swift that casualties were surprisingly low.* S.Sgt. W. W. Frank. (Marine Corps)

**1420.** *Marine infantrymen take cover behind a tank while it fires on Communist troops ahead.* Hongchon Area, May 22, 1951. Sgt. John Babyak, Jr. (Marine Corps)

**1421.** *Men of the 9th Inf. Regt. man an M-26 tank to await an enemy attempt to cross the Naktong River.* September 3, 1950. Cpl. Thomas Marotta. (Army)

**1422.** *United Nations troops fighting in the streets of Seoul, Korea.* September 20, 1950. Lt. Robert L. Strickland and Cpl. John Romanowski. (Army)

**1423.** *Leathernecks lead patrol between destroyed buildings in "mop-up" of Wolmi Island, gateway to Inchon.* September 15, 1950. Sgt. Frank C. Kerr. (Marine Corps)

**1424.** *Marine Pvt. 1st Class Luther Leguire raises U.S. Flag at American consulate in Seoul, while fighting for the city raged around the compound. September 27, 1950. Sgt. John Babyak, Jr. (Marine Corps)*

**1425.** *Leatherneck machine gun crew dug in for the night in Korea. Ca. 1950. (Marine Corps)*

**1426.** *Fighting with the 2nd Inf. Div. north of the Chongchon River, Sfc. Major Cleveland, weapons squad leader, points out Communist-led North Korean position to his machine gun crew. November 20, 1950. Pfc. James Cox. (Army)*

**1427.** *Infantrymen of the 27th Infantry Regiment, near Heartbreak Ridge, take advantage of cover and concealment in tunnel positions, 40 yards from the Communists. August 10, 1952. Feldman. (Army)*

**1428.** *Paratroopers of the 187th RCT [Regimental Combat Team] float earthward from C-119's to cut off retreating enemy units south of Munsan, Korea. March 23, 1951. Cpl. P. T. Turner. (Army)*

**1429.** *Men and equipment being parachuted to earth in an operation conducted by United Nations airborne units. Ca. 1951. Defense Dept. (USIA)*

**1430.** *U.S. Marines of the First Marine Div. Reconnaissance Co. make the first helicopter invasion on Hill 812, to relieve the ROK Eighth Div., during the renewed fighting in Korea. September 20, 1951. T. G. Donegan. (Navy)*

**1431.** *Men of the 19th Inf. Regt. work their way over the snowy mountains about 10 miles north of Seoul, Korea, attempting to locate the enemy lines and positions. January 3, 1951. Pfc. James J. Jacquet. (Army)*

**1432.** *U.S. Marines move forward after effective close-air support flushes out the enemy from their hillside entrenchments. Billows of smoke rise skyward from the target area. Hagaru-ri. December 26, 1950. Cpl. McDonald. (Marine Corps)*

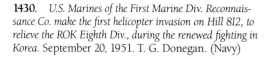
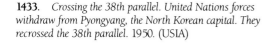

**1433.** *Crossing the 38th parallel. United Nations forces withdraw from Pyongyang, the North Korean capital. They recrossed the 38th parallel. 1950. (USIA)*

**1434.** *Commandoes of the 41st Royal British Marines plant demolition charges along railroad tracks of enemy supply line which they demolished during a commando raid, 8 miles south of Songjin, Korea. April 10, 1951. (Navy)*

**1435.** *Pfc. Roman Prauty, a gunner with 31st RCT (crouching foreground), with the assistance of his gun crew, fires a 75mm recoilless rifle, near Oetlook-tong, Korea, in support of infantry units directly across the valley. June 9, 1951. Peterson. (Army)*

**1436.** *Men of the 4.2 mortar crew, 31st Heavy Mortar Co. fire at enemy position, west of Chorwon, Korea.* February 7, 1953. Sgt. Guy A. Kassal. (Army).

**1437.** *The Rockets Red Glare — U.S. Marines launch a 4.5 rocket barrage against the Chinese Communists in the Korean fighting.* Ca. 1951. (Marine Corps)

**1438.** *Near Song Sil-li, Korea, a tank of 6th Tank Bn. fires on enemy positions in support of the 19th RCT.* January 10, 1952. Pfc. Harry M. Schultz. (Army)

**1439.** *Night view of the First Rocket Battery, 11th Marine Regiment, firing a night mission, somewhere in the Marines front line sector.* April 15, 1953. M.Sgt. Eugene C. Knauft. (Marine Corps)

**1440.** *Navy Sky Raiders from the USS* Valley Forge *fire 5-inch wing rockets at North Korean communist field positions.* October 24, 1950. PhoM3c. Burke. (Navy)

**1441.** *Lt. R. P. Yeatman, from the USS* Bon Homme Richard, *is shown rocketing and bombing Korean bridge.* November 1952. (Navy)

**1442.** *Navy AD-3 dive bomber pulls out of dive after dropping a 2000 lb. bomb on Korean side of a bridge crossing the Yalu River at Sinuiju, into Manchuria. Note: anti-aircraft gun emplacement on both sides of the river.* November 15, 1950. (Navy)

**1443.** *Supply warehouses and dock facilities at this important east coast port feel the destructive weight of parademolition bombs dropped from Fifth Air Force's B-26 Invader light bombers. Wonsan, North Korea. Ca. 1951.* Air Force. (USIA)

**1444.** *A 16-inch salvo from the USS* Missouri *at Chong Jin, Korea, in effort to cut Northern Korean communications. Chong Jin is only 39 miles from the border of China.* October 21, 1950. (Navy)

# AID & COMFORT

*Photographs 1446–1474*

**1445.** *The USS* Missouri *fires 16-inch shell into enemy lines at Hungnam. A 16-inch 3-gun salvo is on its way to commies.* December 26, 1950. (Navy)

**1446.** *Buddies aid wounded man of 24th Inf. Regt., after a battle 10 miles south of Chorwon, Korea. April 22, 1951.* Cpl. Tom Nebbia. (Army)

**1447.** *In bitter fighting on Hook Ridge, Marines threw back 800 screaming, bugle-blowing Chinese. A wounded Marine is given a drink of water by buddies as he lies awaiting evacuation to a rear area aid station. November 1952. T.Sgt. Robert Kiser. (Marine Corps)*

**1448.** *A wounded U.S. Marine awaiting transportation back to a field hospital after receiving first-aid at the battle zone.* Defense Dept. (USIA)

**1449.** *Pfc. Thomas Conlon, 21st Inf. Regt., lies on a stretcher at a medical aid station, after being wounded while crossing the Naktong River in Korea. September 19, 1950. Cpl. Dennis P. Buckley. (Army)*

**1450.** *Wounded American soldiers are given medical treatment at a first aid station, somewhere in Korea. July 25, 1950. Pfc. Tom Nebbia. (Army)*

**1451.** *A wounded American is lifted onto a helicopter at the 21st Inf. Regt. collecting station at Painmal, Korea, one mile south of the 38th Parallel, for evacuation to a base hospital. April 3, 1951. H. W. Holbrook. (Army)*

**1452.** *Crew members of Co. D, 89th Tank Bn., give first aid to wounded soldier, during action against the Chinese Communist forces north east of Seoul, Korea. May 1, 1951. Pfc. Charles Fabiszak. (Army)*

**1453.** *U.S. Marines wounded at Kari San Mountain are evacuated via helicopter and flown to hospital in rear areas for treatment. Navy Corpsmen prepare three wounded Marines for evacuation. May 23, 1951. N. H. McMasters.* (Navy)

**1454.** *Pfc. Orvin L. Morris, 27th Regiment, takes a much deserved rest during his evacuation to Pusan, Korea, on a hospital train. He was wounded by enemy mortar fire on front lines. July 29, 1950. Sgt. Dunlap.* (Army)

**1455.** *General view of the 3rd ROK Mobile Army Surgical Hospital, Wonju, Korea. September 1951.* (Army)

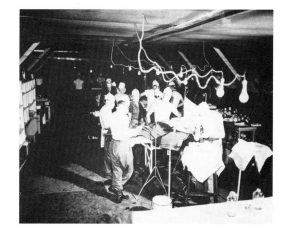

**1456.** *M/Sgt. George Miller selects human blood for patient at the 8076th Mobile Army Surgical Hospital at Kunu-ri, Korea. November 27, 1950. Cpl. Fred Rice.* (Army)

**1457.** *Personnel and equipment needed to save a man's life are assembled at HQs of the 8225th Mobile Army Surgical Hospital, Korea. October 14, 1951. Cpl. Charles Abrahamson.* (Army)

**1458.** *An operation is performed on a wounded solider at the 8209th Mobile Army Surgical Hospital, twenty miles from the front lines. August 4, 1952. Feldman.* (Army)

**1459.** *A grief stricken American infantryman whose buddy has been killed in action is comforted by another soldier. In the background a corpsman methodically fills out casualty tags, Haktong-ni area, Korea. August 28, 1950. Sfc. Al Chang. (Army)*

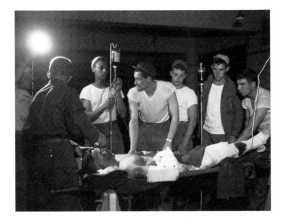

**1460.** *Seriously wounded soldier of the 116th Engineers, prior to his operation at the 121st Evacuation Hospital, in Yongdong-pu.* August 17, 1951. G. Dimitri Boria. (Army)

**1461.** *Wounded soldiers use wheelchairs and crutches until they learn how to walk with a synthetic limb. Pfc. Charles Woody, injured near Taegu, walks on crutches. Walter Reed Mil. Hosp.* Washington, DC, December 8, 1950. T.Sgt. Trehearne, USAF; PhoM2c. Knudsen, USN. (USIA)

**1462.** *A young Marine finds a moment of quiet and solitude in which to offer up a prayer for the safety of himself and his comrades. Minutes later, the 1st Marine Division launched an offensive against entrenched communist troops.* Ca. 1951. Cpl. Eugene Suarez. (Marine Corps)

**1463.** *Chaplain Kenny Lynch conducts services north of Hwachon, Korea, for men of 31st Regt.* August 28, 1951. Pvt. Jack D. Johnson. (Army)

**1464.** *Chaplain Dennis Murphy celebrates mass for the men of 65th AAA Bn., at Bolo Point, Okinawa.* July 19, 1951. Nelse Einwaechter. (Army)

**1465.** *Men of 92nd Engineer Searchlight Company focus on Yodeler Elton Britt during Camel Caravan variety show at Hongchon, Korea.* June 9, 1951. Pfc. R. J. McKinney. (Army)

**1466.** *Marilyn Monroe, motion picture actress, appearing with the USO Camp Show, "Anything Goes," poses for the shutterbugs after a performance at the 3rd U.S. Inf. Div. area.* February 17, 1954. Cpl. Welshman. (Army)

**1467.** *Marilyn Monroe sings several songs for an estimated 13,000 men of the First Marine Division. Miss Monroe stopped at the First Marine Regiment on her tour of the military units in Korea.* February 16, 1954. Cpl. Kreplin. (Marine Corps)

**1468.** *Al Jolson entertains U.S. troops at Pusan Stadium during his visit to the fighting front. He died shortly after his return from Korea where he gave of his talent untiringly and unceasingly. He made the trip at his own expense.* September 17, 1950. Kondreck. (Army)

**1469.** *Bob Hope, radio and screen star, sits with men of X Corps, as members of his troupe entertain at Wonsan, Korea.* October 26, 1950. Cpl. Alex Klein. (Army)

**1470.** *Audience reaction to the Bob Hope show at Seoul, Korea.* October 23, 1950. Capt. Bloomquist. (Army)

**1471.** *USO Troupe — Mickey Rooney and members of his show feed troops chow; right to left are: Dick Winslow, Mickey Rooney, Deenah Prince, Alice Tyrrell, and Red Barry.* October 12, 1952. Cpl. John Scoblic. (Marine Corps)

**1472.** *These men of the Heavy Mortar Co., 7th Inf. Regt., go native, cooking rice in their foxhole in the Kagae-dong area, Korea.* December 7, 1950. Pfc. Donald Dunbar. (Army)

**1473.** *A soldier of the ROK Army eating lunch in a war-destroyed house in Munsan-ni, Korea, as a field ration made in Japan for the ROK Army is shown unpacked.* July 17, 1951. G. Dimitri Boria. (Army)

**1474.** *Carrying a full load of beer donated by the Marine Corps League for Marines in Korea, is Cpl. R. L. Quisenberry, Dayton, Ohio.* July 25, 1951. Cpl. William Goodman. (Marine Corps)

# CIVILIANS & REFUGEES

*Photographs 1475–1487*

**1475.** *United Nations flag waves over crowd waiting to hear Dr. Syngman Rhee speak to the United Nations Council in Taegu, Korea.* July 30, 1950. Sgt. Girard. (Army)

**1476.** *Refugees crowd railway depot at Inchon, Korea, in hopes they may be next to get aboard for trip further south and safety from communist hordes.* January 3, 1951. C. K. Rose. (Navy)

**1477.** *Long trek southward: Seemingly endless file of Korean refugees slogs through snow outside of Kangnung, blocking withdrawal of ROK I Corps. January 8, 1951. Cpl. Walter Calmus. (Army)*

**1478.** *Refugees streaming across the frozen Han River on the ice as they flee southward before the advancing tide of Red Chinese and North Korean Communists. Shattered bridges are shown in the background. January 1951. INP. (USIA)*

**1479.** *Korean natives prepare to board an LST during the evacuation of Hungnam, while other refugees unload some of their meager belongings from an ox-cart and load them on a fishing boat. December 19, 1950. (Navy)*

**1480.** *North Korean refugees use anything that will float to evacuate Hungnam. Here they jam the decks of a South Korean LST and many fishing boats. December 19, 1950. (Navy)*

**1481.** *A refugee family from Ching Pung Men near Masan, now living in a refugee camp at Changseung-po, Korea. October 1950. United Nations. (USIA)*

**1482.** *Miss Mo Yun Sook, famed Korean poetess, is telling how she escaped the Communist-led North Koreans when they captured Seoul, by hiding in the mountains until the U.N. forces liberated the city. November 8, 1950. Cpl. Robert Dangel. (Army)*

**1483.** *An old Korean man takes a rest on the street in front of destroyed buildings, in Seoul. August 20, 1951. G. Dimitri Boria. (Army)*

**1484.** *A Korean orphan boy adopted by a motor pool battalion at Inchon, Korea and nursed back to health. He is called "Number One" by the boys of the motor pool. June 6, 1951. (Navy)*

**1485.** *With her brother on her back a war weary Korean girl tiredly trudges by a stalled M-26 tank, at Haengju, Korea. June 9, 1951. Maj. R. V. Spencer, USAF. (Navy)*

**1486.** *A small South Korean child sits alone in the street, after elements of the 1st Marine Div. and South Korean Marines invaded the city of Inchon, in an offensive launched against the North Korean forces in that area. September 16, 1950. Pfc. Ronald L. Hancock. (Army)*

**1487.** *Homeless, this brother and sister search empty cans for morsels of food, and try to keep warm beside a small fire in the Seoul, Korea, railroad yards. November 17, 1950. Pfc. Fulton. (Army)*

# PRISONERS

*Photographs 1488–1498*

**1488.** *A U.S. Marine tank follows a line of prisoners of war down a village street.* September 26, 1950. S.Sgt. John Babyak, Jr. (Marine Corps)

**1489.** North Korean prisoners, taken by the Marines in a foothills fight, march single file across a rice paddy. 1950. (Marine Corps)

**1490.** U.S. Marines guarding three captured North Koreans, ca. 1950. Sgt. W. M. Compton. (Marine Corps)

**1491.** *North Korean prisoner of Marines who rolled enemy back in Naktong River fighting. He wears a "Prisoner of War" tag and was treated in accordance with United Nations' rules of international warfare.* September 4, 1950. S.Sgt. Walter W. Frank. (Marine Corps)

**1492.** *Three Korean Communists in a fishing boat are captured by the USS* Manchester *off the coast of Korea.* May 10, 1951. (Navy)

**1493.** *Men of the 1st Marine Division capture Chinese Communists during fighting on the central Korean front.* Hoengsong, March 2, 1951. Pfc. C. T. Wehner. (Marine Corps)

**1494.** *Two North Korean boys, serving in the North Korean Army, taken prisoner in the Sindang-dong area by elements of the 389th Inf. Regt., are interrogated by a U.S. soldier shortly after their capture. September 18, 1950. Pfc. Francis Mullin. (Army)*

**1495.** *Communist guerrillas and their families, captured and brought down from Mt. Chirisan, by elements of the ROK Capitol Division, are fed in the POW stockade, Kurije, Korea. December 12, 1951. Cpl. Paul E. Stout. (Army)*

**1496.** *At the United Nations' prisoner-of-war camp at Pusan, prisoners are assembled in one of the camp compounds. The camp contains both North Korean and Chinese Communist prisoners. April 1951. Gahn, State Dept. (USIA)*

**1497.** *This anti-Communist North Korean just released from a prisoner of war camp is serving as a kind of cheerleader for fellow ex-POW's as they shout their joy of reaching Seoul. The flags are of the Republic of South Korea. Ca. 1953–54. Gravy. (USIA)*

**1498.** *Return of POW's during Operation "Big Switch," Panmunjom, Korea. Communist POW's ripped off their clothing and strewed it along the road. Some of the clothing is burning. August 12, 1953. Larsen. (Navy)*

# DEATH & DESTRUCTION

*Photographs 1499–1514*

**1499.** *The wreckage of a bridge and North Korean Communist tank south of Suwon, Korea. The tank was caught on a bridge and put out of action by the Air Force.* October 7, 1950. Marks. (Army)

**1500.** *Wreckage of big transport which North Koreans hit while it was on Kimpo Airfield, is again in friendly hands, upon recapture of field.* September 18, 1950. Sgt. Frank C. Kerr. (Marine Corps)

**1501.** *Scene of war damage in residential section of Seoul, Korea. The capitol building can be seen in the background (right).* October 18, 1950. Sfc. Cecil Riley. (Army)

**1502.** *ROK military police pose before the ruins of a devastated building in Pohang. Most buildings that housed red troops were destroyed.* October 17, 1950. (Navy)

**1503.** *Korean women and children search the rubble of Seoul for anything that can be used or burned as fuel.* November 1, 1950. Capt. F. L. Scheiber. (Army)

**1504.** *An aged Korean woman pauses in her search for salvageable materials among the ruins of Seoul, Korea.* November 1, 1950. Capt. C. W. Huff. (Army)

**1505.** *General view of buildings in the suburbs of Seoul, Korea, destroyed by artillery and air strikes.* August 20, 1951. G. Dimitri Boria. (Army)

**1506.** *A Chinese soldier, killed by Marines of the 1st Marine Division in Korea during attack on Hill 1051, on Kari San Mountain. Killed by air support.* May 23, 1951. N. H. McMasters. (Navy)

**1507.** *Korean civilians fleeing from the North Korean forces, killed when caught in the line of fire during night attack by guerrilla forces near Yongsan.* August 25, 1950. Cpl. Ingram. (Army)

**1508.** *Koreans from Hamhung identify the bodies of some 300 political prisoners who were killed by the North Korean Army by being forced into caves which were subsequently sealed off so that they died of suffocation.* October 19, 1950. Lt. Winslow. (Army)

**1509.** *A Korean family mourns their murdered father, victim of the wholesale murder at Chonju by North Koreans.* September 27, 1950. M.Sgt. E. T. Tarr. (Army)

**1510.** *One of four Americans of the 21st Inf. Regt. found between the forward observation post and the front line. The men were probably captured the night of July 9th, and shot thru the head with their hands tied behind their backs.* July 10, 1950. Cpl. Robert Dangel. (Army)

**1511.** *How a man died on the way to Maeson Dong.* September 2, 1950. Sgt. Turnbull. (Army)

**1512.** *A wounded chaplain reads a memorial service over the snow-covered bodies of dead Marines. Koto-ri, Korea.* December 3, 1950. Cpl. W. T. Wolfe. (Marine Corps)

**1513.** *Cpl. Charles Price sounds "Taps" over the graves of fallen Leathernecks during memorial services at the First Marine Division cemetery at Hungnam, following the division's heroic break-out from Chosin Reservoir.* December 13, 1950. Cpl. W. T. Wolfe. (Marine Corps)

**1514.** *Marines of the First Marine Division pay their respects to fallen buddies during memorial services at the division's cemetery at Hamhung, Korea, following the break-out from Chosin Reservoir.* December 13, 1950. Cpl. Uthe. (Marine Corps)

# PEACE

*Photographs 1515–1522*

**1515.** *Panmunjom, Korea, the site of military armistice negotiations between representatives of the Communist forces fighting in Korea, and United Nations forces representatives.* November 1, 1951. Capt. Edward W. Plummer. (Army)

**1516.** *Col. James Murray, Jr., USMC, and Col. Chang Chun San, of the North Korean Communist Army, initial maps showing the north and south boundaries of the demarcation zone, during the Panmunjom cease fire talks.* October 11, 1951. F. Kazukaitis. (Navy)

**1517.** *Gen. W. K. Harrison, Jr., signs armistice ending 3-year Korean conflict. Gen. Harrison, left table, and North Korean Gen. Nam Il, right table, sign documents.* July 23, 1953. F. Kazukaitis. (Navy)

**1518.** *U.N. correspondents at the armistice building, Panmunjom, Korea.* July 23, 1953. Weber. (Navy)

**1519.** *The families of the returning POW's waving and greeting the ship the* General Nelson M. Walker *as it docks at Fort Mason, California.* August 23, 1953. Pfc. Brink. (Army)

**1520.** *1st Lt. Alvin Anderson, one of the many repatriated POW's to return home aboard the USNS* Marine Phoenix, *embracing his mother and sister as other members of his family look on.* Fort Mason, CA, September 14, 1953. Herb Weiss. (Army)

**1521.** *Repatriated POW Capt. Frederick Smith is greeted by his father on his arrival at Fort Mason, Calif., on board the USNS* Marine Phoenix. *September 14, 1953.* Herb Weiss. (Army)

**1522.** *A little Korean girl places a wreath of flowers on the grave of an American soldier, while Pfc. Chester Painter and Cpl. Harry May present arms, at the United Nations cemetery in Pusan. April 9, 1951.* Cpl. Alex Klein. (Army)

# SELECTED SOURCES AND FURTHER READING

American Battle Monuments Commission. *American Armies and Battlefields in Europe: A History, Guide, and Reference Book.* Washington, DC: U.S. Government Printing Office, 1938.

*The American Image: Photographs from the National Archives 1860–1960.* New York: Pantheon Books, 1979.

Barnard, George. *Photographic Views of Sherman's Campaign.* 1866. Reprint. New York: Dover Publications, 1977.

Beckett, C. Tucker. "Military Photography in Mexico." *The Camera* (November 1916): 599–616.

Beede, Benjamin R. *Intervention and Counterinsurgency: An Annotated Bibliography of the Small Wars of the United States, 1898–1984.* New York: Garland Publishing, 1985.

Best, James J. *American Popular Illustration: A Reference Guide.* Westport, CT: Greenwood Press, 1984.

Bourke-White, Margaret. *Dear Fatherland, Rest Quietly.* New York: Simon and Schuster, 1946.

———. *Portrait of Myself.* New York: Simon and Schuster, 1963.

———. *Purple Heart Valley.* New York: Simon and Schuster, 1944.

Capa, Robert. *Slightly Out of Focus.* New York: Henry Holt, 1947.

*The Civil War.* 28 vols. Alexandria, VA: Time-Life Books, 1983–87.

*The Coast Guard at War.* 31 monographs. Washington, DC: Historical Section, Public Affairs Division, U.S. Coast Guard, 1946–.

Conrat, Maisie and Richard Conrat. *Executive Order 9066: The Internment of 110,000 Japanese Americans.* San Francisco, CA: California Historical Society, 1972.

Crawford, Anthony R., ed. *Posters of World War I and World War II in the George C. Marshall Research Foundation.* Charlottesville, VA: University Press of Virginia, 1979.

Cresswell, Donald H., ed. *The American Revolution in Drawings and Prints.* Washington, DC: Library of Congress, 1975.

Darrah, William C. *The World of Stereographs.* Gettysburg, PA: William C. Darrah, 1977.

Davis, William C., ed. *The Image of War, 1861–1865.* 6 vols. Garden City, NY: Doubleday, 1981.

Duncan, David Douglas. *This is War! A Photo-Narrative in Three Parts.* 1951. Reprint. New York: Bantam Books, 1967.

Dupuy, R. Ernest, and Herbert L. Bregstein. *Soldiers' Album.* Boston: Houghton Mifflin, 1946.

Ebert, John, and Katherine Ebert. *Old American Prints for Collectors.* New York: Scribners, 1974.

Eichberg, Robert L., and Jacqueline M. Quadow. *Combat Photography.* Washington, DC (Signal Corps Historical Monograph F-2b), 1945.

Faber, John. *Great News Photos and the Stories Behind Them.* 2d ed., rev. and enl. New York: Dover Publications, 1978.

Fielding, Mantle. *American Engravers Upon Copper and Steel.* Philadelphia, 1917. Supplement to Stauffer, *American Engravers.*

Fralin, Frances. *The Indelible Image: Photographs of War — 1846 to the Present.* New York: Harry N. Abrams, 1985.

Freidel, Frank. *Over There: The Story of America's First Great Overseas Crusade.* Boston: Little, Brown & Co., 1964.

———. *The Splendid Little War.* Boston: Little, Brown & Co., 1958.

Gardner, Alexander. *Gardner's Photographic Sketch Book of the Civil War.* 1866. Reprint. New York: Dover Publications, 1978.

George, Albert E., and Capt. Edwin H. Cooper. *Pictorial History of the Twenty-Sixth Division.* Boston: Ball Publishing Co., 1920.

Gernsheim, Helmut, and Alison Gernsheim. *Roger Fenton, Photographer of the Crimean War.* London: Secker and Warburg, 1954.

Gidal, Tim N. *Modern Photojournalism: Origin and Evolution, 1910–1933.* New York: MacMillan, 1972.

Gurney, Gene. *A Pictorial History of the United States Army.* New York: Bonanza Books, 1966.

Hannah, S.Sgt. Dick. *Tarawa: The Toughest Battle in Marine Corps History.* New York: U.S. Camera, 1944.

Hannavy, John. *Roger Fenton of Crimble Hall.* Boston: David R. Godine, 1975.

Heitman, Francis B. *Historical Register and Dictionary of the United States Army.* Washington, DC: U.S. Government Printing Office, 1903.

*Historical Sketch of the Signal Corps (1860–1941).* Fort Monmouth, NJ: Eastern Signal Corps Schools, U.S. Army, 1942.

Horan, James D. *Mathew Brady, Historian With a Camera.* New York: Crown Publishers, 1955.

*International Center of Photography Encyclopedia of Photography.* New York: Crown Publishers, Pound Press, 1984.

Johnson, Rossiter. *Campfires and Battlefields: A Pictorial Narrative of the Civil War.* New York: Gallant Books, 1960.

Lesy, Michael. *Bearing Witness: A Photographic Chronicle of American Life, 1860–1945.* New York: Pantheon Books, 1982.

Leventhal, Albert R., and Del Byrne. *War. The Camera's Battlefield View of Man's Most Terrible Adventure from the First Photographer in the Crimea to Vietnam.* New York: Ridge Press, 1973.

Lewinski, Jorge. *The Camera at War: A History of War Photography from 1848 to the Present Day.* New York: Simon and Schuster, 1978.

Library of Congress. *Exhibition of Prints Relating to Early American History.* Washington, DC: U.S. Government Printing Office, 1931.

*LIFE's Picture History of World War II.* New York: Time, Inc., 1950.

MacDonald, Gus. *Camera: Victorian Eyewitness. A History of Photography: 1826–1913.* New York: Viking Press, 1980.

Maloney, Tom, ed. *U.S. Camera Annual 1951.* New York: U.S. Camera, 1950.

————, ed. *U.S. Camera Annual 1952.* New York: U.S. Camera, 1951.

————, ed. *U.S. Camera Annual 1953.* New York: U.S. Camera, 1952.

————, ed. *U.S. Camera Annual 1954.* New York: U.S. Camera, 1953.

Maloney, Tom, and Edward Steichen, eds. *The U.S.A. at War: U.S. Camera 1944.* New York: U.S. Camera, 1943.

————, eds. *The U.S.A. at War: U.S. Camera 1945.* New York: U.S. Camera, 1944.

————, eds. *U.S. Camera 1946 — Victory Volume.* New York: U.S. Camera, 1945.

Maurer, Maurer. *The U.S. Air Service in World War I.* Washington, DC: Office of Air Force History, 1978.

Mercey, Arch A., and Lee Grove, eds. *Sea, Surf and Hell: The U.S. Coast Guard in World War II.* New York: Prentice-Hall, 1946.

Meredith, Roy. *Mr. Lincoln's Camera Man Mathew B. Brady.* New York: Charles Scribner's Sons, 1946.

Miller, Francis Trevelyan. *Original Photographs Taken on the Battlefields During the Civil War of the United States By Mathew B. Brady and Alexander Gardner.* Hartford, CT: Edward B. Eaton, 1907.

————. *The Photographic History of the Civil War.* 10 vols. New York: The Review of Reviews Co., 1911–12.

Morison, Samuel Eliot. *History of United States Naval Operations in World War II.* 14 vols. Boston: Little, Brown & Co., 1947–62.

National Portrait Gallery. *Permanent Collection Illustrated Checklist.* Washington, DC: Smithsonian Institution Press, 1980.

O'Sheel, Patrick, and Gene Cook, eds. *Semper Fidelis: The U.S. Marines in the Pacific, 1942–1945.* New York: William Sloane Associates, 1947.

Olds, Irving S. *Bits and Pieces of American History as Told by a Collection of American Naval and Other Historical Prints and Paintings.* New York, 1951.

Peters, Harry T. *America on Stone.* Garden City, NY: Doubleday, Doran & Co., 1931.

————. *Currier & Ives: Printmakers to the American People.* Garden City, NY: Doubleday, Doran & Co., 1929.

Phillips, Christopher. *Steichen at War.* New York: Harry N. Abrams, 1981.

*Regulations Governing Correspondents and Photographers with the United States Army.* Washington, DC: U.S. Government Printing Office, 1918.

*Reporting to Remember — Unforgettable Stories and Pictures of World War II by Correspondents of the Associated Press.* New York: Associated Press, 1945.

Robertson, Peter. "Canadian Photojournalism During the First World War." *History of Photography,* vol. 2, no. 1 (January 1978): 37–52.

Russell, Andrew J. *Russell's Civil War Photographs: 116 Historic Prints.* New York: Dover Publications, 1982. Reproduces a scrapbook entitled "United States Military Railroad Photographic Album" (verso t.p.), ca. 1865–66.

Scherman, David E., ed. *LIFE Goes to War: A Picture History of World War II.* New York: Pocket Books, 1977.

*Soldiers of the American Revolution: A Sketchbook.* Washington, DC: Center of Military History, 1976.

Stauffer, David McNeely. *American Engravers Upon Copper and Steel.* New York: The Grolier Club, 1907.

Steichen, Edward. *A Life in Photography.* Garden City, NY: Doubleday, 1963.

———. *The Blue Ghost — A Photographic Log and Personal Narrative of the Aircraft Carrier U.S.S. Lexington in Combat Operation.* New York: Harcourt, Brace & Co., 1947.

———, comp. *Power in the Pacific. A Pictorial Record of Navy Combat Operations on Land, Sea and in the Sky.* New York: U.S. Camera, 1945.

———. *US Navy War Photographs, Pearl Harbor to Tokyo Harbor.* New York: U.S. Camera, 1946.

Taft, Robert. *Photography and the American Scene.* 1938. Reprint. New York: Dover Publications, 1964.

Thompson, George R., and Dixie R. Harris. *United States Army in World War II — The Technical Services, The Signal Corps: The Outcome.* Washington, DC: Office of the Chief of Military History, 1966.

Townsend, George Alfred. "Still Taking Pictures. Brady, the Grand Old Man of American Photography." *The World* (New York), 12 April 1891, p.23.

*United States Army in World War II.* 61 vols. Washington, DC: Army Historical Division, Office of the Chief of Military History, and Center of Military History, 1947–77.

*War Department Annual Reports, 1919. Report of the Chief Signal Officer.* 66th Cong., 2d sess., H. Doc. 426. Washington, DC: U.S. Government Printing Office, 1920.

War Department. *Catalogue of Official A.E.F. Photographs Taken by the Signal Corps, U.S.A.* Washington, DC: U.S. Government Printing Office, 1919.

———. *Combat Photography.* Washington, DC: U.S. Government Printing Office (War Department pamphlet no. 11-5), 1945.

———. *List of the Photographs and Photographic Negatives Relating to the War for the Union, Now in the War Department Library.* Washington, DC: U.S. Government Printing Office, 1897.

Westover, John G. *Combat Support in Korea.* U.S. Army in Action Series. Reprint. Washington, DC: Center of Military History, 1987.

Wilkerson, Marcus M. *Public Opinion and the Spanish-American War. A Study in War Propaganda.* Baton Rouge, LA: Louisiana State University Press, 1932.

Willoughby, Malcolm F. *The U.S. Coast Guard in World War II.* Annapolis, MD: U.S. Naval Institute, 1957.

Witkin, Lee D., and Barbara London. *The Photograph Collector's Guide.* Boston: New York Graphic Society, 1979.

*World War II.* 35 vols. New York and Alexandria, VA: Time-Life Books, 1976–83.

# LIST OF RECORD GROUPS

# LIST OF NEGATIVE NUMBERS

1. 208-LU-25K-4
2. 069-N-4877-C
3. 148-GW-439
4. 148-GW-437
5. 148-GW-436
6. 208-FS-3200-3
7. 148-GW-335
8. 208-FS-3200-5
9. 200-JH-3
10. 148-GW-475
11. 127-N-521360
12. 111-SC-94758
13. 148-GW-441
14. 148-GW-454
15. 148-GW-448
16. 148-GW-571
17. 148-GW-459
18. 148-GW-587
19. 030-N-31-170
20. 148-GW-662
21. 148-GW-1141
22. 111-SC-92968
23. 208-LU-25K-10
24. 148-GW-1209
25. 391-AR-2-1
26. 127-EX-1-27
27. 148-GW-594
28. 148-GW-174
29. 066-G-15D-25
30. 148-GW-580
31. 148-GW-332
32. 148-GW-331
33. 016-AD-8
34. 148-GW-201
35. 148-GW-184
36. 148-GW-189
37. 148-GW-923
38. 066-G-5-106
39. 066-G-5-107
40. 208-LU-25K-7
41. 148-GW-164
42. 148-GW-390
43. 019-N-9977-A

44. 148-GW-461
45. 148-GW-462
46. 208-LU-25K-14
47. 019-N-10430
48. 127-N-A408767
49. 127-N-529413
50. 016-AD-60
51. 148-GW-344
52. 148-GW-396
53. 148-GW-334
54. 148-GW-179
55. 016-AD-61
56. 148-GW-1073
57. 148-GW-474
58. 019-N-1583
59. 148-GW-76A
60. 148-GW-611
61. 111-SC-92025
62. 148-GW-617
63. 111-BA-1073
64. 148-GW-811
65. 148-CC-11-3
66. 208-PU-104HH-4
67. 148-CD-4-23
68. 148-CD-4-18
69. 148-GW-566
70. 208-PR-10J-1
71. 019-CN-12348
72. 127-N-526627
73. 030-N-31-105
74. 208-LU-25F-10
75. 208-LU-25H-5
76. 208-LU-25H-2
77. 019-N-12435
78. 127-N-308820
79. 148-GW-488
80. 127-N-302108
81. 208-LU-25H-6
82. 111-SC-92653
83. 127-N-302099
84. 111-SC-96966
85. 111-SC-96968
86. 111-SC-96967

87. 127-N-515040
88. 111-SC-92715
89. 148-GW-478
90. 066-G-21C-31
91. 111-SC-104311
92. 111-SC-90818
93. 111-SC-96970
94. 208-PR-10P-2
95. 111-SC-96965
96. 111-SC-83420
97. 127-N-308884
98. 111-SC-96978
99. 111-SC-99035
100. 111-SC-96984
101. 111-SC-96979
102. 111-SC-96992
103. 111-SC-96986
104. 111-SC-96983
105. 111-SC-96985
106. 127-N-306076
107. 208-PR-10E-7
108. 208-PR-10Q-2
109. 165-JT-230
110. 111-B-4687
111. 111-BA-2145
112. 111-B-5240
113. 200-FL-22
114. 127-N-521396
115. 079-CWC-3F-10
116. 208-N-25004
117. 111-B-3656
118. 111-B-6348-A
119. 165-SB-23
120. 111-B-4975
121. 111-B-4975
122. 111-B-36
123. 200-CC-730
124. 111-B-55
125. 111-B-1769
126. 111-B-4282
127. 111-B-4624
128. 111-B-3698
129. 111-B-64

130. 165-B-1921
131. 111-B-4146
132. 111-B-1564
133. 111-B-1867
134. 064-M-9
135. 064-M-184
136. 111-BA-1226
137. 208-PR-10J-2
138. 111-B-5348
139. 165-JT-302
140. 111-B-5454
141. 111-B-250
142. 111-B-256
143. 111-B-499
144. 165-SB-76
145. 111-B-157
146. 111-B-484
147. 111-B-247
148. 111-B-215
149. 111-B-1048
150. 111-B-446
151. 111-B-375
152. 111-B-5886
153. 165-WHC-80
154. 111-B-4482
155. 165-C-692
156. 111-B-487
157. 111-B-54
158. 066-G-22J-1
159. 121-BA-914A
160. 111-B-4858
161. 064-CV-335
162. 111-B-333
163. 111-B-486
164. 165-C-729
165. 200-CC-375
166. 064-CV-304
167. 077-HL-99-1
168. 165-SC-39
169. 111-B-523
170. 111-B-559
171. 077-AG-1-8
172. 200-CC-306

173. 165-SB-19
174. 165-SC-16
175. 111-B-438
176. 200-M-276-2
177. 111-B-98
178. 111-B-127
179. 165-SB-63
180. 045-X-10
181. 111-BA-1917
182. 064-CC-63
183. 200-CC-486
184. 019-N-33D-1
185. 019-N-16139
186. 165-C-630
187. 111-B-620
188. 111-B-2016
189. 111-B-5234
190. 111-B-448
191. 111-B-296
192. 111-B-2011
193. 111-B-411
194. 111-B-182
195. 111-B-473
196. 165-C-592
197. 165-C-752
198. 111-B-40
199. 200-CC-103
200. 111-B-5514
201. 111-B-82
202. 111-B-400
203. 165-C-655A
204. 165-C-647A
205. 077-F-194-6-80
206. 077-F-194-6-21
207. 165-WHC-115
208. 111-B-801
209. 111-B-185
210. 165-C-714
211. 165-C-474
212. 165-SB-64
213. 111-B-512
214. 079-TP-2148
215. 111-B-1857

| | | | | |
|---|---|---|---|---|
| 216. 111-B-2112 | 264. 111-BA-2034 | 312. 111-RB-1298 | 360. 395-SE-7060 | 408. 306-MVP-22-11 |
| 217. 111-B-327 | 265. 200-KWG-12 | 313. 165-FS-16-13634 | 361. 111-SC-152780 | 409. 306-MVP-6-9 |
| 218. 165-C-403R | 266. 200-KWG-31 | 314. 111-AGA-3-7 | 362. 165-WGZ-4H-1 | 410. 306-MVP-6-8 |
| 219. 111-B-173 | 267. 200-KWG-42 | 315. 111-AGA-6-573 | 363. 111-SC-152798 | 411. 306-MVP-10-9 |
| 220. 079-TP-2265 | 268. 200-KWG-22 | 316. 111-AGA-3-317 | 364. 111-SC-161688 | 412. 306-MVP-10-2 |
| 221. 165-C-100 | 269. 200-KWG-10 | 317. 111-AGA-4-423 | 365. 111-SC-62503 | 413. 306-PSC-66-3211 |
| 222. 200-CC-1051 | 270. 111-SC-94543 | 318. 111-AGA-3-22 | 366. 165-WW-489A-22 | 414. 306-MVP-21-1 |
| 223. 066-G-22A-1 | 271. 019-N-19-9-17 | 319. 391-PI-34 | 367. 127-EX-1-1 | 415. 306-MVP-21-2 |
| 224. 077-F-194-6-62 | 272. 019-N-2454-S | 320. 111-RB-1633 | 368. 127-N-520276 | 416. 306-MVP-14-28 |
| 225. 165-C-571 | 273. 165-IWN-5-1 | 321. 165-FS-16-13733 | 369. 127-N-519742 | 417. 306-MVP-15-14 |
| 226. 165-SB-22 | 274. 111-RB-2806 | 322. 395-PI-1-50 | 370. 127-N-519898 | 418. 306-MVP-25-2 |
| 227. 016-AD-2 | 275. 111-SC-94469 | 323. 111-SC-94360 | 371. 127-EX-1-6 | 419. 306-MVP-25-1 |
| 228. 111-B-680 | 276. 111-SC-113505 | 324. 111-SC-95130 | 372. 127-N-523733 | 420. 306-MVP-5-3 |
| 229. 111-B-683 | 277. 111-RB-2747 | 325. 077-CR-301 | 373. 127-N-527091 | 421. 306-MVP-5-4 |
| 230. 111-B-5393 | 278. 127-N-302104 | 326. 111-SC-88858 | 374. 127-N-526273 | 422. 306-PSC-68-58 |
| 231. 111-BZ-11 | 279. 111-AGA-2-149 | 327. 127-N-515634 | 375. 127-N-531216 | 423. 306-MVP-4-4 |
| 232. 200-CC-2288 | 280. 111-AGA-1-118A | 328. 111-RB-3659 | 376. 127-N-516038 | 424. 306-MVP-4-19 |
| 233. 111-B-497 | 281. 111-AGA-1-59 | 329. 111-RB-3688 | 377. 306-ST-503-58-14398 | 425. 306-MVP-4-11 |
| 234. 165-A-445 | 282. 111-RB-1337 | 330. 165-CR-4B-1 | 378. 306-DR-2-8 | 426. 306-PSC-66-1047 |
| 235. 165-A-446 | 283. 111-AGA-1-37 | 331. 111-SC-83087 | 379. 306-PSC-65-2029 | 427. 306-MVP-4-8 |
| 236. 064-CC-58 | 284. 111-AGA-2-165 | 332. 127-N-515039 | 380. 306-PSC-65-2011 | 428. 165-WW-447A-4 |
| 237. 165-C-172 | 285. 111-AGA-1-77 | 333. 077-CR-103 | 381. 306-DR-20-33 | 429. 004-P-55 |
| 238. 165-WHC-111 | 286. 111-AGA-1-48 | 334. 127-N-519234 | 382. 306-PS-54-10014 | 430. 004-P-52 |
| 239. 165-C-777 | 287. 127-N-302102 | 335. 165-CB-2175 | 383. 306-PS-55-10516 | 431. 004-P-8 |
| 240. 165-SC-44 | 288. 111-SC-101564 | 336. 094-UM-199925 | 384. 306-PS-54-11793 | 432. 165-WW-61-2 |
| 241. 111-B-4748 | 289. 111-RB-4033 | 337. 094-UM-199912 | 385. 306-PSC-54-17567 | 433. 165-WW-420-P379 |
| 242. 165-SC-38 | 290. 111-SC-94528 | 338. 094-UM-203865 | 386. 080-G-644449 | 434. 019-N-11381 |
| 243. 165-C-793 | 291. 111-RB-2839 | 339. 094-UM-195397 | 387. 306-PSA-68-3528 | 435. 165-WW-474E-18 |
| 244. 165-C-780 | 292. 111-SC-94503 | 340. 165-CB-3559 | 388. 306-SSM-8K-2 | 436. 165-WW-598B-7 |
| 245. 111-B-4667 | 293. 111-SC-94508 | 341. 165-CB-2233 | 389. 306-MVP-18-13 | 437. 165-WW-481B-3 |
| 246. 165-SC-55 | 294. 111-SC-113552 | 342. 165-CB-3560 | 390. 306-MVP-8-4 | 438. 165-WW-483A-1 |
| 247. 165-SB-18 | 295. 111-SC-84810 | 343. 165-CB-3596 | 391. 306-MVP-8-5 | 439. 165-WW-476-13 |
| 248. 165-SB-88 | 296. 165-SW-8B-1 | 344. 094-UM-204047 | 392. 306-MVP-8-6 | 440. 111-SC-8218 |
| 249. 165-SB-91 | 297. 111-SC-89751 | 345. 165-CB-3450 | 393. 306-PSC-64-5382 | 441. 165-WW-479A-23 |
| 250. 111-B-112 | 298. 165-IWN-5AB | 346. 165-CB-2938 | 394. 306-SSM-8H-SVN-2-25 | 442. 165-WW-256A-6 |
| 251. 111-B-137 | 299. 306-ST-505-58-4822 | 347. 094-UM-195542 | 395. 306-SSM-8H-SVN-2-21 | 443. 165-WW-474B-1 |
| 252. 111-B-562 | 300. 165-SW-12A-9 | 348. 165-CB-3963 | 396. 306-MVP-10-8 | 444. 165-WW-119A-1 |
| 253. 165-SB-36 | 301. 086-G-7U-1 | 349. 165-CB-3539 | 397. 306-MVP-14-6 | 445. 165-WW-113A-5 |
| 254. 165-SB-41 | 302. 111-SC-94538 | 350. 165-UM-43 | 398. 306-MVP-17-3 | 446. 165-WW-126-22 |
| 255. 165-SB-40 | 303. 111-SC-113614 | 351. 165-UM-21 | 399. 306-MVP-16-8 | 447. 165-WW-114B-3 |
| 256. 111-B-65 | 304. 111-SC-94441 | 352. 165-CB-H.8 | 400. 306-MVP-15-10 | 448. 165-WW-151B-8 |
| 257. 111-B-74 | 305. 111-SC-94475 | 353. 165-CB-H.26 | 401. 306-MVP-14-31 | 449. 165-WW-146B-16 |
| 258. 165-SB-94 | 306. 042-M-G-42 | 354. 165-WW-558C-4 | 402. 306-PSC-65-4106 | 450. 165-WW-147B-15 |
| 259. 165-SB-99 | 307. 111-RB-1705 | 355. 165-WW-558C-3 | 403. 306-PSC-61-9069 | 451. 165-WW-321D-1 |
| 260. 066-G-22B-1 | 308. 111-RB-1317 | 356. 395-SE-5047 | 404. 306-MVP-16-1 | 452. 165-WW-321D-8 |
| 261. 200-CC-3404 | 309. 165-FS-16-13638 | 357. 395-SE-7024 | 405. 306-MVP-22-6 | 453. 165-WW-328A-1 |
| 262. 064-M-20 | 310. 111-RB-1341 | 358. 165-WW-489A-89 | 406. 306-MVP-22-9 | 454. 111-SC-7045 |
| 263. 111-BA-1653 | 311. 111-RB-1327 | 359. 395-SE-7097 | 407. 306-MVP-22-10 | 455. 165-WW-332D-16 |

| | | | | |
|---|---|---|---|---|
| 456. 165-WW-115A-1 | 504. 165-WW-199A-3 | 552. 165-WW-189C-3 | 600. 111-SC-26545 | 648. 111-SC-13224 |
| 457. 165-WW-288A-19 | 505. 165-WW-399A-3 | 553. 004-P-306 | 601. 018-E-3996 | 649. 165-WW-472A-7 |
| 458. 004-G-40-1 | 506. 111-SC-11259 | 554. 165-WW-217A-2 | 602. 165-GB-14009 | 650. 111-SC-158424 |
| 459. 111-SC-19653 | 507. 165-WW-343A-6 | 555. 165-WW-350-1 | 603. 111-SC-2913 | 651. 111-SC-158426 |
| 460. 165-WW-288C-9 | 508. 165-WW-521B-1 | 556. 165-WW-350-5A | 604. 111-SC-46154 | 652. 111-SC-27518 |
| 461. 165-WW-476-21 | 509. 165-WW-458C-20 | 557. 045-WP-296 | 605. 018-E-4292 | 653. 111-SC-27413 |
| 462. 165-WW-289C-7 | 510. 165-WW-235D-3 | 558. 165-WW-11A-7 | 606. 018-E-6233 | 654. 165-WW-465C-4 |
| 463. 165-WW-289B-3 | 511. 165-WW-232B-19 | 559. 004-G-67-302 | 607. 111-SC-51107 | 655. 111-SC-21766 |
| 464. 111-SC-89398 | 512. 165-WW-235D-2 | 560. 004-G-31-2 | 608. 165-WW-63C-40 | 656. 165-WW-127-49 |
| 465. 111-SC-16567 | 513. 165-WW-243-108 | 561. 004-G-4-3 | 609. 018-E-5456 | 657. 111-SC-23400 |
| 466. 111-SC-89541 | 514. 111-SC-16561 | 562. 165-WW-172-1 | 610. 111-SC-18580 | 658. 165-WW-43A-11 |
| 467. 165-WW-332A-1 | 515. 111-SC-16569 | 563. 111-SC-9869 | 611. 165-WW-232A-11 | 659. 165-WW-259-60 |
| 468. 165-WW-321A-2 | 516. 111-SC-7268 | 564. 165-WW-581A-1 | 612. 165-WW-63C-10 | 660. 165-WW-56-1 |
| 469. 165-WW-332D-43 | 517. 165-WW-61-34 | 565. 004-G-10-1 | 613. 111-SC-16566 | 661. 165-WW-39B-3 |
| 470. 165-WW-321C-1 | 518. 165-WW-61-8 | 566. 165-WW-169B-4 | 614. 165-BO-717 | 662. 165-WW-578B-2 |
| 471. 018-E-3893 | 519. 165-WW-232B-13 | 567. 165-WW-233A-4 | 615. 111-SC-18672 | 663. 165-PP-1-1 |
| 472. 018-E-3850 | 520. 165-WW-61-62 | 568. 004-G-25-3 | 616. 111-SC-13501 | 664. 165-BO-562 |
| 473. 165-WW-417-37 | 521. 165-WW-578B-6 | 569. 004-G-24-8 | 617. 111-SC-23112 | 665. 111-SC-16352 |
| 474. 165-PP-17-1 | 522. 053-LL-12-1 | 570. 165-WW-600D-5 | 618. 111-SC-29652 | 666. 111-SC-12151 |
| 475. 165-WW-127-114 | 523. 165-WW-463A-51 | 571. 165-WW-170C-1 | 619. 165-WW-286-36 | 667. 111-SC-24942 |
| 476. 165-WW-127-4 | 524. 165-WW-463A-5 | 572. 004-P-61 | 620. 111-SC-94980 | 668. 165-WW-566B-23 |
| 477. 165-WW-334A-4A | 525. 053-LL-8-1 | 573. 004-P-136 | 621. 111-SC-19753 | 669. 111-SC-24719 |
| 478. 165-WW-335A-48 | 526. 053-WP-4C | 574. 165-WW-309D-6 | 622. 111-SC-8716 | 670. 165-WW-247B-10 |
| 479. 165-WW-334A-7 | 527. 053-WP-14 | 575. 165-WW-315A-18 | 623. 111-SC-20906 | 671. 111-SC-14647 |
| 480. 165-WW-321C-3 | 528. 004-P-200 | 576. 111-SC-8271 | 624. 165-WW-286-16 | 672. 165-WW-265B-45 |
| 481. 165-WW-324C-56 | 529. 045-WP-182 | 577. 165-WW-313A-4 | 625. 111-SC-23134 | 673. 165-WW-248M-7 |
| 482. 165-WW-339C-9 | 530. 045-WP-596 | 578. 165-WW-64A-26 | 626. 165-WW-286-6 | 674. 165-WW-265B-17 |
| 483. 165-WW-334A-23 | 531. 053-WP-10B | 579. 111-SC-8445 | 627. 165-WW-286-32 | 675. 045-WP-343 |
| 484. 019-N-12344 | 532. 004-P-193 | 580. 004-G-36-1 | 628. 165-BO-402 | 676. 165-WW-489B-10 |
| 485. 165-GP-3068 | 533. 053-WP-2B | 581. 165-WW-192B-3 | 629. 165-BO-601 | 677. 165-WW-180A-41 |
| 486. 165-GP-3001 | 534. 165-WW-509B-4 | 582. 111-SC-337 | 630. 111-SC-22334 | 678. 165-WW-179C-2 |
| 487. 165-GP-3002 | 535. 165-WW-509A-9 | 583. 165-WW-326B-1 | 631. 111-SC-23674 | 679. 165-WW-179C-11 |
| 488. 019-N-11434 | 536. 165-WW-595E-7 | 584. 111-SC-19271 | 632. 111-SC-14654 | 680. 165-WW-181B-3 |
| 489. 165-GB-2146 | 537. 165-WW-509B-2 | 585. 111-SC-20902 | 633. 165-WW-287A-2 | 681. 165-WW-179A-14 |
| 490. 111-SC-26646 | 538. 086-G-11F-7 | 586. 111-SC-24644 | 634. 111-SC-24936 | 682. 165-WW-179B-19 |
| 491. 165-GB-1000 | 539. 165-WW-491B-1 | 587. 165-BO-577 | 635. 111-SC-107 | 683. 111-SC-32080 |
| 492. 111-SC-23921 | 540. 165-WW-491C-31 | 588. 111-SC-44921 | 636. 165-BO-590 | 684. 111-SC-20917 |
| 493. 127-N-306713 | 541. 165-WW-492A-9 | 589. 111-SC-27163 | 637. 165-WW-286-51 | 685. 165-BO-637 |
| 494. 165-WW-431-P1487 | 542. 165-EO-2C-1 | 590. 111-SC-10302 | 638. 111-SC-97271 | 686. 111-SC-23442 |
| 495. 165-WW-428-P1135 | 543. 165-WW-595D-14 | 591. 111-SC-18846 | 639. 111-SC-23094 | 687. 165-WW-461D-3 |
| 496. 165-WW-434-P1775 | 544. 111-SC-35757 | 592. 111-SC-29656 | 640. 052-S-2303 | 688. 165-WW-A161-4 |
| 497. 242-HB-1103 | 545. 111-SC-31731 | 593. 165-WW-432-P1529 | 641. 052-S-2296 | 689. 165-WW-157A-1 |
| 498. 111-SC-49191 | 546. 165-WW-229D-50 | 594. 165-WW-432-P1524 | 642. 111-SC-10879 | 690. 165-WW-164B-6 |
| 499. 111-SC-89677 | 547. 086-G-8B-162A | 595. 018-E-5228 | 643. 165-WW-286-34 | 691. 165-WW-179A-8 |
| 500. 208-PU-93Y-4 | 548. 165-WW-228B-12 | 596. 165-WW-432-P1523 | 644. 111-SC-20936 | 692. 111-SC-33408 |
| 501. 165-WW-442B-2 | 549. 165-WW-59C-6 | 597. 165-WW-428-P1284 | 645. 004-G-21-4 | 693. 165-WW-539A-4 |
| 502. 165-WW-420-P323 | 550. 165-WW-570A-3 | 598. 200-GS-13 | 646. 165-WW-471A-3 | 694. 111-SC-16568 |
| 503. 165-WW-127-91 | 551. 165-WW-202E-3 | 599. 111-SC-23128 | 647. 165-WW-341A-44 | 695. 165-WW-538A-11 |

696. 165-FC-13-1
697. 111-SC-23669
698. 111-SC-23877
699. 111-SC-28224
700. 111-SC-31945
701. 165-WW-182A-2
702. 111-SC-42258
703. 111-SC-25357
704. 018-E-5114
705. 018-E-3228
706. 117-MP-3-7
707. 117-MC-28-4
708. 111-SC-74402
709. 208-PR-10K-1
710. 165-WW-77C-17
711. 111-SC-25684
712. 111-SC-33075
713. 111-SC-50086
714. 111-SC-50082
715. 165-WW-78A-2
716. 111-SC-67079
717. 165-WW-127-12
718. 165-WW-127-2
719. 287-L.1.9:P26
720. 165-WW-127-27
721. 165-WW-80A-8
722. 111-SC-55456
723. 111-SC-159294
724. 111-SC-159296
725. 111-SC-46155
726. 004-P-208
727. 165-WW-139C-3
728. 044-PA-71
729. 044-PA-24
730. 044-PA-820
731. 111-SC-148129
732. 080-G-468549
733. 080-G-475237
734. 080-G-475184
735. 026-G-3154
736. 226-FPL-MH-126
737. 226-FPL-MH-23
738. 226-FPL-MH-48
739. 080-G-300215
740. 080-G-43078
741. 080-G-21861
742. 208-N-5704
743. 079-AR-82

744. 026-G-3584
745. 080-G-331330
746. 242-EB-7-38
747. 111-SC-134627
748. 306-NT-1391-7
749. 080-G-239549
750. 111-SC-260486
751. 208-YE-182
752. 111-SC-210621
753. 208-PU-154F-5
754. 208-PU-153C-14
755. 111-SC-192258
756. 080-G-294122
757. 080-GK-14036
758. 111-SC-232989
759. 080-G-324556
760. 208-PU-195GG-1
761. 044-PA-191
762. 044-PA-245
763. 044-PA-777
764. 044-PA-1966
765. 044-PA-246
766. 179-WP-278
767. 044-PA-531
768. 044-PA-120
769. 044-PA-935
770. 026-G-4548
771. 208-AMC-3D-9
772. 210-G-2A-35
773. 210-G-2C-261
774. 210-G-2C-455
775. 210-G-3B-424
776. 210-G-2C-153
777. 210-G-3C-310
778. 210-G-2A-6
779. 210-G-3A-204
780. 210-G-3B-414
781. 210-G-2B-29
782. 210-G-3C-302
783. 210-CC-S-26C
784. 210-G-3C-334
785. 210-G-3C-594
786. 210-G-10C-839
787. 044-PA-1688
788. 208-PU-91 B-5
789. 208-AMC-3D-1
790. 188-FS-7-100
791. 208-AA-3221-2

792. 208-AA-322H-1
793. 208-AA-322H-7
794. 208-COM-482
795. 208-COM-1084
796. 208-COM-1179
797. 208-COM-1135
798. 179-WP-1563
799. 208-AA-352W-4
800. 208-AA-352X-1
801. 208-AA-352V-4
802. 208-AA-352QQ-5
803. 080-G-412756
804. 086-WWT-3-67
805. 080-G-412645
806. 208-AA-352OO-1
807. 208-NP-1KKK-3
808. 080-G-412633
809. 086-WWT-85-35
810. 086-WWT-78-30
811. 086-WWT-46-9
812. 086-WWT-33-58
813. 086-WWT-85-16
814. 086-WWT-33-41
815. 080-G-468489
816. 080-G-468488
817. 208-AA-352AA-5
818. 080-G-412639
819. 080-G-475980
820. 080-G-468517
821. 080-G-68535
822. 044-PA-885
823. 179-WP-860
824. 044-PA-115
825. 179-WP-672
826. 208-X-6177-D
827. 044-PA-230
828. 044-PA-1748
829. 044-PA-146
830. 044-PA-82
831. 044-PA-578
832. 179-WP-1401
833. 064-M-276
834. 080-G-343666
835. 080-G-468222
836. 080-G-475186
837. 080-G-475182
838. 080-G-472528
839. 127-N-126413

840. 080-G-472661
841. 080-G-468134
842. 080-G-280710
843. 080-G-472555
844. 080-G-472556
845. 080-G-468179
846. 306-NT-1285F-3
847. 026-G-3423
848. 226-FPL-4-13
849. 226-FPL-4-10
850. 208-AA-324A-1
851. 226-FPL-4-17
852. 080-G-166952
853. 111-SC-195512
854. 208-YE-2B-7
855. 026-G-3056
856. 026-G-4098
857. 026-G-3892
858. 026-G-2840
859. 127-N-72208
860. 080-G-413414
861. 208-YE-138
862. 111-SC-257350
863. 111-SC-206125
864. 111-SC-200408
865. 111-SC-211318
866. 111-SC-174073
867. 111-SC-185284
868. 111-SC-189623
869. 111-SC-191760
870. 127-GR-84-68407
871. 111-SC-221867
872. 080-G-335388
873. 080-G-475164
874. 127-N-97628
875. 127-N-85221
876. 080-G-472498
877. 080-G-472195
878. 080-G-468523
879. 111-SC-172004
880. 080-G-280693
881. 127-N-118933
882. 127-N-110104
883. 127-GR-97-124581
884. 080-G-417628
885. 026-G-2074
886. 026-G-032344(2)
887. 080-G-700302

888. 111-SC-203553
889. 080-G-281781
890. 080-G-281784
891. 080-G-471841
892. 226-FPK-22-11
893. 111-SC-198675
894. 080-G-468492
895. 080-G-470222
896. 208-NP-6LL-11
897. 080-G-475089
898. 080-G-475096
899. 080-CASA-618
900. 208-AA-2F-20
901. 208-N-3581
902. 111-SC-203412
903. 127-N-138204
904. 111-SC-193249
905. 111-SC-210796
906. 112-SGA-43-2000
907. 080-G-415477
908. 127-G-110244
909. 208-YE-22
910. 026-G-3531
911. 127-N-126599
912. 111-SC-213198
913. 127-G-63454
914. 111-SC-180534
915. 026-G-3122
916. 080-G-328610
917. 111-SC-198263
918. 111-SC-187247
919. 112-SGA-43-531
920. 112-SGA-44-11664
921. 112-SGA-44-10842
922. 319-CE-124-237580
923. 080-G-413963
924. 080-G-346694
925. 112-SGA-45-2386
926. 026-G-3345
927. 208-AA-1H-14
928. 111-SC-208582
929. 026-G-4677
930. 127-N-95743
931. 127-N-82262
932. 080-G-238322
933. 080-G-329299
934. 111-SC-206681
935. 080-G-218861

936. 080-G-468151
937. 080-G-468123
938. 080-G-415475
939. 080-G-468312
940. 080-G-469993
941. 080-G-53871
942. 080-G-468316
943. 080-G-468099
944. 080-G-11258
945. 080-G-468645
946. 080-G-468524
947. 080-G-468153
948. 080-G-281662-6
949. 080-G-272803
950. 080-G-281718
951. 026-G-2140
952. 080-G-53855
953. 080-CASA-443A
954. 080-G-470720
955. 080-G-59525
956. 080-G-301351
957. 080-CASA-71
958. 080-G-419959
959. 080-G-470985
960. 080-CASA-706
961. 080-G-204747A
962. 080-G-427475
963. 080-G-376123
964. 080-G-205473
965. 080-G-266523
966. 080-G-54288
967. 080-G-475071
968. 080-G-468604
969. 080-G-431073
970. 026-G-1517
971. 080-G-474168
972. 080-G-17054
973. 080-G-59493
974. 080-G-415001
975. 080-G-238363
976. 080-G-17489
977. 080-G-20989
978. 080-G-274266
979. 080-G-273880
980. 080-G-323712
981. 242-HAP-1928-46
982. 200-GR-14
983. 200-GR-12

984. 131-GR-164-2
985. 306-NT-178018
986. 208-N-39840
987. 208-N-39835
988. 208-N-39843
989. 242-HLB-2658-16
990. 242-JRPE-44
991. 238-OR-143-23
992. 306-FS-326-24
993. 208-PP-10A-2
994. 200-SFF-57
995. 208-PP-10A-1
996. 242-GAP-286B-4
997. 208-PP-10A-3
998. 242-HLB-5073-20
999. 242-EB-7-35
1000. 306-NT-901B-3
1001. 306-NT-901-73
1002. 306-NT-3146V
1003. 306-NT-3173V
1004. 306-NT-2743V
1005. 306-NT-901C-7
1006. 306-NT-901-19
1007. 306-NT-901C-11
1008. 306-NT-3176V
1009. 306-NT-3163V
1010. 306-NT-901-69
1011. 306-NT-901-71
1012. 306-NT-901-72
1013. 306-NT-3170V
1014. 306-NT-901C-20
1015. 111-SC-179564
1016. 242-EAPC-6-M713a
1017. 208-PU-138LL-3
1018. 111-SC-182245
1019. 226-FPL-2626
1020. 226-FPL-2599
1021. 226-FPL-2557
1022. 226-FPL-2665(A)
1023. 111-SC-180476
1024. 111-SC-246532
1025. 111-SC-178198
1026. 111-SC-179879
1027. 208-NP-6XXX-1
1028. 111-SC-187126
1029. 111-SC-187704
1030. 111-SC-205289
1031. 111-SC-337154

1032. 111-SC-195385
1033. 111-SC-188691
1034. 111-SC-205602
1035. 306-FS-326-33
1036. 026-G-2326
1037. 226-FPL-MH-109
1038. 226-FPL-T-25
1039. 111-SC-190504
1040. 111-SC-194399
1041. 026-G-2343
1042. 111-SC-190366
1043. 111-SC-189910
1044. 026-G-2397
1045. 026-G-2441
1046. 026-G-2513
1047. 111-SC-191933
1048. 111-SC-192224
1049. 112-SGA-44-12123
1050. 111-SC-193970
1051. 208-YE-68
1052. 111-SC-196728
1053. 208-YE-54
1054. 208-AA-19Z-1
1055. 208-AA-217401
1056. 208-MFI-5H-1
1057. 111-SC-193008
1058. 208-MFI-3B-1
1059. 111-SC-193197
1060. 111-SC-193997
1061. 111-SC-193835
1062. 111-SC-193903
1063. 208-AA-56T-4
1064. 111-SC-199803
1065. 111-SC-210047
1066. 111-SC-354702
1067. 111-SC-194568
1068. 111-SC-197367
1069. 111-SC-197455
1070. 111-SC-197561
1071. 111-SC-198240
1072. 111-SC-222396
1073. 111-SC-197861
1074. 111-SC-199295
1075. 111-SC-198849
1076. 111-SC-199296
1077. 111-SC-198534
1078. 111-SC-324556
1079. 111-SC-199406

1080. 111-SC-199639
1081. 306-NT-1334B-11
1082. 111-SC-201973
1083. 208-YE-193
1084. 111-SC-197661
1085. 208-YE-133
1086. 208-YE-132
1087. 208-YE-7
1088. 111-SC-197660
1089. 306-NT-901-74
1090. 111-SC-197261
1091. 111-SC-206235
1092. 239-PA-70-4
1093. 111-SC-203836
1094. 111-SC-205298
1095. 111-SC-205778
1096. 111-SC-205228
1097. 208-AA-342BB-1
1098. 111-SC-203308
1099. 111-SC-204516
1100. 111-SC-209154
1101. 239-PA-6-34-2
1102. 111-SC-264918
1103. 111-SC-204480
1104. 111-SC-203416
1105. 208-AA-206K-31
1106. 111-SC-206379
1107. 111-SC-203648
1108. 111-SC-206391
1109. 111-SC-208199
1110. 111-SC-266491
1111. 111-SC-203466
1112. 111-SC-204810
1113. 111-SC-203475
1114. 111-SC-203590
1115. 111-SC-203572
1116. 111-SC-205480
1117. 111-SC-204811
1118. 111-SC-264811
1119. 111-SC-203771
1120. 111-SC-203464
1121. 111-SC-203456
1122. 111-SC-203461
1123. 111-SC-207193
1124. 111-SC-264895
1125. 111-SC-266656
1126. 111-SC-266662
1127. 111-SC-205315

1128. 111-SC-206611
1129. 111-SC-206193
1130. 111-SC-206406
1131. 208-AA-132N-2
1132. 080-G-30549
1133. 080-G-30550
1134. 080-G-19948
1135. 080-G-16871
1136. 080-G-32420
1137. 080-G-19947
1138. 080-G-19943
1139. 080-G-32915
1140. 111-SC-334265
1141. 111-SC-249636
1142. 208-AA-80B-1
1143. 111-SC-334296
1144. 127-N-114541
1145. 208-AA-288BB-2
1146. 208-N-8480
1147. 080-G-12076
1148. 080-G-41196
1149. 208-AA-12X-21
1150. 208-N-15394
1151. 111-SC-197901
1152. 111-SC-360599
1153. 226-FPK-19-45-745
1154. 226-FPK-19-45-743
1155. 226-FPK-18-45-726
1156. 111-SC-197939
1157. 111-SC-201144
1158. 111-SC-208807
1159. 111-SC-197483
1160. 226-FPK-45-426
1161. 226-FPK-45-352
1162. 026-G-2925
1163. 026-G-2839
1164. 026-G-3183
1165. 026-G-2682
1166. 026-G-3289
1167. 111-SC-183574
1168. 111-SC-191475
1169. 127-N-68998
1170. 026-G-2658
1171. 026-G-4718
1172. 111-SC-192796
1173. 111-SC-190968
1174. 127-GR-113-83260
1175. 127-N-83261

1176. 080-G-52573
1177. 127-N-88073
1178. 127-N-95249
1179. 127-N-63458
1180. 127-GR-119-64002
1181. 080-G-48359
1182. 080-G-48358
1183. 127-N-63472
1184. 026-G-3364
1185. 111-SC-189099
1186. 127-N-71981
1187. 111-SC-212770
1188. 127-GR-114-83270
1189. 127-N-91366
1190. 127-N-151749
1191. 208-N-29695
1192. 127-N-72050
1193. 127-N-82619
1194. 080-G-475159
1195. 080-G-475093
1196. 026-G-2708
1197. 080-G-476304
1198. 026-G-3394
1199. 026-G-3166
1200. 080-G-205686
1201. 080-G-294131
1202. 026-G-3539
1203. 080-G-47471
1204. 208-AA-86M-1
1205. 026-G-3537
1206. 026-G-3856
1207. 111-SC-407101
1208. 026-G-3566
1209. 080-G-272632
1210. 026-G-3738
1211. 111-SC-205918
1212. 026-G-3558
1213. 026-G-4650
1214. 026-G-4774
1215. 127-G-142484
1216. 080-G-474953
1217. 127-N-110249
1218. 127-N-109619
1219. 026-G-4122
1220. 026-G-4474
1221. 080-G-413988
1222. 026-G-4140
1223. 127-N-109624

1224. 127-GR-97-126420
1225. 111-SC-211476
1226. 026-G-4426
1227. 127-N-122154
1228. 127-N-123170
1229. 127-N-120562
1230. 127-GR-95-122119
1231. 127-N-119485
1232. 127-N-127910
1233. 127-N-117054
1234. 111-SC-209070
1235. 127-G-118775
1236. 127-N-120807
1237. 127-N-123169
1238. 080-G-490232
1239. 080-G-413915
1240. 208-LU-13H-5
1241. 127-N-136176
1242. 208-N-43888
1243. 077-AEC-52-4457
1244. 077-MDH-6.55b
1245. 077-AEC-48-27
1246. 077-AEC-52-4459
1247. 080-G-473743
1248. 080-G-473755
1249. 208-AA-132N-4
1250. 111-SC-227909
1251. 111-SC-212513
1252. 111-SC-256688
1253. 111-SC-212111
1254. 112-SGA-44-11702
1255. 111-SC-191728
1256. 111-SC-170234
1257. 111-SC-193132
1258. 111-SC-202857
1259. 111-SC-193785
1260. 080-G-474128
1261. 111-SC-178801
1262. 111-SC-207907
1263. 111-SC-208042
1264. 026-G-4730
1265. 111-SC-192535
1266. 026-G-3698
1267. 127-GR-113-83266
1268. 026-G-2528
1269. 127-GR-99-122422
1270. 226-FPK-15-1
1271. 127-N-138676

1272. 242-HLB-3609-25
1273. 242-HLB-3609-32
1274. 242-HLB-3609-34
1275. 242-HB-47721-306
1276. 131-NO-29-16
1277. 238-NT-281
1278. 238-NT-293
1279. 238-NT-288
1280. 238-NT-282
1281. 026-G-1583
1282. 208-NP-6QQQ-1
1283. 208-YE-105
1284. 111-SC-339075
1285. 080-G-54412
1286. 026-G-2391
1287. 112-SGA-44-14053
1288. 112-SGA-44-7879
1289. 111-SC-341504
1290. 260-MGG-1061-1
1291. 208-YE-145
1292. 111-SC-206078
1293. 111-SC-193010
1294. 111-SC-231809
1295. 111-SC-233010
1296. 238-NT-592
1297. 238-NT-612
1298. 111-SC-225295
1299. 111-SC-206395
1300. 306-PS-55-21266
1301. 111-SC-333290
1302. 319-PW-67A
1303. 127-N-64363
1304. 026-G-4669
1305. 080-G-469956
1306. 080-G-468228
1307. 127-N-125719
1308. 080-G-490488
1309. 127-N-70216
1310. 080-G-490317
1311. 080-G-324478
1312. 080-G-490320
1313. 111-SC-201182
1314. 080-G-490444
1315. 080-G-418331
1316. 080-G-43376
1317. 080-G-273768
1318. 080-G-474900
1319. 111-SC-209733

1320. 026-G-3000
1321. 342-CGA-66
1322. 208-EX-249A-27
1323. 306-NT-3157V
1324. 226-FPL-VBD-13
1325. 226-FPL-CP-385
1326. 208-YE-122
1327. 208-AA-207L-1
1328. 239-RC-24-28
1329. 239-PA-6-48-1
1330. 200-HC-79
1331. 026-G-3577
1332. 226-FPK-45-497
1333. 127-N-137017
1334. 208-PR-10L-3
1335. 127-GR-106-121116
1336. 208-N-39903
1337. 111-SC-206174
1338. 200-HC-78
1339. 111-SC-198245
1340. 111-SC-232557
1341. 112-SGA-44-30564
1342. 080-G-57405
1343. 127-N-84864
1344. 026-G-3182
1345. 111-SC-204462
1346. 208-YE-148
1347. 111-SC-196741
1348. 111-SC-207902
1349. 111-SC-190597
1350. 026-G-3971
1351. 026-G-2330
1352. 026-G-4739
1353. 111-SC-206292
1354. 111-SC-205398
1355. 226-FPK-45-411
1356. 079-AR-508Q
1357. 111-SC-210208
1358. 080-G-377094
1359. 111-SC-329414
1360. 208-N-43468
1361. 111-SC-210644
1362. 111-SC-210626
1363. 080-G-348366
1364. 127-G-146818
1365. 111-SC-207868
1366. 208-AA-1H-12
1367. 080-GK-5645

1368. 208-AA-1H-3
1369. 208-AA-2H-1
1370. 080-G-421130
1371. 080-G-490487
1372. 306-PS-50-16807
1373. 306-PS-50-15266
1374. 111-SC-348438
1375. 306-PS-51-10432
1376. 111-SC-365348
1377. 306-PS-51-6988
1378. 306-PS-51-15870
1379. 111-SC-351591
1380. 306-PS-50-10792
1381. 306-PS-50-10828
1382. 111-SC-345283
1383. 111-SC-363216
1384. 111-SC-351458
1385. 111-SC-343967
1386. 306-PS-50-11298
1387. 306-PS-50-9064
1388. 111-SC-410209
1389. 306-PS-51-9709
1390. 080-G-625791
1391. 127-N-A156980
1392. 127-N-A4852
1393. 111-SC-356309
1394. 111-SC-358355
1395. 111-SC-384231
1396. 306-PS-50-10721
1397. 111-SC-358042
1398. 127-N-A345138
1399. 111-SC-387519
1400. 127-N-A1285
1401. 127-N-A9345
1402. 111-C-7226
1403. 306-PS-50-12226
1404. 111-SC-344307
1405. 111-SC-355021
1406. 080-G-420027
1407. 111-SC-410709
1408. 111-SC-344946
1409. 127-N-A131033
1410. 127-N-A131970
1411. 306-PS-51-13676
1412. 127-N-A131445
1413. 306-PS-51-9760
1414. 080-G-433002
1415. 080-G-423206

1416. 127-N-A2716
1417. 111-SC-FEC-53-402
1418. 127-N-A3189
1419. 127-N-A3191
1420. 127-N-A8585
1421. 111-SC-347856
1422. 111-SC-351392
1423. 127-N-A2739
1424. 127-N-A3386
1425. 127-N-A2888
1426. 111-SC-353469
1427. 111-SC-410716
1428. 111-SC-362121
1429. 306-PS-51-5924
1430. 080-G-433340
1431. 111-SC-355544
1432. 127-N-A5439
1433. 306-FS-259-21
1434. 080-G-428242
1435. 111-SC-369801
1436. 111-SC-415620
1437. 127-N-A156882
1438. 111-SC-389600
1439. 127-N-A171006
1440. 080-G-422387
1441. 080-G-639948
1442. 080-G-422112
1443. 306-PS-51-10303
1444. 080-G-421049
1445. 080-G-426954
1446. 111-SC-365537
1447. 127-N-A166426
1448. 306-PS-52-1237
1449. 111-SC-348678
1450. 111-SC-344399
1451. 111-SC-362636
1452. 111-SC-366309
1453. 080-G-429571
1454. 111-SC-345322
1455. 111-SC-380826
1456. 111-SC-354716
1457. 111-SC-382662
1458. 111-SC-409689
1459. 111-SC-347803
1460. 111-C-6620
1461. 306-PS-50-16899
1462. 127-N-A156900
1463. 111-SC-378917

1464. 111-SC-378561
1465. 111-SC-369730
1466. 111-SC-452342
1467. 127-N-A365478
1468. 111-SC-348605
1469. 111-SC-351586
1470. 111-SC-351580
1471. 127-N-A166304
1472. 111-SC-354103
1473. 111-C-6560
1474. 127-N-A156550
1475. 111-SC-344511
1476. 080-G-425418
1477. 111-SC-356475
1478. 306-PS-52-2719
1479. 080-G-424096
1480. 080-G-424513
1481. 306-PS-51-17008
1482. 111-SC-352692
1483. 111-C-6787
1484. 080-G-429675
1485. 080-G-429691
1486. 111-SC-348594
1487. 111-SC-353947
1488. 127-N-A3810
1489. 127-N-A3242
1490. 127-N-A3597
1491. 127-N-A2122
1492. 080-G-428666
1493. 127-N-A6759
1494. 111-SC-348805
1495. 111-SC-386498
1496. 306-PS-51-7134
1497. 306-PS-54-1497
1498. 080-G-626977
1499. 111-C-6143
1500. 127-N-A2812
1501. 111-SC-351356
1502. 080-G-420652
1503. 111-SC-351697
1504. 111-SC-351700
1505. 111-SC-386809
1506. 080-G-429573
1507. 111-SC-347020
1508. 111-SC-351359
1509. 111-SC-350339
1510. 111-SC-343302
1511. 111-SC-347826

1512. 127-N-A5552
1513. 127-N-A5421
1514. 127-N-A5426
1515. 111-SC-383310
1516. 080-G-437021
1517. 080-G-625728
1518. 080-G-625785
1519. 111-SC-425769
1520. 111-SC-431161
1521. 111-SC-431160
1522. 111-C-6425

# ARTIST INDEX

*Item number follows artist's name.*

# PHOTOGRAPHER INDEX

*Item number follows photographer's name.*

Abrahamson, Cpl. Charles, 1457
Acme, 753, 760, 814, 817, 900, 987, 1150, 1372, 1377, 1403
Albers, Clem, 778, 779, 780, 781
Albert, Pfc. John F., 1158
Allen, Sgt. E. R., 1115
Allen, Henry, 1151
American Red Cross, 658, 659, 660, 672, 676, 677, 678, 680, 850
Andrejka, Cpl. J. F., 1190
Anker, Gerald C., 1171
Associated Press Ltd., 1290
Augustine, Sgt. Bill, 1289
Babyak, Sgt. John, Jr., 1420, 1424, 1488
Bailey, Pvt. Bob, 1229
Barnard, George N., 164, 168, 174, 210, 240, 241, 242, 246
Barnett, Sgt. Thomas D., Jr., 911
Barry, T4c. George J., 1258
Battersby, Lt. R. J., 1333
Batts, 1177
Baum, T4c., 925
Beckett, C. Tucker, 335, 340, 342, 343, 345, 346, 348, 349
Beebe, Spencer, 809
Belfer, Cpl. Edward, 1124
Benrud, 1352
Benson, 1033
Binford, Ens. Thomas, 968
Birmingham View Co., 661
Black Star, 1381
Blau, T4c. Sidney, 1118, 1129
Blomgren, 1298
Bloomquist, Capt., 1470
Bonnard, 1029
Boria, G. Dimitri, 1388, 1402, 1407, 1460, 1473, 1483, 1505
Bowen, 853
Boyle, 1028

Brady, Mathew, 122
Bransford, 905
Braun, 1077
Breeding, 1385
Brenner, 1186, 1192
Brink, Pfc., 1519
Bristol, Lt. Comdr. Horace, 835, 841, 845, 898, 937, 945, 962, 1306
Brown, Lt. J. S., 671
Buckley, Cpl. Dennis P., 1449
Bull, 1030, 1034
Burke, PhoM3c., 1440
Burns, Sgt. James L., 1174, 1175, 1193
Calmus, Cpl. Walter, 1477
Castle, Lt. Ivor, 635
Caverly, Q.M. Sgt. Leon H., 579, 666
Central News Photo Service, 366, 470, 494, 612, 619
Chancellor, Cpl. James L., 1395
Chang, Sfc. Al, 1397, 1459
Chichersky, Pfc. W., 1120, 1122
Chorlest, T.Sgt., 1235
Christ, Pfc. Emerich M., 1405
Cirzan, L. F., 965
Cissna, T3c. A., 934
Clayton, T4c., 865
Clements, Cpl. H. H., 874
Clemmer, T4c. Jack, 1123, 1337
Clover, Harold W., 1330, 1338
Cohen, Pvt. L., 650, 651
Cohn, 1364
Compton, Sgt. W.M., 1490
Cook, George S., 134
Cooke, Sgt. Bob, 1223
Cooper, Lt. Edwin H., 622
Cooperman, CPhoM. Alfred N., 974
Cordray, 1187
Cote, PH1. Jean C., 391
Cox, Pfc. James, 1426
Crowe, Cpl., 1408

Cudabac, PhoM1c. R. N., 1317
Cunningham, 755, 920
Curtis, C., 654
Cusack, Robert M., 1227
Dangel, Cpl. Robert, 1482, 1510
Dargis, 1167
Davis, Capt. Charles, 375
deBerri, Lt. Edmond M., 516
Delano, Jack, 826
DeMarco, Sgt. J. A., 1341
D'Emidio, T4c. Ernani, 868
Diers, PhoM3c. D. C., 960
Dinwiddie, William, 299
Donegan, T.G., 1430
Dorsey, Lt. Paul, 873, 1194
Downey, John, 1058
Dreyfuss, 1217, 1218
Drummond, A., Jr., 1128
Duff, Lt. Adrian C., 630, 665, 669, 683
Dunbar, Pfc. Donald, 1472
Duncan, Lt. David D., 839, 1224, 1335
Dunlap, Sgt., 1382, 1454
Duthewich, Lt., 655
Eastman, Cpl., 1236
Edgren, 1073
Edwards, J. D., 167
Eikleberry, Sgt. Gideon J., 592, 703
Einwaechter, Nelse, 1464
Eldridge, Capt. Fred L., 747
Emanuel, Bert, 377
England, Sgt. Howard S., 881
Estep, Lt. Ralph, 492
Fabian, Cpl. John, 1309
Fabiszak, Pfc. Charles, 1394, 1396, 1452
Feldman, 1427, 1458
Fennel, 438
Fineberg, Sfc. Morris, 712
Fitzgerald, T.Sgt. Glen A., 1269
Forney, Pvt. Ralph, 1106, 1108